My Music in London

1945-2000

This book is for Pauline Del Mar, good friend and lovely person.

With thanks also to my angels:

Cris Fleming
The Rev. and Mrs John Wates
Roger Tanner

My Music in London
1945–2000

John Amis

AMISCELLANY
BOOKS

Copyright © John Amis 2006
First published in 2006 by Amiscellany Books
Flat R, 17 Eccleston Square
London SW1V 1NS

Reprinted 2008

Distributed by Gardners Books, 1 Whittle Drive, Eastbourne, East
Sussex, BN23 6QH
Tel: +44(0)1323 521555 | Fax: +44(0)1323 521666

www.amolibros.com

British Library Cataloguing in Publication Data
A catalogue record for this book is available from
the British Library.

ISBN 978-0-9551580-0-1

Typeset by Amolibros, Milverton, Somerset
This book production has been managed by Amolibros
Printed and bound by T J International Ltd, Padstow, Cornwall, UK

Contents

List of Illustrations

Foreword

This book has an unusual structure. It begins with a review of the first concert given by the Amadeus Quartet and ends over fifty years later in 1999. What lies in between is a review of the postwar period in music mostly in London as seen and heard through the eyes and ears of one person. It is not a *comprehensive* review or an history. During these years I had various jobs (Gemini is my star sign): critic, broadcaster, administrator, concert manager, lecturer, singer and I was a constant opera- and concert-goer. The management side began for me during the war, helping to run the National Gallery Concerts, an Arts Club for the London Philharmonic, the music section of the Institute of Contemporary Arts, the Summer Schools of Music at Bryanston (1948-52) and Dartington (1953-81), editor of music television programmes for the BBC; what with those and interviewing over a thousand musicians for the BBC, in particular its Transcription Service (1958-90) and World Service (1975-85), I met or worked with nearly all the important and less important (though not less interesting) musicians of our time. From 1948 to 1965 I was London Music Critic of *The Scotsman* and a contributor to other newspapers and journals – and since 1988 I have been Music Critic of *The Tablet*. I appeared for some eighteen years (ten on telly) in the BBC programme *My Music* with Frank Muir, Denis Norden, Ian Wallace and Steve Race as quiz-master.

Part one consists mainly of reviews of those golden times when the gods had names like Callas, Flagstad, Heifetz, Horowitz, Beecham, Bruno Walter and Klemperer. These reviews, mostly written on the night, tell their own story of the times although I have sometimes filled in the background or added anecdotal material; these additions I have marked in the text with the initials HS for hindsight. Tempting though it was occasionally to touch them up a little I have not done so. *The Scotsman* was generous, not with 'bawbies', but with space. But having space meant that I had to work at my scores to cope with the wide variety of music that came my way. At that time I was virtually the only critic to attend rehearsals but I found it was essential to do so where new music was concerned; I covered the premieres (absolute or British) of such works as: Britten's *The Turn of the Screw, Let's Make an Opera, Chinese Songs, Winter Words* and *Noye's Fludde;* Tippett's *The Midsummer Marriage,* first and second symphonies and Piano Concerto; Walton's *Troilus and Cressida,* Cello Concerto and second symphony; Constant Lambert's *Tiresias,* Janacek's *Kat'a Kabanova,* Messiaen's *Turangalila* and Schönberg's *Moses und Aron.* The Edinburgh paper kindly paid expenses for me to go out of town so that I could cover events at Glyndebourne, Aldeburgh, Bath, Cheltenham and abroad at Brno, Lyons, Wexford and Zurich. The reviews are re-printed here with the kind permission of *The Scotsman,* all reviews are from that newspaper except where otherwise stated.

Part two deals with the last decades of the twentieth century and what I was up to: lecturing, travelling, writing and listening to music; and a few other topics. Events provide pegs for slices of life and profiles of, for instance, Messiaen, Tippett, Britten, Milhaud, Poulenc, Copland, Enescu, Tcherepnin, Ireland, and many others. It was a pleasure to have written about some musicians who were not so well-known when I wrote about them but gradually became so; Tippett was one such, likewise Colin Davis, Alfred Deller, the Amadeus and Joan Sutherland. The financial and political aspects of music do not, I find, make for interest on the whole so I have left them out, also sex, meals and dreams. In the more autobiographical parts of this volume I have rarely, I think, duplicated any of my previous book *Amiscellany* (Faber and Faber, 1985).

The period I write about in this book has been full of stress but also great artistic joys. It was wonderful, for example, to have been alive and around when Britten and Tippett wrote their great works and I was lucky enough to know them and call them friends. Things like that, the music I have heard, good friends and (usually) just enough money have made my life a happy one. This book is an attempt to share some of these good things with you...and to keep you informed.

John Amis

PART ONE – (Reviews)

STRING QUARTETS:
New Talent at Wigmore Hall   14.1.48

Two string quartets new to the public have made their debut in London at the Wigmore Hall this week. To give a Wigmore Hall recital, the booking has to be made about a year in advance, so great is the demand from new artists. Pianists appear in dozens, there is a superfluity of fiddlers, and singers are two a penny. But the appearance of a new string quartet is a comparative rarity.

The Hurwitz String Quartet played Haydn in D, Op.20, No. 4; Bartok No. 1; Rawsthorne's Theme and Variations and Beethoven's Op. 95 in F minor. The programme was too long and only their obvious long acquaintance with the last work carried them through that difficult piece.

The ensemble of the Hurwitz is very good; they obviously think about what they are playing. Technically, individual playing lacks a little here and there, always with the exception of the fine 'cellist, Terence Weil, who achieves a beautiful tone. The early Bartok was clean and clear and only needed a little more vigour. The Haydn was perhaps the best performance of the evening.

The Amadeus String Quartet is even better. It played to a packed house Mozart in D minor K. 421, the Verdi and Beethoven's third quartet of the Op. 59, in C major.

The performance of the Verdi placed this quartet right at the top of the tree; technically, intellectually and musically it was superb. This charming and passionate offspring of Verdi's old age, companion of *Otello* and *Falstaff,* is a ticklish thing to play: nasty unison passages and difficult phrases which have to be played *pianissimo:* the Amadeus managed everything with ease.

The Mozart and Beethoven were both good even if the standard of the Verdi was not quite equalled. The leader of the quartet is Norbert Brainin, for whom I predict a great future as a solo violinist. I must also mention Peter Schidlof for his lovely viola tone. The standard of playing in both these quartets is very high and we must welcome their appearance warmly for the shortage of good quartets is acute.

HS: For various reasons the life of the Quartet which Emanuel Hurwitz led was short. The Amadeus reached the pinnacle of quartet playing lasting until Schidlof's heart attack and death in 1987, upon which the quartet was no more. Peter was a lovely man and a consummate musician – I think his sound on the viola was the most beautiful I ever heard.

The shortage of good quartets in the UK was over by the '60s and by the '80s there was a plethora of good ones: Lindsay, Chilingirian, Allegri, Brindisi, etc. Part of the reason was the coaching they received, in particular from Sidney Griller, former leader of a British quartet bearing his name, the best in the late '30s and early '40s, at the Royal Academy of Music in London. Also there were competitions offering prizes and universities offering a living.

MEWTON-WOOD:
Wigmore Hall Recital   18.3.49

Last night Mewton-Wood, the Australian born pianist, gave a recital at the Wigmore Hall. His programme consisted of the Schubert Sonata in A minor, Op.42; the Beethoven Variations on an original theme, Op. 34; and the Sonata in E flat, Op. 27, No. 1; Hindemith's Second Sonata; and a Nocturne and Ballade by Chopin.

I find Noël Mewton-Wood by far the best of the young pianists in this country. Technically he is superbly equipped and nothing daunts him, from the Diabelli Variations to the Busoni Concerto, which, characteristically enough, he played from memory last week at Chelsea. Intellectually he is far above the average pianist.

He has the vitality which, allied to a high degree of concentration, never allows him to give a sloppy performance. Also he has great integrity, musically and technically.

What stops him from being a world beater then? Firstly, he has not yet reached full maturity. When he has, he may be. He is only twenty-six years of age. Secondly, his temperament. In his best mood, he is one of the best pianists in the world, but he has other times when things go wrong for various reasons. And when things go wrong inaccuracy sets in and he can bang the piano unmercifully. It happened at his recital at the Wigmore.

There were fine things in his Schubert last night. The Trio was played with a rare feeling of repose, and a *rubato* so subtle that one could scarcely detect it. The finale showed the clear line there is between Schubert and Mahler. The Beethoven Variations have always seemed to me unjustly neglected and the shock of the change of keys of each variation was as great as ever.

Perhaps the finest playing of the evening was in the Hindemith. It may sound a strange thing to say of a work by this composer, but it was a very imaginative reading that read much between the lines; and read things I never knew were there. This Sonata is much the easiest of the three for the listener and contains one of Hindemith's rare purple passages in the slow movement.

HS: In some cases, artists I reviewed were friends. If I knew that my thoughts were too adverse I did not write. Sometimes I chanced it and hoped that my critiques would not impair a friendship. Only once did it do so.

Noël Mewton-Wood (1922-53) was the progeny of a father who was never mentioned and a mother called Dulcie who could have been a prototype of Edna Everage and came from Melbourne, what's more. She willed Noël into being a musician (just as that other powerful Melbourne mum did with her child, Percy Grainger) but would not let him go. Noël was partly taught by Artur Schnabel who no doubt fixed for the beautiful infant to play Beethoven 3 with Beecham. Noël corrected Sir Thomas at rehearsal who conceded the point with the remark, 'You see, gentlemen, out of the mouths of babes and sucklings.'

He managed to get out of Ma's clutches (although she lived in London, and had a dress shop in Bond Street at one time), was a great friend of his uncle, writer and critic W. J. Turner (who bequeathed him his considerable collection of pictures) but most of his friends were homosexual. In his early twenties, when I first met him, he was living in the country at Eridge near Tunbridge Wells as a sort of lodger, doted on by Nancy Eckersley. She had little to do with her husband, Roger, who had at one time been BBC Controller and spent her time researching Christopher Marlowe and breeding Alsatian dogs helped by Noël. He was open to all the arts, read voraciously, composed a bit but not successfully except for the film score for Bernard Miles' feature film *Tawny Pipit* (1944), and was conversant with all the arts, knew a lot about medicine, made and operated toy theatres and was the only pianist I have known who could (and did) mend a piano string. He was self-conscious in his body language and at that time it was not obvious that he was queer. That is, until he fell in love with Bill Fedricks, a British Council man. They moved in together to a house on Hammersmith Terrace of Félice Dubuis (another mothering would-be lover) and became a couple. Noël had a good career – was a great favourite of Tippett and Britten, constantly playing at Aldeburgh and took over recitals with Peter Pears when Ben was too busy or, later, incapacitated – Noël had regular recitals at the Wigmore Hall and Proms, made wonderful recordings but he never became a top pianist. And when Bill, always a hypochondriac, died Noël blamed himself and, together with what he saw as his career failure and the fact that he was prone to suicide, he had three shots and finally succeeded in killing himself with cyanide. He left me his Steinway concert grand and we had an hour's conversation on the phone the night before – no hint of what was to happen.

It was one of the best friendships I ever had, he was the most encouraging duet player and made me play better than I could, he was fresh, funny and serious; we often talked far into the night and walked the dogs far into the day. Later on, I teased him when he showed signs of 'mincing' and he teased me about being straight; when I could not see the attraction of some man he would say: 'Trouble with you, Johnnie, is, you haven't got the bugger's eye.'

MOZART FESTIVAL:
Sir Thomas Beecham at Glyndebourne   25.4.49

John Christie and Sir Thomas Beecham are now near neighbours in Sussex, and, like good neighbours, they decided to get together for a little music-making, Beecham with his Royal Philharmonic Orchestra at Christie's Opera House at Glyndebourne. The first of three miniature festivals took place this weekend, devoted to the works of Mozart, an appropriate choice on the eve of the conductor's seventieth birthday.

This is perhaps the right occasion to express thanks to a great conductor who has spent a lifetime making music in a wonderful way. Beecham is a difficult man to thank, and perhaps the best way to do so would be for the State to give his orchestra a substantial grant so that it and Beecham could devote more time to Mozart and other of his favourites and less to Tchaikovsky.

For Beecham has spent too much time recently peddling the latter composer's over-played works in large London cinemas.

When Sir Thomas comes on to the platform these days you may think he looks nearly his age, but once he starts conducting the years drop from him. I have scarcely ever seen such an exhibition of exuberant conducting as we had on Saturday night during the finale of the Symphony No. 34 in C. And every three or four bars there was a furious shout exhorting the players to more lively attack. But the gestures and shouts were only the trappings of the most superb performance.

It is hopeless to try to describe Beecham at his best in Mozart or to explain how he obtains his results, but part of his secret must surely be the extraordinary care he takes in marking the parts. If you were to look at any orchestral part of a Mozart work which Beecham has played for years you might have difficulty in discovering the printed notes because of the profusion of phrasing marks, dynamic markings, and other nuances. His task on the platform at the performance is to see that he gets what is written in the Beecham parts, plus the mood, energy, and the elegance of the gallant style.

The wind, brass, and percussion do not come in for much of the extortion for they are mostly famous men in the orchestral world and often distinguished for their solo and chamber music playing. There may be better single woodwind players in other orchestras in this country, but there is no team capable of such fine ensemble playing. No, it is the strings which come in for Sir Thomas's particular attention The performance of the slow movement of the famous *Eine kleine Nachtmusik* was quite ravishing, owing to his encouragement.

Apart from the two works I have already mentioned, there were superlative performances of the Symphonies numbered 39 and 29 and the overture to *The Magic Flute*. Gioconda de Vito is a fine violinist but seemed to me unsuited stylistically for Mozart, whose G major Concerto she played.

The rest of the orchestral programmes included performances of portions of the *Haffner Serenade* and the Divertimento No. 17 for strings and two horns, K.344, which sounded, I regret to say, unrehearsed.

The next two festivals take place in May and June. In May we are promised three concerts of Haydn, and included among the attractions is Mr Christie himself performing on the hurdy-gurdy in a Divertimento for two instruments of that noble species.

HS: Alas, Mr Christie never made music with Sir Thomas and I didn't hear that Divertimento until the Aldeburgh Festival of 1999 – and a jolly boring number it is too.

Sir Thomas Beecham was born in Lancashire in 1879 with a golden (eponymous) pill in his mouth and bought his way into conducting with the help of his father's money. What pleased him often pleased others and we owe him a debt of an even greater size than the debts he incurred pleasing himself and us. There have been many articles, programmes and books about him and no doubt there will be more if and when the surviving, third Lady Beecham releases or makes public the archives. Shirley doesn't want the Beecham name to be besmirched which it surely would be if certain letters, papers, etc. were made public. So perhaps I should only write here about my personal dealings with him. He had a public persona and a private one. The private person had some intimate friends, not too many I would guess; he was, for example, friendly with his orchestra and with people like myself on the staff but not chummy. After many years as his assistant conductor, Norman was always *Mister* Del Mar; likewise I was Mister Amis, both to Sir Thomas and to the horrible second Lady Beecham, Betty. She was on drugs; her upper right arm looked like a much used dartboard. Drugs had turned a bouncing, buxom, agreeable young woman (as William Glock knew her before the war when he often played duets in public with her) into a manipulating, malicious scarecrow of a woman (as all knew her after her return to the UK as No. 2). By this time Sir Thomas was easy-going and rarely lost his cool; I saw lapses of temper three times only: once when an American company issued a Beecham

8

record album with an advertisement on the back for Toscanini (who had once called Sir Thomas a clown, 'punchinello'); once at Eastbourne when he couldn't open a door ('stand clear, dearest, I am going to break the door down') which opened easily enough once it was seen to be a sliding door; and once, before the whole Royal Philharmonic when he decided to dress down myself and the general manager, Charles Cannon, for some slips up of the orchestral personnel fixer lady. He made a show of it for the benefit of the players, gradually worked himself up from cool to hot in sixty seconds, even though everybody knew where the fault lay – it was a political move.

I found that there was a kind of glass or perspex wall between Beecham and world. He didn't want people to know that he worked exceedingly hard at his scores and the preparation of the orchestral parts. Very British that, like the schoolboy who makes a century at the match but professes never to go to net practice. And talking of British, Sir Thomas was proud of being British, no matter how many times he excoriated the British. I think he was also a shy man and that is why he summoned up his public persona wit to protect himself.

It was magnanimous of John Christie to invite Beecham to do concerts at Glyndebourne. Beecham habitually attacked institutions which did not include him. The Royal Festival Hall aroused his ire because he was not invited to take part in the opening concerts in 1951. Likewise he attacked Covent Garden after the war, having expected to be asked to run the Opera House; most nastily he attacked its music director, Rafael Kubelik, even on racial grounds, he was a *foreigner*, dammit. And Glyndebourne he had attacked before the war, foreigners again, you know: 'Mozart, like good wine, needs no Bus(c)h', a dig at Fritz Busch, Glyndebourne's music director.

The tie-up with Beecham came partly because I had worked as Beecham's concert manager in 1947-8 and partly because of my friendship with Glyndebourne's manager, Moran Caplat. The playing of the London Philharmonic, Glyndebourne's first resident orchestra, had got a bit lackadaisical; Caplat and I connived to get the Royal Philharmonic Orchestra to take over; this was Beecham's new orchestra, formed after he had parted company with the LPO which he had formed in 1932. Since the RPO was already now in the Glyndebourne pit it seemed natural, Beecham willing, to have some concerts on Sunday afternoons, with Sir Thomas conducting, not in the pit of course, but on the stage. There were Mozart mini-festivals, with Haydn and Schubert sharing the honours. Beecham was living nearby so for a couple of seasons things went well. Christie and Beecham dined and smoked together but two king-sized personalities did not dine and smoke for long in the same house (any more than Christie and Benjamin Britten dined together for long). But it was nice while it lasted.

John Christie, 1882-1962, was an eccentric Englishman with an amazing ability to get things done. A former housemaster at Eton he married, age forty-nine, a soprano called Audrey Mildmay. As she was not getting enough work JC decided to build an opera house in his garden in the heart of the Sussex Downs. He did it properly and got two German refugees, Fritz Busch and Carl Ebert, to be his music director and producer. The opera house at Glyndebourne specialized in Mozart but also put on Rossini, Verdi and Donizetti. New standards were set and the seasons are always booked out to this day. After John's death his son, George, took charge, successfully rebuilt the opera house in the '90s and music and opera are still greatly in the debt of this magnificent example of private enterprise.

Carl Ebert, 1887-1980, started off as an actor, working mainly in Frankfurt and his native Berlin, later directed the theatre in Darmstadt and the State Opera in Berlin, the Turkish National Opera 1937-47, he was Glyndebourne's producer from the start in 1934 and after the war 1947-59. He and Busch worked marvellously together and the Christies clearly thought he was a god, if not God. If Ebert's productions in the '30s were as good as his *Idomeneo* in '51 – and I am sure they were – then he was epoch-making. After the war his Mozart became stale with repetition (all frills and hiding behind screens, know what I mean?), but *Idomeneo* for the first time was certainly making an epoch.

There is more about Glyndebourne in part 2.

TURANDOT – WITH EVA TURNER
Puccini's Last Opera   30.5.48

Last night saw the première of the Covent Garden production of Puccini's opera *Turandot*. Musically, Puccini's last essay in this form is superior to its predecessors but development of the characters is absent. In fact only Liu comes to life. For the rest, the piece relies on magnificent full-blooded singing and spectacle.

The spectacle was well handled by the producer, Michael Benthall. Leslie Hurry designed some of his fantastic, sprawling, surrealist-touched sets and costumes to match.

Turandot's trains are usually a feature of this opera, and the designer had realised two enormous affairs for the occasion. These costumes caused the singer some difficulties. Robust though Eva Turner is in physique and voice alike, she looked many times as though she were going a purler.

There were various other little hindrances to enjoyment. Things like the banners waved in Act II in time to the music in intention, but always ragged and late. Glyndebourne has shown us that even glasses should be clinked on the beat.

The singing was disappointing on the whole, with the exception of the chorus, which maintains a high standard always. Eva Turner's was the only voice big enough to fill Covent Garden, and it was truly astonishing to hear her dominating large chorus and full orchestra, all sounding the same notes. Her intonation was faulty, but she somehow carried the part and the audience loved her, despite her rudimentary acting.

Indeed, the standard of acting was very low throughout the company. The part of Liu should be played with pathetic and *petite* charm. Vera Terry lacks the physical attributes necessary for this interpretation, but sang well.

Walter Midgley, as the Prince, had the singing style but not the necessary quality of voice. Constant Lambert conducted a performance which was alert and accurate, but rarely moved the emotions.

HS: Eva Turner (1892-1990) was a great dramatic soprano. In full flood her voice could cut like a laser to dominate chorus and orchestra. At her memorial service in Westminster Abbey her c.1929 recording of 'In questa reggia' from *Turandot* was played and it was thrilling to hear the truly vital way she blotted out the trumpets and horns singing in unison with her. But she could also melt your heart with her way of turning a *pianissimo* phrase as Aida, the third act aria in Verdi's opera, which begins 'O patria mia' (also on an ancient Columbia 78). She conquered the home country and she conquered Italy where she was a favourite at La Scala, Milan in the later '20s and '30s. But she was one of those unfortunate artists whose career was robbed of its triumphal last period by the '39-'45 war. In 1947-8 she made her final appearances at Covent Garden as Turandot. My first sentence is correct even if the word 'dramatic' applied to the category of her voice rather than her acting ability.

Dame Eva (as she suitably became) was a formidable creature by the time I got to know her, kind but downright in the way that Lancashire people can be. She was spreading in her figure but her face, especially the eyes, dominated any social scene she was in. She was determined that the Italian language should be correctly pronounced and to that end she rolled her 'r's like a drill and exaggerated double consonants quite monstrously – once you heard her mention her tenor colleague Giovannnnni Martinellllli you stored it in your memory for future imitations. She was strongly religious and obviously had a private line to the Almighty. Once we were on a jury together for a singing competition and, having cast her vote, she then expressed to me that she wondered whether she had voted correctly. Since she had been previously saying that God always directed her actions I teased her by asking if God then had changed her mind. I was reprimanded in suitable Lancastrian terms by this great dame who once told me that she sometimes regretted having sacrificed domestic happiness to the demands of her career.

THE ELGAR FESTIVAL:
Jascha Heifetz and Pierre Fournier   8.6.49

The Elgar Festival is now in full flood; every major work and many minor ones of this unexportable composer are being played.

Interest ran high when the festival was mooted, for every violinist and cellist in town wanted to know who would be chosen to play the concertos for those two instruments. Some were disappointed that British artists were not chosen. Elgar is so English, they said, how can you expect a Russo-American Jew to interpret the mind and work of an Edwardian Catholic Englishman from the Midlands?

No doubt the organisers of the festival would reply that the choice of Jascha Heifetz and Pierre Fournier was made, firstly, because these two artists are the best available in the world; secondly, because of their eminence they might fill the hall; and thirdly, because engaging these two artists might encourage them to try and convince the rest of the world that Elgar is exportable after all.

Heifetz played the Elgar Violin Concerto on Sunday afternoon with the London Symphony Orchestra, under Sir Malcolm Sargent. The music of the first movement completely eluded Heifetz, and he seemed utterly at odds with it. The slow movement he took faster than usual, and it sang sweetly without clogging itself with sentimentality. The last movement I never expect to hear better played. It is, of course, a very florid part, full of arabesque, but the appalling difficulties were made to seem like an easy exercise. At one point, the blaséness with which he played a fiendish set of octaves made a violinist sitting next to me exclaim with mingled admiration and chagrin.

Was the experiment of Heifetz a success? The general opinion seemed mixed. The Elgarians felt disappointed, the Heifetz admirers were transported, whilst the present writer steered a middle course somewhere between the two.

But the experiment of engaging Pierre Fournier to play the Cello Concerto last night with the BBC Symphony Orchestra, under Sir Adrian Boult, was a great success. Unlike Heifetz, who has played the Violin Concerto in America, Fournier was keyed up by natural feelings of anxious anticipation, but his first performance and his playing had the stamp of greatness about it.

It was a reading that even flattered the work a little, for Fournier prevented the last movement from sounding trivial, which can happen so easily. His tone was noble, his pizzicato especially full-sounding, and the technical execution well-nigh perfect. Not the least admirable part of the performance was Boult's accompaniment, which made one marvel anew at the way in which the orchestration allows every note of the solo part to be heard.

This Cello Concerto, a work of Elgar's later years that may reasonably be described as 'introvert', contrasted vividly with the work which preceded it last night, the overture *In the South*, an extrovert piece which swaggers about making much the same gestures as the *Don Juan* of Richard Strauss. The orchestra gave fine performances of both this and the Symphony No. 1, thanks to Sir Adrian's obvious sympathy and enthusiasm for the works.

HS: Violinists often bewail that the first two movements of the Elgar Concerto are difficult enough but that then they are faced with a finale of even greater technical difficulty. To this challenge Heifetz rose like a soaring eagle, as his recording shows.

Somewhere around these years Heifetz gave a recital at Drury Lane when the encores were superbly alive but the main items, a Bach Suite, a Mozart Concerto (with piano) and the Brahms D minor Sonata were thrown off rather perfunctorily – as was Sonata No. 2 by the Northern Ireland composer Howard Ferguson. The composer knew nothing of the impending performance of his work until the programme was announced. He went to the concert with Myra Hess but the performance of the sonata was such that the composer could scarcely recognise the music as his own. Neither he nor Myra could face going round after the recital to utter the required insincerities so they just went home.

Jascha Heifetz (1901-1987) was, in most people's ears, including mine and any fiddler I ever knew, the world's greatest violinist. It was not only how he played the notes but how he got from one note to the next; he was a master of the portamento and the way he played the first note of a phrase could turn your head and your heart upside-down. He had a cold side to him but the more I hear his recordings the more that coolness seems to have a warm centre. Violinists have said that part of his greatness was that physically he was exactly the right shape for the violin.

Brooks Smith told me once that after he had been Heifetz's accompanist for seven or eight years and therefore with him constantly in cars, trains, planes as well as on the concert platform and his frequent companion at meals and receptions, he suggested that perhaps he could drop the 'Mister' and call him Jascha. 'Oh, I don't think so,' said the Maestro. And when they had played their last concert together many years later, Brooks stammered out his thanks for everything, Heifetz said, 'O.K., well, goodbye then; and don't forget to return my piano part of *Lotusland.'* [An encore piece by Cyril Scott.]

Pierre Fournier (1906-86) was a distinguished cellist indeed, one of the half-dozen best of the century. Not quite at the summit, perhaps, but he certainly made the final camp before the peak. Did he hold back just that little bit with his refinement and sensibility? Was his clubfoot a spur to make him more determined to get to the top or did it hamper his emotions? Idle question perhaps; Fournier was a great cellist and a great musician. A great teacher as well, and, so said a beautiful cellist friend of mine (daughter of Augustus John), a great lover.

PHILADELPHIA ORCHESTRA:
16.6.49

The Philadelphia Orchestra played its London farewell concert at Haringay on Tuesday, and after a few more provincial concerts will say goodbye to Britain. London has been fortunate in having a dozen chances to hear this 'wondrous machine', and there are many like myself, students of orchestral playing who have found that the playing of this orchestra has provided a major and unforgettable experience in their musical lives.

Its playing provides a criterion by which all other orchestral playing, in the past or in the future, is to be judged. So far, at any rate, no orchestra that I have heard in the flesh has come near the excellence of the Philadelphia; certainly not those from London, Turin, Manchester, Berlin, Paris, Prague, Vienna or Amsterdam.

Certainly I have not so experienced the sheer, sensual sound of the various instruments playing in consort, the violins, the horns, the 'cellos, and double-basses especially, since I first heard an orchestra. The sounds that the Philadelphia Orchestra makes have, as it were, re-educated my ears, presenting me with what I recognise to be the true sound of an orchestra, just as if I had been listening all these years with my ears imperfectly tuned.

Not only is the sound of this orchestra truly beautiful, but its players are virtuosos who are enthusiastic in their work, who listen to each other, and, being disciplined, their ensemble resembles that of a string quartet.

Eugene Ormandy, the conductor, is a man who knows what he wants, and knows how to get it. What he wants is tone, volume, balance, precision, all the effects that are known in orchestral writing and lively playing.

Unfortunately, he seems not to be a highly gifted musician, but a virtuoso conductor of some importance. Thus, at the farewell concert at the Royal Albert Hall, his interpretation of the Symphony by César Franck was clogged with sentimentality. But the second half was a rising crescendo of excitement and sound.

Bartok's suite from the unsavoury *The Miraculous Mandarin* ballet is a collection of 'modern' noises that conquered the ear by sheer battery and incredulousness that an orchestra could play it; for Bartok writes for the trombones as if they were clarinets.

With Respighi's *Fountains of Rome* orchestral chemistry persuaded the audience that it had deserted Kensington Gore in favour of the Appian Way. But Richard Strauss's tone poem *Death and Transfiguration* proved to be Ormandy's favourite party-piece. Climax succeeded climax, and still the tone stayed golden and increased in volume, until one felt it would almost be a relief if the Albert Hall exploded.

Joy at such playing was finally tempered with regret at the departure of this noble orchestra and chagrin at the thought of how many times I am going to bore my readers in the future with the odious comparison 'It was not as good as the Philadelphia.'

HS: I wrote a review in similar terms of a concert conducted by Ormandy during an Edinburgh Festival. I was reading my review next day in a plane just before take-off for London when a small round man settled into the seat beside me. With horror I realised it was Eugene Ormandy so I quickly stuffed *The Scotsman* under my seat and, after a bit, chatted with my neighbour. He was nice and not a bit big-time.

PELLÉAS ET MÉLISANDE: 21.6.49

The operatic diet at Covent Garden this season has contained no French fare but *Carmen*. To make up for this deficiency the management has just given us three performances of Debussy's only opera *Pelléas et Mélisande*.

The chorus and orchestra of Covent Garden were conducted by Roger Désormières. Not only the conductor, but also the singers, and décor were from the Opéra Comique, Paris.

Debussy's opera is not for everyone; it is not so much an opera as a series of tableaux or stage-pictures. The only truly dramatic scene is that in which Golaud uses the young boy, Yniold, to spy on the lovers up in the room above. The use of a child as innocent dupe was ever one of Maeterlinck's pathetic devices, as witness the unfortunate *Tintagiles*.

The music is restrained to the utmost. There is no Wagnerian 'beating about the bush', rather a lepidopterous fluttering. It is evocative music which rarely traces dramatic tension. But some of the most beautiful sounds in all music are contained in the score.

It is clear that *Pelléas* must be carefully staged, and exquisitely played and sung. But alas, the décor by Valentin Hugo was a stylistic mix-up, that started with a sub-aqueous pink forest and continued with a pantomime castle. And, for once in London, one has to complain of a stage too light. Maeterlinck in the text, specifies continuous darkness where the light never penetrates.

Of the singers H. B. Etcheverry must be mentioned first of all for his superb singing and portrayal of Golaud; a real voice and a real artist. The Mélisande of Irène Joachim moved me not at all, though she was accurate (as they all were, these French singers).

Her acting was of the order that is so restrained as scarcely to be called acting at all. She gave little more than an animated concert performance. Surely Mary Garden or Maggie Teyte must have infused some magic into this difficult part.

Jacques Jansen (Pelléas) sang clearly with the good diction that all the cast seemed to possess, but the occasional bursts of lyrical fervour escaped him.

The chief honours went to Roger Désormières, who made certain that every orchestral detail was put across without sacrificing the general effect. The orchestra played splendidly and with the necessary subtlety.

HS: Déso (1898-1963), as everyone called him, was a most agreeable man, a very fine conductor; he was slim, wiry but relaxed. Alas, he had a car smash in 1952 from which he emerged paralysed. Irène Joachim, descendant of the violinist, had been his girl-friend for many years and she staunchly looked after him after the accident. They came to the Summer School in Bryanston in 1950 when in its early years. Déso conducted the Kalmar orchestra and Irène sang. Déso also gave great encouragement to Colin Davis, then in his early twenties, who was clarinettist in the Kalmar Orchestra but did some of his first conducting here.

NEW BRITTEN OPERA
An Entertainment for Young People. Cheltenham Festival 20.7.49

The new Britten opus is called *Let's Make an Opera*. It is an entertainment in two parts designed for children. The scheme is an opera within a play, for the first part is a play showing a dress rehearsal of what is to be the second part, a tiny opera, *The Little Sweep*.

The play is generally considered to be too long, and a revised version is expected. Perhaps in the reconstruction more attention will be paid to strictly operatic techniques and less to stagecraft, for at the moment the first part might almost be called *Let's Make a Play*.

The opera itself (libretto by Eric Crozier) is concerned with a sweepboy called Sammy. Some young children kidnap him from his unkind master, bath, feed, clothe him, and eventually smuggle him away to a happier life.

The forces employed are five grown-ups, two of them very young members of the Group, and six children, string quartet, two players at one piano, percussion, and a conductor, who not only has to conduct but to act and to rehearse the audience in four songs.

These four songs serve as opening and final choruses, and interludes between scenes; they are all in unison except for the lovely

Night Song when the audience is divided into four groups of birds: owls, turtle-doves, chaffinches and herons.

Audience-participation is a common occurrence in the music-hall, but this must be its début in opera. It succeeds, as it always does, in breaking down the barrier between the two sides of the footlights. Norman Del Mar's charm and skill in conducting and rehearsing the audience have been rightly praised as an important factor in the success of the opera.

Of the grown-ups, Norman Lumsden gives a fruity display of natural comic acting as the rascally sweep. Anne Sharp, a young member of the Group, shows great talent and a most pleasing voice as Juliet. The children, drawn from schools in Ipswich, are all competent and accurate; and that stated, it goes without saying that they are all quite enchanting to see and hear.

The sets by John Lewis are colourful, the dresses no more than adequate, and the production, by Basil Coleman, well contrived. Since the technical difficulties are so simple, if I may be permitted to lapse into Irish, this opera can, and I hope will, penetrate into every town and village in these isles that has a hall and some children.

The music explores a vein of simple charm, and aubade-like tenderness that is at once endearing and captivating. Like each new work by Benjamin Britten, it is unmistakeably his, yet is unlike anything else he has written. This opera may prove to be a landmark in his career, for even he, with all his well-known skill, moving simplicity, and increasing maturity, has never achieved before such beauty with such economy.

Juliet's little song, 'Soon the coach will carry you away', will serve to illustrate this maturity. It is scored for voice, violin, and piano and, later on, 'cello; a little song which can only be described as having the stamp of lyric greatness, for I cannot conceive that Schubert or Schumann would be ashamed to acknowledge having composed such an exquisite morsel.

There is great skilfulness in the writing of the children's vocal lines, for they have real parts in the ensembles and they are given their notes by the orchestra in a variety of subtle ways.

Britten is famous for his 'passing-the-time-of-day' phrases; think of the number of 'good-mornings' and 'good-nights' in *Grimes*,

Herring and *Lucretia*, but the vernal quality of the children's greetings to Sammy of 'morning' may beat the lot in public estimation.

As with the other Britten chamber operas, the loss of chorus or full orchestra is never felt; the music is truly for the chosen medium and is genuine 'chamber music'.

Though this is a children's opera, and the children at Cheltenham loved it, there can be few grown-ups too sophisticated to enjoy it. And, of course, being Britten, there is plenty for the music student to wonder at.

The audience, for example, has four verses to sing of the opening chorus. The notes are the same throughout, but the accompaniment is in a different key in each verse. The device keeps the song fresh, but I doubt if one in a hundred would notice it; and if you pointed it out they would probably accuse you of being a music critic.

COUNTER-TENOR:
Alfred Deller's Recital   2.10.49

Last week's recital at the Cowdray Hall was chiefly notable for the part played in it by Alfred Deller, the counter-tenor. There is nothing new about the counter-tenor voice, it has been used for centuries in cathedral choirs to sing the alto parts. But until the recent advent of Mr Deller, the voice has not been heard solo for many, many years, because there has been no voice of sufficient quality to be suffered to sing alone.

The word 'suffer' can be used in its other sense in connection with an untrained counter-tenor, as any who have had the misfortune to hear one in action can testify; it is a fruity, warbling noise, reminding one of how 'the voice of the turtle' might sound.

Henry Purcell himself was a skilled counter-tenor. A journal of his time, describing the first performance of one of his Odes to St Cecilia, tells how Mr Purcell sang the solo alto part 'with incredible airs and graces'. But many listeners, including famous musicians, have been slightly taken aback at their first encounter with this voice.

The counter-tenor is, in fact, produced by a species of falsetto. Its inclusion in performances is necessary to give the requisite tone-colour in works by composers like Handel and Purcell in which the voice is indicated.

At the recital, Alfred Deller was heard first of all in songs by John Dowland intended to be sung with lute accompaniment. The lute part was most satisfactorily realised on the guitar by Desmond Dupré. Mr Deller's *tessitura* is of an unusually sweet tone, and his dexterity in moving his voice, his innate sense of style and musicianship make him a singer of rare quality.

Such things as the singing of 'Flow not so fast ye fountains' and the pathos of the last phrase of 'In darkness let me dwell' will not soon be forgotten by those present. We were returned to earth with an enchanting ditty by Morley which begins 'Will ye buy a fine dog with a hole in his head?'

A second group of songs with tasteful harpsichord accompaniment by Walter Bergmann was devoted to Purcell: two songs from *The Fairy Queen*: 'Not all my Torments' and 'Sweeter than Roses'. The singer showed himself capable of appreciating all the 'British Orpheus' melisma and coloratura, and he was able 'to move the heart and excite the passions'.

The concert ended with the first performance of *Three Sixteenth-Century Poems* set for counter-tenor, flute, and guitar by Wilfrid Mellers. They are settings of poems by Strode, Nashe and Skelton. Expertly written for this unusual combination, the songs are attractive and will, I have no doubt, continue to attract so long as Alfred Deller sings; and perhaps longer, for I expect other singers will have the sense to try them.

HS: It now seems that Purcell did *not* sing counter-tenor; the text about him singing 'with incredible airs and graces' was apparently misconstrued. Too bad. Deller's voice had a unique character and sound. There have been some fine subsequent singers using this voice but none has quite equalled Alfred Deller.

BORIS GODUNOV AND BORIS CHRISTOFF: Covent Garden Production   21.11.49

Boris Christoff made his début at Covent Garden on Saturday night in the title role of Mussorgsky's *Boris Godunov*.

There was much debate amongst the elders in the foyer about his being a second Chaliapin. Be that as it may, and granted his voice is exceedingly like the great Feodor's in many ways, the young ones, unfortunate in not having heard Chaliapin in the flesh, will think of the newcomer, rightly, as the first Christoff.

First of all, Christoff possesses a true Russian bass voice capable of sustaining a powerful *legato* as well as a telling *sotto voce*. Secondly, he is an able musician. Thirdly he is a very fine actor, not only visually but, *mirabile dictu*, vocally.

How touchingly Boris laid tender hands on his little son and the fair Xenia! How dramatically he suggested the catalepsy of the Tsar. It was a remarkable and unforgettable performance that made Mussorgsky's score live vividly.

For the rest, Peter Brook's production is little changed from last year. The hallucinations in the clock scene are now rightly left to the imagination. Marina's swing in the Polish scene has gone, but I am glad to say that the horse is retained in the final scene. In fact, one severe critic in the audience, a boy aged ten, remarked after the opera, 'Well, I liked the horse.'

Under Warwick Braithwaite's direction the orchestra played well and the chorus was superb. In some of the Tsar's scenes, the Rimsky-Korsakov version was spatchcocked into the original Mussorgsky scoring.

HS: I went to the Savoy Hotel with my tape-recorder to interview Boris Christoff (1914-93), waited until exactly the hour agreed and asked the desk porter to ring him. The phone was handed to me while the number was ringing. A sepulchral voice answered: 'Am reposing, is coming later.' Eventually the interview took place. He told me how he trained as a lawyer then (he said!) he was in the Bulgarian cavalry; the King of Bulgaria heard him in a concert, was smitten and awarded him money so that he could study in Rome. There he met his future wife, who happened to be the sister of Tito Gobbi. Christoff told me that the number of operatic performances he had seen in his whole life could be counted on his fingers 'and some of those,' he said expiatingly, 'were because my brother-in-law sang in them.' At length the brothers-in-law had a quarrel which lasted some years and this gave a special intensity to some of their duets together, especially ones when they were supposed in the opera to be at odds with one another, such as their duet in Verdi's *Don Carlo*, Christoff the King, Gobbi Posa.

King Philip was one of his two most celebrated roles, the other was Boris Godunov in Mussorgsky's pageant-opera. This last gave him wonderful opportunities which he seized equally wonderfully and the performance continued after the music stopped. His curtain calls were legendary: at first he played being still in the role but gradually Boris or Philip merged into a smiling Christoff. And in case the Covent Garden linkmen might bring the curtains to before he had done all the audience milking he wanted, he would plant one foot on the prompter's box. Nobody did it better: more sincerely yes, but as an extra performance, no. He was a good actor in his roles, his voice was a full, individual one, dark brown with an edge to it, to match the latent menace in the tone.

He was an excellent recitalist too, exploring the Russian repertoire. Chaliapin was his role model but, on records (as it has to be) old Feodor had a better voice; but Christoff was certainly one of the great singers of his day. He took the stage and filled it.

A MOZART MEETING:
Der Schauspieldirektor 23.11.49

The Kalmar orchestra gave a Mozart concert at Crosby Hall, Chelsea, on Monday evening, starting at the late hour of nine o'clock. But it was more than a concert. It was like a musical party, and, moreover, one that Mozart himself would have loved to attend.

The Crosby Hall is a very old hall (moved from the City in 1926-7) that holds about 200 people, and is high enough to have a wooden musicians' gallery. From this gallery the evening's music started. It was the Serenade in E flat, K.375, for a pair each of clarinets, oboes, bassoons and horns, a rough performance.

Then the social side of the evening started – food, drink, smoke, and conversation. In the midst of this a cheerful and comic Trio lasting two minutes was sung, followed later by an excellent performance of the Serenata Notturna, K.239, for two string orchestras, led by Norbert Brainin. After more cakes and ale, the evening ended with a concert performance of *Der Schauspieldirektor*, a one-act comedy, K.486, written while Mozart was completing

Figaro. It consists of a brilliant overture in the master's purest buffo style, two arias to show off the voices of two rival prima donnas, a trio in which the unfortunate impresario tries to placate the two ladies, and a final 'vaudeville'.

The music is delicious Mozart of a good vintage. A skilfully written narration helped us to follow the course of the comedy, which was sung in German. The parts of the two prima donnas are exacting in extreme range and are for this reason well nigh impossible except with freak voices.

Both Inge Markovitz and April Cantelo came near to achieving the impossible, and impressed as being two young singers with style, taste and fine voices.

An excellent clarinettist, Colin Davis, who played in the Wind Serenade, took charge of the orchestra in this opera and made a very good job of it.

HS: When I first met Colin Davis (b.1927) he was trying to make his way as a professional clarinettist in London. He was helped, at that time, with an orchestra partly pros, partly amateurs, named after an oboeist called Peter Kalmar, whose girl friend was a violinist called June Hardy. She had started this little band after her friend's far too early death. June lived in a barn-like place off Holland Park Avenue where she had musical parties; this abode could comfortably seat about forty people. The first one I went to contained about sixty or seventy and we sloshed through Bach's *St Matthew Passion*, chorus, soloists and orchestra; I was a tenor in the chorus and I recall that we tenors sprawled in an upper bunk of a wooden bed. It was fun and uplifting at the same time. Here it was that I first met Colin Davis, also his friend, critic and Berlioz biographer David Cairns. There were also chamber music evenings; I recall Schubert's Octet and other works. Colin played chamber music well although he never made a success in the big symphony orchestras. I was living at that time in Hampstead Garden Suburb as a lodger in the house of a widow of a composer named William Busch. Occasionally we too had chamber music parties in a roof studio and I asked Colin if he would play the Mozart Quintet with a group of chaps I knew who eventually became a professional quartet with the name of Amadeus. Colin played most beautifully that evening.

The Summer School of Music started round about this time (1948) and the next year I persuaded William Glock that we should invite the Kalmar down to Bryanston to do some concerts conducted by Roger Désormières. Colin had by now shown signs of wanting to conduct and in my mind's eye I can see (aided by a photograph) the Kalmars rehearsing *al fresco* with Colin having a go at Stravinsky's *Dumbarton Oaks* Concerto. This was almost his first paid job as a conductor.

He had a girl friend, a lovely girl called April Cantelo, a soprano who joined Alfred Deller's Consort of Singers. She soon joined Colin as his wife and they had two children. A bit later they had a Persian au-pair girl whom Colin eventually married, and with whom he had a host of children. With this second marriage Colin withdrew from his previous circle of friends. His life changed, he had a big chance to conduct *Don Giovanni* when Klemperer was ill. By that time he had also frequently conducted the Chelsea Opera Group in many operas (including Mozart's *Zaide* in which I sang the solo tenor part. I wasn't good enough but Colin was, and, as they in the penultimate chapter of detective stories, 'the rest you know' – about him, that is). He is now, of course, Sir Colin Davis and musical director and chief conductor of the London Symphony Orchestra.

MORLEY COLLEGE CONCERT:
Gieseking and The Royal Philharmonic Orchestra   6.2.50

The Morley College Concert Society provided a three-hour feast on Wednesday night in the Central Hall. The artists were Walter Gieseking, the Royal Philharmonic Orchestra, and the Morley College Choir, conducted by Walter Goehr.

The programme was over long, but it provided some fascinating contrasts in style and period. There were five works: the outer choral shell was Italian, firstly Monteverdi's *Sonata Sopra Sancta Maria*, and finally excerpts from Verdi's *Quattro Pezzi Sacri*; the inner shell was two piano concertos, Mozart's in C major, K.467, and Beethoven's in G major, No. 4, Op. 58; whilst the nut, which required a good deal of chewing, was Michael Tippett's Symphony.

In spite of everything, I think that most of the audience would agree with me that the feature of this concert we shall remember

25

longest was the most familiar work in the programme, because of Gieseking's superlative playing. His performance of the Mozart Concerto was only a little less wonderful.

Faulty balancing and choral flatness marred the performance of Walter Goehr's new edition of the Sonata taken from the Vespers of 1610.

The difficult acoustic of the hall may have been responsible for both defects; when singing or playing in this hall it is sometimes impossible to hear what is going on fifteen or twenty yards away.

The Verdi items were the unaccompanied Ave Maria and the Te Deum for chorus and orchestra, written when the composer was eighty-five years of age.

It is a commonplace of music criticism to say that the *Quattro Pezzi* are inspired by Verdi's life-long devotion to Palestrina. However, I always find the Ave Maria, with its stunning harmonic modulations, more in the spirit of Gesualdo. The Te Deum provided a suitably gorgeous finish to the concert.

Michael Tippett has provided a helpful set of hieroglyphs for the four movements of his Symphony [No. 1]; for the opening *allegro*, an arrow, to denote forward impulse; for the slow movement devised on a ground bass, a circle, the music turning in on itself; for the hocquet-like scherzo, a star; for the fugal finale, a question mark.

The performance under Walter Goehr's direction was the best of his that I have heard. But even so, the work failed to come off, maybe it never will come off.

Why? Because it is difficult to play and to listen to; sometimes for the same reason, that pure counterpoint is not suited to the medium of the full orchestra. It takes a genius of orchestration to bring it off; which I submit, Tippett is not.

The Symphony, part failure though it is, is an important work that should be widely heard and studied. Its form is masterly, and there are some passages of unforgettable beauty in it.

HS: Walter Gieseking (1895-1956) was just about the best pianist for Debussy that the world has ever heard. He was good too in Ravel, Beethoven and Brahms. He was a fabled sight-reader, is known to have made recordings *sight-reading*. He was German and known to be a Nazi supporter.

COVENT GARDEN, OTELLO:
La Scala Opera Season   13.9.50

After concerts by the chorus and orchestra of La Scala, Milan, at the Edinburgh Festival, the entire company, including technicians, has assembled for a two weeks season in London at Covent Garden Opera House.

The season will consist of two Verdi operas, *Otello* and *Falstaff* and Donizetti's *L'Elisir d'Amore*, with choral and orchestral concerts of works already heard at Edinburgh.

The season opened on Tuesday night with *Otello* and scarcely ever can operatic expectations have run so high in post-war years.

Orchestrally we were not let down. The very first chord nearly raised the roof; it was an orchestral chord with an attack and full-toned volume that has not been heard at Covent Garden since the Vienna Philharmonic Orchestra played for performances of Strauss's *Salome*. Orchestrally, the evening was one of splendour.

The first performance of *Otello* was at La Scala sixty-three years ago and the orchestra plays this work as if it owns it. Victor de Sabata is one of the world's supreme bandmasters and every note was in the right place with perfect balance and length – with the possible exception of the last two chords of the opera. But the sounds were not only correct, they were exciting and thrilling; brilliant fiddle passages, the divided cellos in the first act love duet, trumpets playing quick chromatic runs, brass chords; all these things will become vivid memories.

The chorus work, too, was very fine and the highest praise is due to its members. If praise for the choir takes up less space than praise for the orchestra, that is because we are used to good chorus work at Covent Garden from our own resident body.

So far performance had equalled expectation; but thus far only. The chief reason for disappointment was the quality of the solo singers.

The role of Otello is one of the most exacting that a dramatic tenor can essay. Ramon Vinay, who took the part on Tuesday night, is a lyric tenor with a pleasing voice, especially in its lower register. At all times he sang in tune and musically. Scarcely ever did he suggest, vocally or dramatically, the dominating character that Verdi has portrayed so powerfully.

Gino Bechi's Iago was downright second-rate.

Of the three principal roles, the Desdemona of Renata Tebaldi was far the most convincing as regards fulfilling Verdi's vocal and musical requirements. But pathos was completely lacking from her histrionic gamut in the last act.

The production was fair enough though by no means outstanding, the acting poor, the costumes goodish but inclining towards the vulgarity of the sets.

The extraordinary emotional, pathetic, and grand qualities of Verdi's masterpiece were by no means fully realised, and the solo singers, the production, and the conductor must all take their measure of blame.

HS: I was particularly saddened by Gino Bechi because on records he was, and remains, one of my favourite singers. He could act with the voice, had a wonderful sense of line and could portray evil as no other, not even Tito Gobbi. His records of Iago and Anckarstroem (in *Ballo*) are unequalled, likewise his Gérard in *Andréa Chénier*. But at Covent Garden he was a shadow of his former excellent self. The performances by La Scala company got almost universally adverse reviews. Constant Lambert was so incensed by this that he wrote a letter to *The Times* saying that the critics were a bunch of elderly die-hards, suggesting that after the performance they sat at their desks over which there was a big sign written in gothic script saying 'above all, no enthusiasm'.

DER ROSENKAVALIER:
Erich Kleiber at Covent Garden   9.12.50

Erich Kleiber conducted Richard Strauss's *Der Rosenkavalier* on Wednesday night at Covent Garden. Dr Kleiber has been engaged as guest conductor for the next three months, during which he will also direct performances of *The Magic Flute, Carmen, Rigoletto,* and *Pique Dame.*

It is difficult not to believe that the performance on Wednesday night was the beginning of a new epoch. For, under a great operatic conductor, it seems that the Covent Garden company and orchestra can give a truly first-rate performance. On Wednesday night only

Uta Graf, the Sophie, was not a Britisher and a member of the Covent Garden Company.

The performance was not perfect but it was not far off; the orchestral playing was extremely good. Apart from a few tiny 'fluffs', the playing was virtuosic and the clarity of texture exemplary. The string tone was golden, luxuriant, and noble. The full-blown double forte was a splendid assault on the ear, but the singers were never drowned. The whole performance was superbly shaped and the climaxes were unfailingly right.

Sylvia Fisher's Marschallin improves every time – a most moving and distinguished performance. Constance Shacklock's Octavian would be even better if she eliminated the occasional wobble in her voice. Howell Glynne is vocally satisfactory, though his Ochs is not dramatically correct. Uta Graf came into her own in the trio, where her voice blended admirably.

HS: I wrote to Erich Kleiber in 1950 while he was directing eye-opening and heart melting performances of *Rosenkavalier* at Covent Garden. Soonish after the war it was for many of us the first intimation of what string sound should really be. Beecham always favoured a rather thin though not under-nourished sound. Barbirolli could sometimes produce a creamier sound but Kleiber gave us the true article. My letter to Kleiber asked if he would take a conducting class at Bryanston Summer School. He sent a message that I should come to see him in his conductor's room during the break of a rehearsal at the Royal Opera House. The great little man, bald-headed, looked like a Swiss banker in his respectable suit, only the eyes promised more than a business executive, opened the door for me and sat me down opposite him. 'Mr Amis, thank you for asking me and for coming to see me. Conducting…now I learned in the first place from Nikisch,' (here he made a gesture of a beat of a span of seven or eight inches) 'then I was influenced by the conducting of Richard Strauss,' (here another movement of the right arm, about three or four inches) 'and finally,' (pressing his right thumb hard down on the table) 'from Toscanini I learned the WILL. Now you will understand that cannot be taught to young conductors. Goodbye, Mr Amis.'

The orchestral manager and former trombonist at the Garden

29

told me over tea and chicken, his favourite meal, that the day Kleiber had arrived, he, Maurice Smith, had shown him his room and how to get to the orchestral pit. Rather nervous of the great man Maurice said several times, 'I hope there won't be any trouble, Dr Kleiber.' After the third time Kleiber interrupted him: 'Look here, Mr Smith, if there is no trouble, I make it.'

And he did too. The conductor always took the part of the artists against the management. David Webster, who was the management, said no, the auditorium could not be heated for rehearsals. 'All right,' said Kleiber, 'musicians must not be treated like that; no heating, no rehearsal.' The heating was turned on. Like Beecham, Kleiber treated his singers and players as responsible equals. He also worked very hard and unsparingly to coax good performances from the company. Not as wonderful maybe as some singers from outside would have been, but good, even very good. Some of the locals achieved things that were scarcely recognizable either to themselves or the public. *Carmen, Elektra, Rigoletto, Tristan, Queen of Spades* and, above all, his electrifying *Wozzeck*. Finally he couldn't stomach David Webster any more so he quit Covent Garden for ever in 1953. He died three years later (in his bath).

TIRESIAS:
New Constant Lambert Ballet 12.7.51

The Festival gala performance at the Royal Opera House, Covent Garden, last night, in the presence of Her Majesty the Queen in aid of the Sadler's Wells Ballet Benevolent Fund, included a new ballet, *Tiresias*, danced by the resident company.

The scenario and music are by Constant Lambert, the scenery and costumes by his wife Isabel, with choreography by Frederick Ashton.

The ballet follows the story of Tiresias – 'In Crete, there lies the scene' – who was privileged to be turned from man to woman and back again. Zeus and Hera, each saying that the other sex was happier, called upon Tiresias for a decision. For saying that he preferred his life as a woman Tiresias was struck blind by the angry god. By way of compensation Hera gave Tiresias the gift of second sight.

The ballet is divided into three long scenes which together take fifty minutes to play.

The action is neither entertaining nor morally uplifting. On the contrary, it is enervating and decadent, glorying in the more unpleasant side of physical intercourse. Mr Ashton has played with this theme before, in *Les Illuminations*, and this time he has explored it further. The choreographic invention has faded in the attempt. Apart from a scarf dance for Margot Fonteyn, there is little to recommend in the gymnastics and physical writhings. Tiresias the man is athletically played by Michael Soames. Tiresias the woman is Margot Fonteyn, sympathetic and beautiful as ever. Some of the corps de ballet seemed a little ragged. The décor hovers between pre-civilisation and 1951; the mountain backcloth was certainly effective.

Perhaps the saddest aspect of the new ballet was the score, a sorry rehash of the same elements that have made up so many of Constant Lambert's previous works. The faded jazz chords and off-beat rhythms of the '20s together with the angular harmonies and ugly counterpoint of the '30s, mixed with some parallel sevenths that once served Stravinsky well; Lambert dispenses with violins and violas, and tries to make up for their loss with a solo piano and his old love, the cow bell.

There seems no doubt that Lambert is going through an unfortunate phase in his career as a composer. Here's to his complete recovery.

HS: Alas, it did not happen, there wasn't time; and we critics were accused by Sir Osbert Sitwell of having hastened Lambert's untimely death a few months later on 21 August. He may well have been right although I think we all liked Lambert personally, admired many things he had achieved, and wished him well, but of course we had to say what we thought of his latest work.

I gather that it was a tremendous struggle to meet the deadline and several of his friends were called in to help with the orchestration, among them Elisabeth Lutyens, Alan Rawsthorne, Denis ApIvor, Gordon Jacob, Humphrey Searle and Robert Irving. Everything was done under Lambert's supervision.

Constant Lambert (1905-51) was composer, conductor, pianist, music critic and the author of one of the most witty and penetrating books, sometimes right-headed but always provocative, called *Music Ho!* His *Rio Grande* is one of the little masterpieces of the twentieth century, a capsule of the '20s with a spicy mix of jazz as fermented by a 'straight' musician. The trouble was Lambert never managed to come up with anything as good, despite several ballet scores and an impressive choral Elizabethan *Summer's Last Will and Testament.* Somehow it all sounded the same, except when he aped other composers, as he did Stravinsky in his last ballet *Tiresias.* He could conduct brilliantly, mostly off-beat repertoire and certainly not classics like Brahms (whom he accused of composing, not from the piano, but from the double-bass). He boozed himself out of his job as music director of Sadler's Wells Ballet where over a long period his advice had been of inestimable value, not least because his knowledge was not confined to music but ranged over the visual arts, literature and drama.

HOROWITZ AT ROYAL FESTIVAL HALL: 10.10.51

Horowitz has returned to London for the first time since before the war. He is to play two recitals following his only concerto appearance last Monday night, all three events taking place in the Royal Festival Hall. The concerto chosen was Rachmaninov's Third in D minor, in which Horowitz made his London debut and his concerto-recording debut.

Horowitz's many admirers were there on Monday night to be thrilled afresh at his fantastic technique, and his firm, unsentimental control of the music. It was in the *scherzando* section of the finale that his playing was most breath-taking. His fingers, so long that he plays the black notes right up at the wood, seemed to be made of steel and, for all his delicacy, it must be admitted that his tone sounded metallic.

He played some parts of the concerto that the composer himself cut in performance and made some changes in tempo foreign to the composer's intentions.

Walter Süsskind accompanied the soloist well, but the London Philharmonic Orchestra's playing was something less than adequate to the occasion.

HS: Rachmaninov suffered from king-sized depressions and, amazingly enough, was not confident of his ability as a pianist. When he heard the young Horowitz play his Third Concerto, he more or less gave up playing the work himself. But the recordings show that he was superior to Horowitz in musicianship and equal in virtuosity even if the younger man sometimes had the edge in sheer dazzle, if not in general, then in some parts of the D minor Concerto. Rachmaninov's repertoire was not large though; he went on year after year playing the same pieces. But how!

Vladimir Horowitz (1904-1989) is often mentioned as the greatest pianist of the twentieth century together with the name of Rachmaninov. He was Russian born and trained, but went to America in 1928 and stayed there, marrying Toscanini's daughter, Wanda. As far as technical matters are concerned he was the tops until his old age; he could make magic with his Scarlatti, Schumann, Liszt and many other composers. Unfortunately there were lengthy periods lasting many years when he did not play.

DIDO AND AENEAS WITH FLAGSTAD: 12.10.51

No 43a Acacia Road, St. John's Wood, London, is the address not only of Bernard Miles, the actor, but also of the Mermaid Theatre which he and his friends have built in the garden. The theatre is a small one, and the stage occupies exactly half its space. It is based on the idea of an Elizabethan stage, a large tiring house that resembles a cabinet with many openings and doors.

A season has just finished which included performances of Shakespeare's *The Tempest* and Purcell's *Dido and Aeneas*.

Bernard Miles himself produced *Dido*, and his production was typical of the whole project: informed, practical, enthusiastic, performed with love and devotion yet without any hint of preciousness. We have seen three *Dido* productions this summer in London and this intimate Mermaid one is surely nearer to the spirit of the music than either that of Sadler's Wells or the English Opera Group.

Dido was played by Kirsten Flagstad, a performance of great distinction and dignity. If not quite what the Purcell scholars would whole-heartedly approve, at least a singer who can utter her 'Remember me' on a top G without fear of strain.

Aeneas was played by Thomas Hemsley, a good young singer of great promise and good appearance. Edith Coates found the Sorceress a part that might have been written for her. She grimaced, cavorted, and was a general picture of malignity; disdaining the masks her witches wore, she easily outstripped their horrors.

The performance was directed by Geraint Jones from a harpsichord. He and the orchestra were placed in a gallery above the actors and the ensemble was effected by mirrors on the backwall of the auditorium.

The whole atmosphere of the Mermaid is so delightful and serious (in the right way) that we look forward to *The Indian Queen* that Mr Miles has promised us next year. In the more distant future Mr Miles promises a three-hour version of Wagner's *Ring*.

HS: Bernard Miles (1907-91), character actor, theatre manager extraordinary and sometime stand-up comedian; in the latter capacity he had the less than endearing habit of growling when he thought he had earned a laugh. Did excellent skits about a plumber seeing *Hamlet* and *Tristan and Isolde* and retelling the plots. He enticed his friend Kirsten Flagstad into singing the role of Dido, the contract stipulating a daily supply of Guinness and the right of the Miles family to examine her larynx at will. Later Miles built and ran the Mermaid Theatre in Blackfriars. Bernard never gave us his abridged *Ring* but others did.

Kirsten Flagstad (1895-1962) had a voice that could only have come from the far frozen north; it had its own kind of warmth, like the sun in a perfect blue sky shining on an expanse of snow and ice. She was in her late thirties before she emerged as a great Wagnerian soprano, the perfect voice for Isolde, Kundry, Brünnhilde and Leonora. She was not a great actress but her simplicity in deportment and her sincerity were enough to complement the beauty of her voice, so that she was a compelling presence on stage. In recital she was totally convincing in the songs of Grieg and Sibelius.

She conquered Europe and America although the latter country was not sympathetic because her husband was accused of being a Quisling during the '39-'45 war. After giving the first performance of Richard Strauss's *Four Last Songs*, and retiring from singing in 1953 she directed the Norwegian State Opera 1958-60. Earlier she was known to be temperamental and 'difficult' but in later life she was a gentle, retiring and modest person. On long inter-continental sea voyages she disliked being overheard exercising her voice so she opened her porthole and sang to the seals and the whales. She emerged from retirement to sing the part of Fricka in the Decca/Culshaw/Solti *Ring*.

PLAYS AND MUSIC AT LYONS:
The Times 23.7.52

Open-air performances were the main attraction of the twenty-day festival of music and drama which has just ended at Lyons and its suburb Charbonnières. The oldest part of Lyons is at the foot and the side of the hill called Fourvière. Here the two Roman theatres have been excavated and both of them pressed into service for the festival. The smaller of the two, the Odéon, has seats for 2,000 persons and was officially opened for some Bach concerts given by the Stuttgart Chamber Orchestra.

These concerts given in the evenings included two complete performances of those works which the French call, so delightfully, 'les concertos Brandenbougeois'. The acoustics of both theatres are perfect, and though Bach is not usually associated with concerts *en plein air* the time passed in perfect peace in the comparative cool of Lyons nights in late June. There were few aircraft and only an occasional high D minor triad – D minor being the key all whistling trains seem to favour in this part of France. Mr Karl Münchinger, conductor of the Stuttgart band, is your true Bachian, and his soloists served him faithfully. The new leader of the orchestra, Mr Werner Krotzinger, is young but promises great things. All the soloists in the concerts were German with the exception of M. Vaillant, the brilliant solo trumpeter of the French National Orchestra.

The larger Roman theatre seats more than 5,000 people and here Molière's *Amphitrion* was performed and *Le Martyre de Saint Sébastien*. The latter, a *mystère* by D'Annunzio with music by Debussy, gains from the apparent lack of theatricality consequent on a performance out of doors. Mme. Véra Korène not only played the principal role of the Saint, created for Ida Rubinstein, but was responsible for production and adaptation of the text: she did not prune, she positively lopped D'Annunzio's flowery play to sensible proportions. She is an actress of considerable stature, both histrionically and physically, and her speaking voice has the beauty and control that we associate with great French acting.

As producer, Mme. Korène used her resources magnificently. Actors and chorus numbering 350 were deployed over a vast area consisting of half the arena, a built-up stage running the length of the diameter of the semi-circular theatre. Underneath the stage was an orchestra of ninety players, and beyond it stretched terraced floodlit gardens backed in the distance by trees. And so when the Messenger, at the beginning, ran through in silence from the trees at the back to the first rows of the audience, the distance was well over 100 yards. Barnard Daydé's *décor* was richly imaginative; the final music, Psalm 150, was sung as Sébastien mounts to a Paradise, where white-robed angels moved among the trees, resembling one of the heavenly scenes painted by Puvis de Chavannes.

Debussy's music made the experience unforgettable. In the concert hall, music of it, though exquisite in detail, can sound dramatically aimless and even a little precious. With the stage action the work revealed itself as a masterpiece. The musical direction was in the eminently capable hands of M. André Cluytens with Mmes. Janine Micheau and Hélène Bouvier as soloists; chorus and orchestra were local.

Just as D'Annunzio's text was sacrificed for the sake of Debussy's music, so the Italian poet's contemporary, Charles Péguy, had his poetic drama *Jeanne d'Arc* cut in order to make a framework for a spectacle. It was enacted in front of the west door of St. John's Cathedral. The spectacle was of a simple character, impressive and dignified.

Charbonnières, with its casino and beautiful gardens and park, seven miles outside Lyons, provided the setting for a number of attractions of a lighter kind, such as Les Petits Chanteurs de la Croix and the ballet company of Janine Charrat.

RIGOLETTO:
19.12.52

A revival at Covent Garden of Verdi's *Rigoletto* on Tuesday night in the presence of the Queen Mother, brought back former members of the company in Paolo Silveri and Walter Midgley. Silveri has gained in stature since he was last with us and his performance as the old jester showed us that his voice is as fine and rich as ever, while his musicianship and dramatic sense have improved enormously. And as he was already one of the best operatic baritones in the world when he came before, you may imagine the high quality of his performance on Tuesday.

It would be wrong to say that Walter Midgley had improved; he remains imperturbably Walter Midgley: capable with his mellifluous, high, lyrical tenor of getting round Verdi's notes with such ease – other tenors have difficulty – that he has time to add a few notes of Midgley here and there. Representing the Duke of Mantua, he certainly suggested a conceited, brash individual, with no real thought but for himself. As for coming from aristocratic stock, Mr Midgley was as noble as the late Sid Field's impersonation of a barrow boy playing King John. But Mr Midgley often sang extremely well, notably in 'Parmi veder le lagrime' at the beginning of act two.

Ilse Hollweg's Gilda, as last year, is a difficult case, musically excellent, vocally sometimes wonderful, sometimes weak, dramatically not very effective; it could be really good but it has not been so. She is at her best in the ensembles, and the duet between her and Rigoletto in the Duke's palace was the highlight of the evening.

John Pritchard's musical direction of *Rigoletto* was more satisfactory than that of any other conductor we have had at the Royal Opera House except Kleiber. Occasionally the orchestra rose to great heights; the furious accompaniment to 'Cortigiani, vil razza dannata', where Rigoletto lashes at the courtiers who will not tell him where his daughter Gilda has been taken, was furious, clear, and yet, *mirabile dictu*, not too loud for the singer.

HS: Midgley was a good lyric tenor, although his tone was his alone and some people hated it. Imitations of him (mine included) always began with a high-pitched whine but somehow it was a mellifluous whine; he was skilled and he phrased well. He was a gor-blimey sort of chap, always quarrelling with conductors and arguing the toss with the management about attendance at rehearsals and which dressing room he had. Still he had his public, including me. So we looked forward to the evening. He started off well with his first number 'Questo é quello'. But when he took a deep breath for his top note at the end, his gauze moustache came unstuck and went down his gullet. End of aria and jolly nearly end of poor old Midgley. Curtain down while he recovered.

I wish I'd seen that performance when Otakar Kraus hoisted Joan Sutherland over his shoulder and the action caused Joanie to break wind downwards con ultima forza. During the subsequent hush an unmistakeable Ozzie voice was clearly heard: 'Sorry, Otto.'

Otakar (fine artist, wonderful singing actor, great stage presence) went on one night as Anklesocks, sorry Anckarstroem, in *Ballo in Maschera* without his contact lenses. In the scene where the conspirators Tom and Ribbing come into Anklestrap's study by a secret door for the who-shall-kill-the-king work-out Otakar was baffled by the door which was so secret because it was in this production painted the same as the neighbouring walls. Without his lenses Otto just could not see the door handle despite encouraging instructions from Mike Langdon and his mate from the other wide of the closed door. 'Bit to your left, Otto. Now up a bit to your right. Hard down six inches.'

It was all to no avail so eventually Tom and Ribbing gave up the door and barged through the fire-place, otherwise they would have missed their cue.

KATHLEEN FERRIER IN ORPHEUS: 7.2.53

It is said that Gluck's *Orpheus* has been mounted anew at Covent Garden so that we might see Kathleen Ferrier in the title rôle. If this is so it showed great wisdom, for Miss Ferrier and Gluck's hero are well suited to each other, as those who attended the Glyndebourne production of 1947 will remember.

On Tuesday night at her first Royal Opera House performance in the part she brought again her warm voice, dignified utterance, radiant looks, and presence. It was a nobly moving performance. Nobility, indeed, is the key to this music, but alas, nobility was present only when Kathleen Ferrier was.

Frederick Ashton was both producer and choreographer. The production was more classical than realistic. The choreography completely missed the point of the music. The heavenly serenity of the Elysian D minor flute solo was shattered by the distracting bobbing about of the otherwise delectable ballerina, Svetlana Beriosova.

The sets and costumes were designed by the late and much lamented Sophie Fedorovitch, who died last week. She was a fine theatre artist and will be remembered for better work than this, which she did not have an opportunity of revising or touching up.

Veronica Dunne made a more favourable impression as Euridice than she had previously as Mimi without rousing much feeling one way or the other. Adèle Leigh sang sweetly and made a delightfully chubby Cupid.

HS: Kathleen Ferrier (1912-53) was perhaps the last of the true contraltos and one of the best. Her career lasted scarcely more than a decade before being struck down by cancer. That early death, her winning looks and the simple sincerity of her character turned her image into an icon, almost as beloved as Jacqueline du Pré or Princess Diana. From being a telephone operator in her native Lancashire she became famous on the concert platform in works like Elgar's *Dream of Gerontius* and Mahler's *Das Lied von der Erde,* and in the stage title-role of Britten's *Rape of Lucretia* and Gluck's *Orfeo.*

Benjamin Britten, Barbirolli and Bruno Walter loved working with her and their recordings together perpetuate that love. As a person she was a simple Lancashire girl at heart and that was partly why she won hearts with her singing which had a touching nobility and, of course, a truly beautiful voice.

My wife and I went to see her in hospital. We knew she was dying and wondered how on earth we could console her or cheer her up. We need not have worried; she cheered us up in a quite wonderful and uplifting way.

39

ELGAR'S CELLO CONCERTO WITH TORTELIER: 13.3.53

The BBC concert on Wednesday night was predominantly a British programme. Sir Malcolm Sargent was in good fettle with the corporation's orchestra in Strauss's *Don Juan* tone-poem.

Tortelier was the soloist in Elgar's Cello Concerto and a remarkably fine one. About six notes were marred by doubtful intonation but these notes only stood out by contrast in an otherwise impeccable performance. His tone was pure and noble, while his technique was formidable to deal with the many difficulties.

It is a commonplace of criticism here to pooh-pooh any foreigner's performance of any native idiomatic work, but it would be pure bias not to accept Tortelier's interpretation. He had the advantage of coming to the work without any preconceived ideas; so that his reading was pleasantly free from sentimentality or the undue lingering which mars so many performances of this beautiful, intimate work. Sir Malcolm's accompaniment was a joy to hear.

The chief item in the programme was Vaughan Williams's *Sinfonia Antartica*. Surely our love and respect for the great man would not be in question if a little discrimination is shown about his compositions? It seems to insult *Flos Campi*, *Job*, the *Tallis Fantasia*, *Riders to the Sea*, the F minor Symphony, and his other masterpieces not to say that this work is rather an unsatisfactory suite of film-music unworthy to be catalogued among his symphonies.

HS: Paul told me that he played the Elgar as early in its life as eleven years old when he was only sixteen years into his life. It was 1930 and he won a competition for it in France – must have quite shaken up les grenouilles. Paul said he chose the Elgar partly because the flashing semiquavers in the scherzo showed up his bowing technique favourably.

Paul Tortelier (1914-84) once played the solo part in Richard Strauss's *Don Quixote* for a television show and the director superimposed Gustave Doré's famous drawing of the Knight of the Sad Countenance over Tortelier's face and person, the one playing a cello, the other riding a horse. The two fitted perfectly for there was, as well as the nobility, a slightly barmy, wild-eyed quality about

Tortelier: he was…quixotic. He wanted to change the world; and he thought he could do it.

He seemed to be more popular in the UK than in his native France. He was good-looking, charming and with a perfectly preserved stage accent in our language, when the word was easily understandable anyway he would pronounce it in the Franch way which everybody adored. His masterclasses on TV were a wow (even though he could be dictatorial) and we loved his bon mots like 'you must be like the skater on the ice: it is necessary to fall sometimes' and 'try to listen to yourself with less sympathy'. Yes, he could boss sometimes and he must have been hell to live with. Once at Dartington he had a row with his pianist, Paul Hamburger, during a public performance. Hamburger stood up to him and they remained friends.

Tortelier's technique was formidable but he always went behind the notes to find the heart of the music. This made his playing very touching. And he always made beautiful sounds. And he could be devastatingly elegant in a work like Tchaikovsky's *Rococo Variations*. He was married to the lovely Maud who sacrificed her own career (cellist) for the sake of the family; their son Yan Pascal gave up the violin to be a talented conductor (for many years with the BBC Philharmonic) and their daughter Maria de la Pau was an excellent pianist (but for many years she was in a deep depression).

Fortunately for us, Paul did not abandon music to better the world, although he did retreat for a year to a kibbutz in Israel. But the demands of his cello and his pen (he was a keen composer on the side) and possibly his family brought him back to his adoring audiences.

GIANELLA DEL MARCO:
Eight-year-old Conductor at Albert Hall   26.3.53

The eight-year-old Italian girl, Gianella del Marco, conducted the London Philharmonic Orchestra on Tuesday night in the Royal Albert Hall. There was no doubt that she was really conducting. The Overture to *The Magic Flute* and the first movement of Beethoven's Fifth Symphony are full of technical traps for the conductor, and when Gianella went wrong, which she did only once, the orchestra was thrown off its balance for a moment.

Such talent as hers is quite remarkable. According to the printed programme the Pope said of her, 'She is a sign from God.' But just what she signifies is indeed difficult to say. Certainly it would be fruitless to expect a grown-up performance; in which case the performance takes on the quality of a freak show. Once you get over the shock of a child actually doing the conducting there is nothing left. The performances are meaningless and the listener is left perhaps to pity the little girl (her face is full of character, and rather touching to see) spending so much time and energy in such an abnormal occupation.

HS: There was quite a rash of infant conductors, mostly Italian I don't know why, just after the war; there was one called Roberto Benzi who was even cleverer than this Gianella moppet. Benzi's talent even reached maturity.

MISCHA ELMAN:
Violinist's Recital in Festival Hall   13.4.53

The small audience in the Royal Festival Hall on Friday night for a violin recital by Mischa Elman suggested that his stock with the general public is not very high nowadays; even though this was his first visit in several years. But though the public seemed to have forgotten, the violinists had not – I have rarely seen so many in one building.

Frankly, I think the violinists enjoyed it more than anyone else, in the interval they were discussing his playing with great interest and much gesticulation.

Stylistically the recital was not fanciful: first, Handel in the nineteenth-century manner and then Beethoven's *Spring* Sonata played quite meaninglessly (something that has to be played before the encores can start). Then came the Mendelssohn concerto with piano accompaniment and with pauses between the movements. What the violinist was thinking of during the slow movement I cannot imagine; it certainly was not the music, nor playing it in tune.

After the interval we expected that Chausson's *Poème* would be given a measure of sensuality, but all passion seemed to have been spent some time ago. The first of the little pieces, a Hebrew melody by Achron, was more convincingly played than anything else in the programme so far.

Elman's playing on Friday night had often a ravishing tonal elegance and evidence of a masterly technique that could be called upon when the artist cared to. Remarkable was his trill, so quick it sounded like an electric bell, and his way of cutting off a top note without giving it either full value or any vibrato, just as if, having reached the note, he was bored with it.

His platform manner was amusing: deep bows to the expensive seats, little nods to the cheaper ones. With both feet together he seemed to wrap his tails around him drawing himself up to his not very full height looking like a vulture with a bald dome. Then with feet apart he would lean forward to the floor. Having avoided looking at the audience during the course of the piece, he would stare hard at the stalls during the last notes, as if to dare them not to applaud.

The pianist was Joseph Seiger, young and very gifted.

HS: There were several stories about Elman's exalted opinion of himself. One time he stopped playing at a rehearsal to say warmly: 'My God, what a tone!' Woman asks: 'What does it feel like to be Mischa Elman?' 'Madam, I sometimes think I'm dreaming!'

BRITTEN'S NEW SONGS:
Settings of Hardy   26.2.54

The English Opera Group presented a programme of British songs on Sunday evening in the Victoria and Albert Museum. Peter Pears has rarely been in such good form, and it was encouraging to see Benjamin Britten at the piano. For some months the composer had been suffering from bursitis in the right arm. It is perhaps typical of him that during this period he learned to write fluently with his left hand.

The skill, charm, and musical mastery of this duo was nowhere more evident than in their performance of Purcell's ditty 'There's not a swain', which takes but thirty seconds. The minute give and take of rhythm, the way in which words and music are given their due, was worthy of universal admiration.

The novelty of the evening was the first London performance of Britten's Op.53 *Winter Words*, lyrics and ballads by Thomas Hardy. It would indeed be interesting to know why the composer chose these poems to set. They do not suit his music well with the exception of the first two of the eight: 'At Day-close in November' and 'Midnight on the Great Western'. That is not to say, of course, that Britten has not set them without skill or interest. He could do a supremely competent job on a telephone directory or a White Paper. But Britten usually chooses his texts with such care and an eye for suitability that one wonders if, for once, he was persuaded into this task. In 'Wagtail and Baby', for example, words and music are as curiously at odds as they would be if Edward Elgar had set T. S. Eliot or Gertrude Stein.

It is impossible, in the present instance, to judge the music apart from the words. Next time we hear the work we should like to hear the words sung in Polish or some other language we do not know, so as to hear the music more or less undistracted by Hardy's words.

In the first two songs, however, the muse seems to burn more brightly than in the later half-dozen. Did Britten's poetical, critical sense begin working at No. 3?

HS: I don't think I ever made such a Charlie of myself as with this notice. I include it here to show that, although I was the only critic to herald Tippett's first opera *The Midsummer Marriage* as a work of genius, I could also make a first-class ass of myself. The way in which Britten could take wonderful words and add something to them shows a mighty imaginative work of creation. Mea maxississima culpa! Interesting, though, about Britten learning to write with his left hand: Shostakovich did the same thing after a stroke.

TURANGALÎLA:
Messiaen's Monster Symphony 13.4.54

At the second of the BBC Third Programme's concerts in the Royal Festival Hall, on Monday evening, Olivier Messiaen's symphony *Turangalîla* was heard in public for the first time in Great Britain. Messiaen (born 1908) is an interesting historical figure, and it is right that his music should be heard. This symphony, written in 1947-8, is his most ambitious work so far, and it was typical of the public's reaction to his music in general that there were both boos and cheers at the close of Monday's performance.

Messiaen's is an extraordinary talent, and whether or not you like his music, it provides an experience; even though one may feel that *Turangalîla* was born on the sinister side of a French organ-loft. For Messiaen is an organ composer, and his music, like Franck's and Bruckner's, betrays the fact, both in orchestration and in a continuity which is improvisational rather than formal.

The composer begins his programme note on *Turangalîla* by saying 'The whole work is a love-song.' Whole is a key-word – the work lasts seventy-five minutes and consists of ten movements.

The orchestra is a mammoth one and includes, besides triple woodwind and the usual brass (with extra trumpets), a large percussion group with maracas and wood-blocks, a keyboard group of glockenspiel, celesta and vibraphone whose function is not unlike the *gamelan* orchestras of Bali, Ondes Martenot (a species of electronic Banshee) and a piano concertante.

These vast resources are used to express musical ideas which are basically simple and easily apprehended. There is nothing symphonic about it; even the movement *Développement de l'amour*, which the composer describes as developing the three cyclic themes of the work, is nothing but repetition. *Turangalîla* is nothing but a gigantic suite.

Messiaen's music has made a great impression in certain quarters because of its fascinating textures, its simple tunes and its harmonies which, though cloying, are based on conventional harmony.

The melodies are often excessively vulgar and not conducive to development, amongst other reasons, because of their tell-tale intervals of the sixth and augmented fourth. These intervals add vulgarity to the harmony, too. Messiaen's preoccupation with oriental music induces repetition of a sort which often approaches a static or even magnetic quality. The result is a sticky glutinous pudding which appals and fascinates at the same time.

Turangalîla is not boring at first hearing because of the obvious sincerity which drives Messiaen to write like this. He seems to be something of a latter-day Scriabin but, perhaps, a more talented one – a curious figure for music to have thrown up at the present time.

The performers (Yvonne Loriod, piano, Ginette Martenot, ondes, the London Symphony Orchestra, Walter Goehr, conductor) were the same who gave the work on the air last year, so they knew their way about. The composer was present both at rehearsals and concert. The only criticism to be made was that the Ondes Martenot were not sufficiently audible (for some).

GUIDO CANTELLI AT FESTIVAL HALL: 28.5.54

Guido Cantelli's concert on Saturday night in the Royal Festival Hall produced some wonderful playing by the Philharmonia Orchestra. But how this young conductor drives an orchestra!

On Saturday Mozart became a tight coil of shining steel, Dukas as overexuberant as a Danny Kaye song-and-dance number, and Tchaikovsky emerged as a mass of hectic hysteria. Mr Cantelli will surely go off 'pop' one day. This would be a pity, because he is a conductor with tremendous talent. He seemed on Saturday to be possessed with the idea of driving the orchestra rather than guiding it. His gestures and his musicianship have lost the restraint which was so noticeable when he first conducted here (although his *La Mer* last week was an honourable exception).

An orchestra must breathe, and in Mozart's Divertimento in B flat, K.287 the strings (reduced) and two horns were scarcely allowed to. They played the notes extraordinarily well – and Mozart never wrote a more difficult first fiddle part – but the essence of Mozart's spirit was absent. The orchestra did not sing from the heart; it played as if hypnotised. Any eight bars of the sublime Adagio under Beecham would have demonstrated the superficiality of Cantelli's performance.

In Dukas's *The Sorcerer's Apprentice* Cantelli followed the Toscanini fashion of playing it too fast. The result sent the audience into raptures but was not, I fancy, what Dukas wanted. Leslie Heward once took seventeen minutes over this work (Cantelli took ten) and revealed many delightful facets of the work unsuspected in the usual high-powered treatment it usually receives.

46

Hysteria is undoubtedly part of the make-up of Tchaikovsky's Fourth Symphony, but Mr Cantelli could well afford to curb his enthusiasm. He chose a tempo for the pizzicato movement, however, which was perfect. The first violins, solo flute, trumpet, horn, and timpani earned special bonuses on Saturday. The piccolo, oboe, clarinet, and bassoon only just earned their keep.

NEW YORK PHILHARMONIC SYMPHONY ORCHESTRA:
Guido Cantelli. n.d.

Is Cantelli going to be just another virtuoso-conductor or is he going to show that making music and communicating its heart to us is his prime concern?

Few can drive an orchestra more surely, few can produce such wonderful sounds from a first-class orchestra, few can package in Cellophane more efficiently such a work as Ravel's *Daphnis and Chloe*. But to do such things as these does not make a great conductor; they are merely attributes of band-mastering on the highest level.

Technical virtuosity, in conducting as in any other form of art, should be only the beginning, the means and not the end.

Can Cantelli enlarge his repertoire (at present we are beginning to know it too well) and broaden his musical horizon? Can he thus acquire a sense of style so that he is not at a disadvantage in music which requires a fastidious sensibility rather than a talent for observing copious directives? Is he, in the last analysis, prepared to put music first and Cantelli (at least) second?

These questions, and many others, were prompted by the Philharmonic Symphony Orchestra of New York's concert with Guido Cantelli in the Usher Hall on Tuesday night. The programme began with an immaculately tailored performance of Rossini's overture *The Siege of Corinth*.

The First Symphony of Brahms was beautifully played, but the performance lacked spontaneity, revealed nothing of head or heart; it was simply a collection of notes.

Debussy and Ravel fared better. *Nuages* and *Fêtes* and the second suite from *Daphnis and Chloe* are more concerned with the sheer magic of sound than Brahms. Certainly the sounds were ravishing, and the effect was quite exciting.

The virtuosity and sonority of this New York orchestra is a joy to hear. The warmth of bowed sound has already been commented on; the wind chorus last night was shown to fine advantage – the first oboe excelled himself. The brass has the usual American sonority, and the trombones enjoy the luxury of a fourth player 'doubling' the first.

HS: Guido Cantelli (1920-56) died in a plane crash thus depriving us of the maturity of a conductor who was already world famous for his concerts and recordings. He was to have been director of La Scala, Milan which was where he had made his debut at the age of twenty-five. Cantelli was a perfectionist and this led him to make enormous demands on his orchestras and on himself. Toscanini was his mentor and he had something of the senior conductor's good and bad qualities: a search for the truth about the music in hand, and a demand for the best his players could give him (driving them sometimes nearly mad in rehearsals), which could lead to performances that often seemed like loveless drill. But what a talent!

IGOR STRAVINSKY:
Composer Awarded R.P.S. Gold Medal   29.5.54

On his first visit to Britain for sixteen years, Igor Stravinsky had time to conduct only one concert. It was quite an occasion; the Royal Philharmonic Society seized the opportunity to present the composer with its gold medal. Sir Arthur Bliss made the presentation and Stravinsky made a short speech of thanks. The great Russian was visibly more nervous at the prospect of speaking than conducting.

If his manner on the podium is not inspiring than it must be said that his beat, though small, was meticulously accurate. The Royal Philharmonic Orchestra made great efforts and the evening was a great success.

The programme was entirely given over to ballet music and there was little to provoke argument. First came the Divertimento extracted from the score of *Le Baiser de la Fée*. This ballet takes

Tchaikovsky's ballets and fragments of his piano pieces as the point of departure. The result is a gentle, melodious and occasionally lush work.

The *Scènes de Ballet* which followed are in much the same vein, although not nearly so directly indebted to Tchaikovsky. Their brilliance and strength were not fully apparent in the performance.

The chief work of the evening was *Orpheus*, which received an excellent performance in spite of a few minor mishaps. The playing of the wind and brass section was a constant delight.

In the suite from *Petroushka* the orchestra was on more familiar ground and was able to relax a little.

At the close, Stravinsky was given an ovation fitting for one who has for more than forty years been at the head of his profession. He has always kept the world guessing, has always been news, and has written masterpiece after masterpiece. Great composers have always been influenced by their environment and by the music they have encountered. Stravinsky, a child of his day, has encountered five centuries of music and been influenced by all of them.

In his efforts to return to classicism he has been accused of writing pastiche, but his greatest works, the Symphony of Psalms, the Symphony in C, the Symphony in Three Movements, *Orpheus* and *Persephone* stand revealed as peaks of our century, not imitation of anything. And the three early ballets, *Firebird*, *Petroushka* and *Rite of Spring* are unsurpassed in their riots of colour and brilliance.

HS: A fine memento of the great Igor is the video of his last concert in London with the BBC Symphony Orchestra in the Royal Festival Hall. The TV director, Brian Large, was severely hampered during most of the concert because the camera placed in the organ loft with a direct frontal shot of Stravinsky was on the blink. But suddenly, towards the end of the final item, the suite from *Firebird*, it unblinked. Brian sensibly decided to use only this camera for the rest of the piece, the Berceuse and Finale. It was a wonderful close-up of Stravinsky with his small body, face (I always thought) not unlike an enlargement of a fly's face and those seemingly overlong arms like a spider's legs. There was in addition a moment when Igor gave a wind player a cue, 'selling him a pup'; the player waited a whole bar and then came in correctly. To which Stravinsky responded with an apologetic yet ravishing smile.

HS: With true hindsight I would add to the list of masterpieces the later ballet *Agon* and *Requiem Canticles*, gold amongst the dross of the later period which is mostly 'dodecaca' (Poulenc's term).

KAT'A KABANOVA:
First Janacek Opera in Britain   2.6.54

Kat'a Kabanova was presented on Tuesday night at Sadler's Wells Theatre. This is the first time that an opera by Janacek has been mounted in this country and Sadler's Wells is to be congratulated on its enterprise. Janacek is a welcome change in our operatic diet.

Janacek (1854-1928) based a good deal of his music on Slavonic folk song and the vocalisation of speech inflection. His music is made up of short phrases which he builds like a mosaic (c.f. Bartok). He may have realised that music built on tiny patterns can tire, for this three-act opera is very short.

The immediate impression, on hearing Janacek, is of freshness, vitality, primary colours, starkness, and a certain roughness. These qualities might be used in describing Mussorgsky: a comparison that is intentional.

Kat'a is based on Ostrovsky's drama *The Storm*, a play we should call 'typically Russian'; strong mother-in-law controlling weak son married to emotion-starved wife (Katya) in love with someone else, feelings of guilt followed by confession and expiation by drowning.

Janacek adds enormously to the drama by his vivid painting of the background, the night scene, the ever-present Volga, and the elements of the heavens.

Janacek's operas are difficult to translate, because of the attention paid to natural speech inflection: to sing, for the same reason and, especially, because of the angularity of the declamation: to play, orchestrally, because he loved quick repetition of a motive of three or four notes, awkward intervals and violins in the highest register, no matter how difficult, technically, the passages were.

Norman Tucker has made an effective translation, the singers sang and acted well, but the orchestra was not up to Janacek's demands, though it played with considerable spirit and enthusiasm.

Charles Mackerras, a young Australian conductor, showed great skill in handling a difficult assignment. Amy Shuard played the title rôle, showing a powerful voice and great musicianship. But the part also called for a first-rate 'heavy' actress and, not being this as yet, she failed to enlist our complete sympathy for the heroine.

Production, by Dennis Arundell, and costumes and sets were all first class.

This review has mentioned several times the various difficulties involved in this production. The whole project was courageous in the extreme, and a few more performances will probably see an enormous improvement on what, even on Tuesday night, was a most exciting event in the annals of opera-going in Britain.

JOHN CAGE:
Music for Prepared Pianos   30.10.54

For many years now there have come across to London reports of an American who makes a curious kind of music by inserting objects of wood, metal, rubber and plastic material into the strings of a grand piano. This American composer, John Cage (born 1912) is now paying a first visit to this country and he presided at a session of his own music and of some *Musique Concrète* on Tuesday night. The occasion was one of the evening 'side-shows' of the fascinating Diaghilev Exhibition at Forbes House to which all London seems to be flocking.

In his charming introduction Mr Cage said that no doubt some of the audience would find that his compositions were not music; in which case – and nothing could be less aggressive than his way of putting it – some other term would have to be found for it. But, as he pointed out, *Musique Concrète* is not a correct description of music written for 'prepared pianos'. *Musique Concrète* consists of 'natural and usually non-musical sounds recorded and filtered on a magnetic tape, thus eliminating the performer and his virtuosity'.

Mr Cage's piece (we were not vouchsafed its title) performed on Tuesday called for two performers of great manipulative dexterity and virtuosity. John Cage was at one prepared piano, David Tudor at the other. The piano strings were littered with little objects, and on a long stool beside each performer was a plethora of percussion sticks, rattles, squeakers, whistles, and worse. They were all used.

An essential element was the stop-watch at the silent behest of which keys were struck and various parts of the structure of the pianos hit. For example, slamming down the keyboard lid with the sustaining pedal on is one of the more startling noises.

The piece lasted over half an hour, and during it we often thought of Hans Andersen's tale of 'The Emperor's New Clothes' and we always agreed with the view that some other term than music must be thought of for this tedious and silly method of wasting time. Since it could never be serious, it ought to be funnier. If a Sousa march or the first prelude of the *Forty Eight* were played on these prepared pianos, then at least an amusing cabaret act might emerge.

HS: John Cage (1912-1992), was a charmer of a man and I think that was the reason why he lasted so long. Directors and organisers of contemporary music found him irresistible. At another Institute of Contemporary Arts programme in Mahatma Gandhi Hall, Fitzroy Square, the noise of clanking cutlery and dishes intruded into the concert-hall where David Tudor was performing (if that is the correct term) a Cage number called 4'33" which consisted of Tudor sitting at a piano, starting a stop watch, not playing a note, and finishing when the specified time had been counted out. As organiser of the concert I rushed out into the nearby kitchen where two earnest Indians were operating a washing-up machine. They would not, could not, stop the machine so, after some fruitless argument, I returned to the concert room by which time the so-called work had finished. I apologised to Cage for the noise but he was delighted with the extra sound and asked me to find out the make and specification of the washing-up machine and its serial number.

ENGLISH OPERA GROUP:
The Turn of the Screw   6.10.54

The English Opera Group is now giving a short season at Sadler's Wells Theatre which includes *The Beggar's Opera, The Rape of Lucretia*, and a double bill consisting of *Love in a Village* (Arthur Oldham's version) and Lennox Berkeley's *A Dinner Engagement.* But the principal attraction, so far, has been the first performance in this country, on Wednesday night, of *The Turn of the Screw*, Benjamin Britten's new opera, which had its première in Venice last month.

In staging *The Turn of the Screw* – and there are many who will say that it should not be attempted – it is clear that an opera can score immeasurably over a play; for imaginative music can do in ten bars the work of two pages of narrative. James's little masterpiece is so effectively disturbing because of its subtle suggestions of the unspeakable. Britten has risen to this challenge; he has caught the atmosphere of Bly, especially a quality of the supernatural in the everyday. It is not so hard to make a stormy night menacing, but to make a sunny morning sinister needs the hand of a master.

There is a flaw, however, in this operatic version; not a fatal one, but a serious one. Granted that the ghosts, Peter Quint and Miss Jessel, must inevitably sing in an opera, but their visibility and audibility should, surely, be more limited than the librettists and producer make them. Dimly visible in his tower, Quint was a horror, but to see him dancing round the stage singing a duet with Miss Jessel rendered the drama less powerful.

This flaw apart, Myfanwy Piper's libretto is both faithful to the original and dramatically telling. The story is told in a prologue and two acts of eight scenes each. Preceding each scene is an orchestral interlude, each of which is a vital part of the structure; as an additional means of providing continuity and increasing the tension Britten has conceived these interludes as a set of variations.

The swiftness of the scene changing calls for expert lighting and the use of gauzes as well as more solid structures. John Piper's sets are among the best he has ever done. Both the production, by Basil Coleman, and the sets notably gather momentum in the second act. In the first act the production is laboured and unsubtle. The plot is so self-explanatory and the music of the prologue so flimsy that one is tempted to think it expendable.

At this stage one would not expect Britten to have much more to add to the noises to be made with the small orchestra that he has already used in his earlier chamber operas. However, this new score is brimming over with new sounds and new textures, and once more he shows himself to be a real composer, an inventor of sounds. In this opera the celesta is added to the instrumentation and the composer also decided that the piano and celesta parts should be entrusted to an extra player instead of being doubled by the conductor. With typical resourcefulness he has made notable use of this extra pair of hands.

One of the most effective scenes in this opera is that in which little Miles plays 'divinely' to the Governess to distract her attention so that his sister may sneak out to meet Miss Jessel. The piano is heard playing snatches of what might be a childish sonatina; the piano part is simple and attractive, yet the accompaniment of the orchestra adds an undercurrent of suspense, and as the little girl is discovered to be missing the scene ends with Miles crashing out some triumphant chords.

Britten has also added another 'Letter Song' to several operatic examples in a hauntingly beautiful and warmly emotional scene for the Governess.

The vocal parts of this opera were, with the exception of the children's parts, tailor-made for each artist, and the result is that Britten has brought out the best in each singer. As the Governess, Jennifer Vyvyan scores an outstanding success in a poignant and beautiful performance. Joan Cross is the housekeeper Mrs Grose, Peter Pears and Arda Mandikian are the two ghosts; all excellent.

It was, perhaps, expecting too much to find a boy who could sing well and portray the possessed Miles. David Hemmings sings touchingly his curious little song 'Malo' which is used so dramatically at the end of the opera. The other child, Flora, is enchantingly played by Olive Dyer.

Benjamin Britten conducted and secured brilliant playing from the English Opera Group Orchestra.

HEIFETZ AT THE FESTIVAL HALL: 20.11.54

These last few weeks London has been a playground for most of the greatest fiddlers of our time – Menuhin, Oistrakh, Szigeti, and Heifetz. The last named gave the first of two concerto appearances on Thursday night in the Royal Festival Hall.

Sir Thomas Beecham conducted the Royal Philharmonic Orchestra in Haydn's Symphony No 40, the Brahms-Haydn

Variations, and the suite extracted from Rimsky-Korsakov's *The Golden Cockerel*. The great conductor was not in his best form; there was a deal of bad balance, and ill-fitting phrasing in the Brahms Variations, together with some splendid patches of brilliance at the end of the suite and some true Beecham stylishness in the Haydn.

Following the American fashion, the second half of the programme was devoted to the concerto: it was the Brahms. Heifetz's own and individual style of playing is apt to suit Chausson, Tchaikovsky, Lalo and Saint-Saëns rather than Bach, Mozart, Beethoven, and Brahms. Last night, in your critic's view, Heifetz came nearer the spirit of Brahms than usual; perhaps it was no coincidence that on this occasion his technique was less perfect than usual. But this remark about technique should be taken *cum grano salis* for, of course, if Heifetz plays two notes out of tune in an evening it is practically a news item.

The opening minutes of the first movement saw the violinist not at ease, but he warmed up and dashed through his own cadenza with typical virtuosity. It was the slow movement, however, which brought forth the most ravishing sounds. Extreme purists will say that he only approached the spirit of Brahms, but it was the kind of fiddle-playing which makes Heifetz unique.

Casting caution aside, we declare that, whatever the merits of the other august persons named above, Heifetz is the greatest violinist, considered purely in terms of violin-playing.

HS: Of course we remember the perfection of Beecham in his later years, so maybe the other side of the coin ought to be mentioned just this once. For example, I remember a shambolic performance of the interludes from *Peter Grimes*. Tommy had no love for Benjamin Britten whom he referred to more than once in my hearing as a 'prominent member of the Girls' Friendly Brigade'. My guess is that Boosey and Hawkes had taken the conductor out to lunch and that the lunch was more Boosey than Hawkes. So he had been persuaded to include the work at an afternoon concert in the Royal Opera House. Sir Thomas could sometimes behave like a naughty boy when faced with something he did not like. So he did not start rehearsing the interludes until after the coffee break at the last rehearsal on the morning of the concert. This was not enough time to deal with a tricky score whose notes were as unfamiliar to the players as they were to the conductor (the work only later became a repertoire piece).

Another disaster occurred during a performance of the second suite from *Daphnis and Chloe*. Beecham often performed Debussy but rarely Ravel. Now Beecham had the most natural sense of rhythm in the world as long as it was two, three or four in a bar or compounds of those tempi. He had learned to cope with the five/ four second movement of Tchaikovsky's *Pathetic* Symphony but switching rapidly from one tempo to another was not within Beecham's idiosyncratic beating. The finale of *Daphnis* has a lot of five in the bar, sometimes mixing with threes. Somehow Beecham threw the orchestra and they stopped playing all except for a single woodwind player (either Jack Brymer or Gerald Jackson) who kept on gamely until others joined in. But it was a near thing; and of course Beecham never conducted any Ravel again. It was the complicated beating that kept Sir Thomas from programming works by his friends William Walton or Igor Stravinsky. During World War One Beecham had contrived to send some money to the Russian who was stuck in Switzerland and hard up (in my hearing Sir Thomas always referred to Stravinsky as being 'a good egg').

TROILUS AND CRESSIDA:
William Walton's New Opera   5.12.54

There are few creative artists in any age who continue, throughout their lives, both to astonish us and to delight us. They are usually the truly great ones, the Stravinskys, the Eliots and the Picassos. Many of the lesser ones continue to delight us even if the sense of wonder, of being led to new adventures, is absent.

Sir William Walton's opera *Troilus and Cressida*, produced at Covent Garden on Friday night, treads the well-worn paths of the later Walton. The flame of the early works has died down into a gentle, warming glow. The music is well put together – the craft of the clever film composer often shows up – and it is strongly lyrical, grateful to sing, lushly orchestrated. It is not likely to make anybody walk out of the opera-house, complaining about modern music.

Christopher Hassall's libretto is well-shaped, his imagery and metaphors apt and unobtrusive. The story flows and the music is always easy on the ear.

Walton has, in fact, written a very late nineteenth-century opera.

But oh! how one wishes he were bolder. The new opera is all gorgeous flesh without solid bones underneath. The vital impulse which would make us come back to the opera time and time again is lacking. The textures, melodic intervals, rhythmic patterns, harmonic fittings are so often clichés taken from earlier Walton.

The casting was, for the most part, excellent. Richard Lewis makes a fine Troilus, singing and acting like a hero. Magda Laszlo's beauty of looks, carriage, and voice are most suitable. But her characterisation is all on the passive side; when she has to move or act swiftly she is less effective in making Cressida a real person. She had gallantly learned to sing in English for the occasion, but sometimes failed to put across either the words or sense of what she sang.

The most successful musical portraiture in the opera is contained in the parts of Pandarus, the elderly epicure, and Diomede, the bluff military man. In the former part Peter Pears held the stage whenever he was on it with his masterly musical and dramatic sense. But for the announcement made before the opera started, no one would have known that he was a sick man, appearing nobly, against doctor's orders. Otakar Kraus played Diomede with brutal solidity – a first-rate performance.

Frederick Dalberg failed to bring alive the traitorous Calkas, but it may be that the part is the least successful character in the opera.

Hugh Casson's sets are impressive and George Devine's production has much to commend it. Sir Malcolm Sargent conducted with his usual energy and skill. The chorus was excellent.

HS: André Previn was to have conducted but it would have been his first time in the opera house and he funked it. Sargent took over, much to Willie Walton's fury, both at rehearsals and performances.

THE MIDSUMMER MARRIAGE:
Michael Tippett's New Opera   28.1.55

Who was it said that you cannot have such a thing as an opera of ideas? Perhaps he was at Covent Garden, London, on Thursday night, joining in the booing of Michael Tippett's new opera *The Midsummer Marriage*.

Certainly this extraordinary work is a failure in terms of theatrical effectiveness. It is difficult to hear the words, easy to appreciate the situations which arise, but difficult to understand the motives for them. The characters do not, on the whole, come to life, so that if the music is not appreciated, the failure is total.

But Tippett's music is so good that, in spite of everything, *The Midsummer Marriage* cannot and must not be written off as a failure. Here is a composer of greatness daring to do something new in the operatic field and doing it with tremendous vitality and virility. We may not immediately understand everything he does, but the quality of the music commands attention.

The story is basically a simple one. A young couple have run away to get married but there are certain obstacles which delay their marriage for twenty-four hours. The action of the opera takes us from dawn on Midsummer's Day to the following dawn. The obstacles are physical, mental, and magical. The place is a clearing in a wood on a hillside with the ruins of a temple visible; the time is the present.

The story is original but not really new; similarly the music springs from the past. But the working out is fresh and peculiar to our time.

The libretto, also by Tippett, shows his wide range of interest and reading; the key to it would embrace a vast bibliography. However, an opera libretto is not meant to be read by itself, and Tippett's music is the real key to it. The music provides the sense but is not always apparent in the goings on on the stage, and in this opera we must concentrate on the music. This advice may seem unnecessary, but recent experience shows that modern audiences look too much and listen too little.

So far as the operatic disposition of the cast is concerned, Tippett's plan is reasonably conventional. Mark and Jenifer are the runaway couple, a dramatic soprano and tenor. Jenifer's father, Kingfisher, is a baritone villain; his secretary, Bella, and her mechanic boy friend, Jack, are the secondary pair of lovers. There are two Ancients, bass and contralto, always ready to emerge from their ruined temple for an Aristophanic contest or arbitration. There is a clairvoyante,

Madame Sosostris, and she is, according to hallowed operatic tradition, a contralto.

Dancing plays an important part in the opera; in fact, the second act is in the nature of an interlude in which three or four ritual dances take place. The chief dancer, Stephon, is integrated into the action by being an attendant on the Ancients.

Theatrical ineffectiveness is comparatively easy to condone in a composer's first opera. What is less easy to forgive is that Tippett has masked his music so often. Surely the experience of his oratorio *A Child of our Time* should have taught him that brass, though an appropriate textural counterpart to a contralto or a baritone voice, will drown it if allowed to play at the same level? Similarly, should not his *Symphony 1944* have taught him that three lines or more of counterpoint, especially when doubled on the modern orchestra, sound dangerously thick. There is a lot of thick or busy counterpoint in this work.

The musical layout of the opera is fascinating; the numbers are largescaled and most of their arias are in three parts like the big Mozart ones. The ensembles are of two kinds; those which carry the action along and those which comment on it or 'crystallise' it.

The chorus, friends of the young couple, have an important part and there are many big concerted numbers. Very little music is repeated, and there is practically no cross-reference of themes or identification of persons or things with themes. The music is rich in melody, warm in harmony, and lively in rhythm. The result of all this is that Tippett has produced a quite unique work, a strange mixture of solidity, fantasy and poetry.

Tippett has been sympathetically served by his collaborators although their contribution varies in quality. Barbara Hepworth's temple is a tower of strength (some wit said it looked like Ben Nicolson in 3D), but her costumes were not so successful. Christopher West's production is capable but not inspired; John Cranko's choreography is sometimes excellent but often misfired completely; but their task was extremely difficult.

There is not space to give due attention to the performers; sufficient to say that Adèle Leigh took the advantage of having the most grateful part, as Bella. Joan Sutherland as Jenifer, Richard Lewis as Mark, John Lanigan as Jack, Otokar Kraus as Kingfisher, and a newcomer, Oralia Dominguez as Sosostris, all sang well.

The chorus and their master, Douglas Robinson, deserve high praise for singing so magnificently what must have been the toughest assignment they have yet had. John Pritchard's conducting showed him completely in command of the difficult score and the large forces.

Covent Garden must be congratulated for having the perception to see the worth of this new opera and for having given its production proper attention. We in the audience must also be perceptive and give our attention to *The Midsummer Marriage*, our reward will be considerable.

OTTO KLEMPERER AT FESTIVAL HALL: 24.4.55

Everybody knows that Beethoven's *Eroica* is a great work. But how often do we hear a great performance of it? To have a performance which matches the work you need a good orchestra, and for a conductor someone who has something of Beethoven in himself; something of the composer's breadth of vision, noble spirit, and indomitable will; besides, of course, all the musicality, interpretative skill, and all the rest of the technical equipment. And then, having assembled all this, the orchestra and conductor have to be in form. Then, with luck, the clouds clash, there is a charge of electricity, the heavens open, and you are vouchsafed a vision of a great *Eroica*.

This is a fanciful way of beginning to explain that there was a performance of Beethoven's Third Symphony in the Royal Festival Hall on Sunday night which was truly a great one. Otto Klemperer conducted the Philharmonia Orchestra.

The performance of the same composer's Eighth Symphony was no less remarkable and that of the overture *Leonora 3* was also very fine.

There were no startling unorthodoxies in interpretation (he did make the basses play their grace-notes on the beat, though, at the beginning of the Funeral March). On the contrary, the text was such that one heard many new things in the score, or rather, one heard them much more clearly. The quality of sound was, it can only be said, intensely Beethoven-like, so unquestionably right. The virtuoso Philharmonia Orchestra was in the hands of a master, but the playing was never inflexible. It was an inspired and inspiring experience, a concert to remember always.

HS: Otto Klemperer had a healthy dislike of his colleagues. Of Szell's recording of Debussy's *La Mer* he said: 'It is not La Mer but "Szell am See".' (Zell-am-See: Austrian lakeside resort.)

After Klemps had severely burned himself and had to cancel a London performance of Beethoven's Symphony No. 9, Walter Legge asked his advice as to a substitute. Klemperer recommended Hindemith. The performance was a minor disaster. When Legge told him this, Klemperer laughed for ten minutes without stopping.

Another time the Doktor went round to the artists' room after hearing Bruno Walter conduct. He hadn't heard B.W. in years. He addressed Walter by his real name Schlesinger, which B.W. hated to hear used, and continued: 'Your conducting is just as good as it ever was.'

Bruno Walter (1876-1952) and Otto Klemperer (1885-1973) were both in the Mahler circle, both conducted his music and yet their performances were almost as different as chalk and cheese, both however sounding authentic. How come? Asked an interviewer of Klemperer. "Well,' said Dr K scornfully, 'Walter is a moralist: I am anti-moralist.' And, I seem to remember, he used the word 'conciliating'. Yet it is not as easy as that, for what is Beethoven's music if not moral? Walter's Beethoven and Mozart were surely less moral than Klemperer's; and more conciliating but, on good days, not weak or wilting.

One thing should be said that has not been said about these great giants from Mittel-Europ. They came, Klemps, Walter, Furtwängler, having done much of their work with German and Viennese orchestras, the Berlin and Vienna orchestras in particular. And even the American orchestras they had conducted were nearer in style to the Mittel-European than the British orchestras of the '40s and '50s with their one or at most two rehearsals and on with the show. They were good sight-readers, yes, but what about style? So these visitors to Albion had to work hard to maintain their standards and to impose their idiosyncratic styles and I think they found it difficult.

It took a long time for Furtwängler to make music his way with the LPO (it suddenly happened one day in the Albert Hall in the middle of the Brahms-Haydn Variations and we realised at last what Furtwängler was about). Walter had difficulties too. Klemperer soon had the advantage of working continuously with the Philharmonia and was able to reveal his full force. And what a force that was: Beethoven that sounded as if the composer himself were conducting: chords at the beginning of the *Eroica* of the right length and weight. Not too much beauty of sound and of course the Beethoven-style spilled out over other composers: Mozart sounded wonderful but rather as if Beethoven were conducting Mozart.

Walter's Mozart was nearer what we knew from Beecham's Mozart but his Beethoven could also be superb. I remember a Pastoral Symphony with the Vienna Philharmonic in Edinburgh that was sublime, also a great Great C major Schubert. And his Mahler…well, I enjoyed Walter's cheese Mahler even more than I enjoyed Klemperer's chalk; both were very fine. What was Mahler's Mahler like? I suspect somewhere between the two other giants mentioned.

BRUNO WALTER'S CONCERTS:
Noble Bruckner   25.5.55

Bruno Walter's four concerts with the BBC Symphony Orchestra in the Royal Festival Hall have given great pleasure to many people, especially to former Germans and Austrians among the enthusiastic audience.

Sometimes we have thought of Walter as a rather easy-going conductor, fond of sensuous sound and a bit sentimental. That he is fond of sensuous sound was shown often, and nowhere more conspicuously (and successfully) than in Richard Strauss's *Death and Transfiguration*.

But the easy-going sentimentalist was not in evidence. In fact, his Brahms Symphony No. 3 was tight-lipped and taut; the climaxes lacked expansion, and the doting orchestra found itself with not quite enough time to play. It sounded as though Toscanini had rehearsed the work but had been obliged to leave before the end of the concert, and Bruno Walter had taken over at the last moment but had not had time to impress his own personality on the performance. It was, therefore, a performance lacking in conviction.

The Mozart Requiem did not flower. The essential warmth seemed to be missing from the phrasing: there was no hurry here, far from it, but the grandeur was often lacking. The same evening (Sunday last) the orchestra played in mediocre fashion in Haydn's *Miracle* Symphony: always excepting Janet Craxton's beautiful oboe playing in the trio.

What will remain in the memory for a very long time was Bruno Walter's inspired performances of Mahler's First Symphony and Bruckner's Ninth Symphony. British listeners may still be impatient with the obvious shortcomings of Bruckner, but the poetic splendours, the sheer magnificence and the masterly scherzo of this last symphony compel the utmost admiration; especially with Bruno Walter at the conductor's desk. This was a great performance.

SIBELIUS SALUTE:
Ninetieth Birthday Concert   10.11.55

The ninetieth birthday of the great Finnish composer was celebrated in the Royal Festival Hall on Thursday night at a concert conducted by Sir Thomas Beecham. The concert was broadcast and the BBC had made special arrangements to ensure that Sibelius himself should be able to hear the programme clearly, listening in his home near Helsinki. During the course of the concert the Finnish Ambassador to the Court of St. James conferred upon Sir Thomas the Order of the White Rose of Finland, Commander First Class. This was in recognition of Sir Thomas's doughty championship of Sibelius's works over the last forty years or more. Sir Thomas generously shared the honour with our orchestral musicians who always play Sibelius's music with such sympathy and relish.

The programme included the twin peaks of Sibelius's music in that world of romantic austerity which, with its peculiar regional over-and-under-tones, has appealed so greatly to the northern races of Europe and America: from the Symphonic Cycle, the Fourth Symphony, and from the tone-poems *Tapiola*.

The beginning of this century saw the expansion to bursting point not only of harmony but of form. Some composers interpreted themselves more in formal reorientation, some in harmonic, some in both. Sibelius's harmony has never been 'difficult', so that his formal experiments have been, thereby, easier to follow. These experiments have been concerned with the dissemination of thematic fragments and their subsequent growth into a logical argument which owes little of its power to the principles of sonata form.

The extent to which Sibelius is indebted to the folk music of his country is arguable, but what is certain is that, as in Bartok's String Quartets, any local material there may be has been integrated into the very bones of the music.

A great part of the appeal of Sibelius lies in his idiosyncrasies, and it is strange when, after frequent hearings of his larger works, one finds the same musical fingerprints in the smaller works where the tension is slack and the subject matter frankly picturesque. This can prove sometimes as disconcerting as it would be if Olivier were to use for the playing of Mr Puff the speech and gestures he reserves for the blinding of Oedipus.

Sir Thomas Beecham mixed the light and the profound works of Sibelius on Thursday night to give us some soft fruits before cracking the hard nuts. On paper it seems sensible to preface the symphony with the incidental music to *Swan White*, the tone-poem with the music for *Pelléas and Mélisande*; (it is also possible that he did this in deference to the composer's well-known affection and concern for his lesser works.) In the event it proved difficult to change the mood from pretty to profound. Their performances were good but not quite worthy of the occasion nor as remarkable as other readings of the same works from Sir Thomas's baton.

HS: In many people's minds at this time were the unforgettable performances by the Old Vic Company at the New Theatre in St Martin's Lane of a double-bill of Sheridan's *The Critic* and the Greek tragedy of *Oedipus Rex*. Laurence Olivier played Mr Puff in the former, the title-role in the latter. Both parts were played to perfection and he was supported in both plays by Sybil Thorndike and the incidental music of Antony Hopkins – hysterical laughter turned to near hysteria. After one matinee I heard one attendant girl say to a hat-check girl, 'I don't sell many boxes of chox after that Greek thing; it's that Mr Olivier's eyes when he's blinded, you know, puts people right off.'

COMPLEX BOULEZ:
Melody-free Music   8.3.56

The Music Section of the Institute of Contemporary Arts organised a recital of music for two pianos at the Wigmore Hall on Tuesday this week. Two-thirds of the programme was Debussy: *Six Epigraphes Antiques* and *En blanc et noir*. Rather odd that, you might think, for the I.C.A., but the Debussy cushioned the centre-piece of the programme which was *Structures* by Pierre Boulez. Boulez was at one piano and Yvonne Loriod, specialist in Messaien, was at the other. Their Debussy was spirited but lacking in subtlety and accuracy of dynamics.

The *Structures* are of such complexity – although only for four hands at two pianos – that it is exceedingly hard even to follow the score. I shared my score, for example, with Norman Del Mar and Sir William Walton; we were often pages out. Alan Rawsthorne and Sir Arthur Bliss were having similar trouble in front of us. How is it that this music is so difficult and what is it like?

It is serial music and totally 'organised'. That is, not only are the notes ordered according to the twelve-note technique but also the duration, pitch, metre, dynamics and, sometimes the method of attacking the notes are organised according to the order and transpositions of the notes and number of the tone-row. There is no governing pulse-factor and therefore, there is no rhythm as such.

Boulez says himself of this piece that 'we are freed from all melody, all harmony and all counterpoint'. If you were to hear this music I do not think you would wish to contradict him.

I can remember a time when I thought Bartok was a senseless noise; I now know better. Therefore I am not going to write off Boulez before I can admit to understanding it. I can only say that there were people in the Hall who actually, and I believe, sincerely enjoyed the *Structures*. For the majority I think the sound proved continually unpleasant and eventually boring.

What I can say, though, is that this is music gradually disappearing into the machine. For electronic machines can perform this sort of mathematical music more accurately than human beings. The violent attacks on single notes which occupy so much of the *Structures* are not only singularly uneasy on the ear but they damage the pianos. One string was broken at a rehearsal and the hammers and felts must have suffered considerably.

HS Pierre Boulez, b.1926, studied with Messiaen and at the age of twenty he became music director of the theatre company formed by Jean-Louis Barrault and his wife Madeleine Renault; from that association he went on to found Concerts Marigny, later called Domaine Musical, introducing not only the work of the Second Viennese School (Schönberg, Berg and Webern) but also his contemporaries such as Stockhausen, Maderna, and Xenakis. His intentions at this period were radical, to start afresh, abandoning the past as much as possible. His chamber piece, *Le Marteau sans maître*, 1955, made him a celebrity; which piece is considered a masterpiece by the avantgarde. From directing chamber-sized ensembles Boulez then took to conducting symphony orchestras. He soon gave up, thank God, Beethoven symphonies, but teamed up with Wieland Wagner at Bayreuth to direct *Parsifal*. From there he moved on to be a specialist, and a mighty impressive if cool, conductor of the world's best orchestras in Debussy, Mahler, Messiaen, Stravinsky, Berg, Webern, Schönberg and similar works. Having once incited people to burn down the opera houses he has become a welcome opera director. His incredible memory and ear, plus a pleasant and practical manner, have made him a welcome guest conductor all over and he worked wonders as chief conductor of the BBC Symphony Orchestra. He has said that no composition is ever complete and he has backed up that statement by constantly revising his own compositions. The later Boulez is less fierce than the younger one. I have met him quite a few times and interviewed him too. His English is still untidy which seems at odds with such a precise composer and conductor. He is a really nice man.

A NEW MICHAEL TIPPETT WORK:
Premiere of Piano Concerto   1.11.56

The John Feeney Charitable Trust has made it possible for three new works by British composers to be commissioned for the City of Birmingham Symphony Orchestra. The first work, *Meditations on a Theme of John Blow* of Arthur Bliss, was performed last year, Edmund Rubbra's Seventh Symphony is on the way, and on Tuesday night, in the Town Hall, Birmingham, the première was given of Michael Tippett's Piano Concerto.

It is strange that both Britten and Tippett at the moment are creating music with a preponderance of the interval of a fourth. With Hindemith this interval has long been a favourite but with our two local composers it has been a recent acquisition. In Britten's *The Turn of the Screw* the fourth dominated the scene; in Tippett's opera *The Midsummer Marriage*, it was the same. Tippett's new concerto also inhabits the world of fourths.

At first hearing, indeed, the concerto may seem to be something like a selection from the opera, arranged for piano and orchestra. But the likeness is only initial. The concerto springs from the same source but its course is different.

The new work lasts just over half an hour and is a true piano concerto. Very striking are, not only its freshness and sense of magical adventure, but its high content of sheer pleasure and the poetic, as opposed to percussive, nature of the piano writing.

'Genius' is a strong word but it cannot be denied Tippett in view of the works which have emerged from his (slow) pen during the last fifteen years. It is a genius hampered by a certain awkwardness of texture and technique that makes every work of his a little more difficult to play and hear than it need be; but it is the awkwardness of a giant. In this concerto, by way of example, there are moments of over-scoring, over-complication, and even miscalculation that obscure the effect. But the strength, individuality, and beauty of the work is of such a quality that the experience of listening is enriching to the mind and the emotions.

The first movement begins with a long tune which uncurls a texture of sheer enchantment. The harmony is typical of the whole piece: the composer's direction 'doux et lumineux' aptly describes the sound.

The piano part contrives through much of the concerto to be a cascade of arpeggios and brilliant scale-work: sometimes the listener is carried away by the rush and sparkle of the stream of notes.

The movement exists for ten minutes with changes of mood but without a real change of material, always returning to the rapt expression of the opening.

The slow movement avoids sonata form, consisting of two sections where canons in the orchestra are heavily decorated by prismatic piano arpeggios, followed by a third in which, as in the corresponding movement of Beethoven's Fourth Concerto, the piano is called upon to calm down an angry orchestra. The movement ends in wonderful peace.

The finale is a rondo whose subjects return to gaiety from episodes which are by turns richly romantic, charmingly capricious, and one containing what would be rather sternly Brahmsian piano chords were they not crystallised by the celesta. Here and elsewhere in the concerto there are concessions to brilliance and tonal indulgencies which are unexpected in Tippett, even after hearing his opera. The concerto may, in the last analysis, lack the fiery urgency of the opera, but there is no doubt that it is the most important British concerto since Walton's equally masterly work for viola.

Tippett was well served by his soloist for Louis Kentner had not only mastered the fantastically difficult notes but had penetrated to the meaning behind the notes. Unfortunately the conductor, Rudolf Schwarz, had not a similar insight into the work nor was the C.B.S.O. able to execute the notes with any great degree of efficiency or proper balance. The music presents difficult problems, not made any easier by the hall's over-resonance. As it was, the work's merits were clearly seen, so conductor and orchestra are to be thanked for their patience, and we can all look forward to frequent rehearings of this fascinating new work.

A TALE OF FOUR OPERAS:
The Spectator   7.12.56

The winning entries in the 1951 Festival of Britain opera competition were Arthur Benjamin's *A Tale of Two Cities*, Alan Bush's *Wat Tyler*, Berthold Goldschmidt's *Beatrice Cenci* and Karl Rankl's *Dierdre of the Sorrows.* The prize was £200 each with no guarantee of performance. The kudos brought frustration in its wake for the four composers, they have been trying ever since to get their operas on to the English stage.

Rankl refused to allow his opera to be broadcast, but he has recently made and performed a concert suite of music taken from it. Substantial extracts from Goldschmidt's work have been heard on the BBC and Benjamin's was given in full this way. *Wat Tyler* is to be broadcast on December 9 and 10 on the Third, but has otherwise been heard only in extract at a concert given, with piano, in the Conway Hall.

Not unnaturally two of these four composers looked towards the Continent. I understand that Benjamin has placed his work at Metz, with a premiere due in March. But the story of Alan Bush and his opera(s) is rather remarkable and deserves to be told more fully. Bush is *persona grata* behind the Curtain and managed to get the East Berlin radio to broadcast *Wat Tyler*. As a result of the performance Leipzig decided to stage the opera in 1953. It was such a success that it was given over twenty times during two seasons and Bush found himself with commissions for three further operas for Rostock, Berlin and Weimar.

HS: I believe Rankl's *Dierdre* was never produced, Benjamin's *Tale* was eventually done at Sadler's Wells in 1957, Bush's *Wat Tyler* likewise, same theatre in 1974, *Beatrice Cenci* was heard in concert during the Goldschmidt flowering of interest in the '90s, and was staged more than once in Germany.

Karl Rankl was a curious man, by no means untalented but over-parted as music director of Covent Garden 1946-51. I believe he knew he was out of his depth and he conveyed his inferiority to his musicians. I suspect that his compositions (eight symphonies as well as an oratorio and *Dierdre*) suffered from being what the Germans call Kapellmeistermusik; that is well made boring music.

L.P.O. in LONDON:
Poulenc's Concerto for Two Pianos   14.1.57

The Liverpool Philharmonic Orchestra paid one of its rare visits to London on Sunday night to give a concert in the Royal Festival Hall. The playing and the programme were of the sort to make one wish that the visits will be more frequent.

John Pritchard has not long been the conductor of this orchestra, but already between them there has been established a *rapport*. There were a few hesitant 'plonks' from the strings during the evening, but otherwise the playing was very good; the standard of wind and brass playing has improved greatly.

The programme seemed to have been devised to contain something for everybody – Wagner, Haydn, Poulenc, Vaughan Williams, and Bartok.

Bartok's decision to rescue an orchestral suite from his ballet *The Miraculous Mandarin* may have been a mistake. The plot of the ballet is so unsavoury that performances of it on the stage must be rare. The music of the suite is continuous, and its eighteen minutes are a protracted crescendo in tension and grim harmonies but not supported by any substantial or even interesting musical ideas.

The Haydn Symphony chosen was one of the few examples of the genre in the minor key: number 80 in D. It is a work full of eccentricity, and well worth playing. The conductor brought an excellent sense of style and wit to the performance.

The Concerto of the evening was Poulenc's for two pianos and orchestra, in which the composer was partnered by Benjamin Britten. This was not the first time they have played their work together. I remember a performance in the Albert Hall some ten years ago. Then, as now, the ear was struck by the Frenchman's cloudy pedalling and the Englishman's cleanness.

As for Poulenc's music, as usual, it is difficult to know what to think; and the best advice when listening to it, perhaps, is – Do not think: let this entertainer divert you.

Debussy wrote of the first Paris performance of *Tod und Verklärung* (I quote from memory): 'In the recipe for jugged hare the directions begin by saying "take a hare". The trouble with Strauss is: he takes anything.'

What would Debussy have thought, then, of Poulenc? For the range of ingredients in Poulenc's dishes (*soufflés surprises*?) is far wider than in Strauss. Poulenc will start off a movement, as he does the middle one of this concerto, with Mozart, go on to 'café chantant', Massenet, Stravinsky; the music swings from one succulent chord to another like Rachmaninov, gives a pat cadence like a music-hall number, then, as if twinged by conscience, behaves austerely for a bar or two. But then it's off in a flash and one feels that Poulenc's facial resemblance to Fernandel is no accident but a reminder not to take him too seriously. At the same time, though, do not laugh out loud because you might miss some flash of wit, a slapstick gesture, a beautiful tune, or an original piece of scoring.

HS: One reason why I remembered the previous (1946) performance of the Concerto was that I turned pages on that occasion for the composer (Marion Stein – later Countess of Harewood and Mrs Jeremy Thorpe – did so for Britten). My remarks about *The Miraculous Mandarin* were belied by its subsequent popular acclaim. I still dislike it.

WALTON'S CELLO CONCERTO:
European Premiere   15.2.57

The Royal Philharmonic Society gave the European première of William Walton's 'Cello Concerto in the Royal Festival Hall on Wednesday. The BBC not only provided its orchestra and conductor, Sir Malcolm Sargent, but also broadcast and televised the occasion.

The work was commissioned by Gregor Piatigorsky, who played the solo part on Wednesday and also last month in Boston at the world premiere. There are three movements: an elegiac slow movement, a typical Waltonish scherzo, and a set of variations.

This new concerto is, I would say, Walton's finest work since the Violin Concerto, for although the new piece is conservative in outlook it does seem to be the result of a genuine impulse rather than – as many felt of the String Quartet, Violin Sonata, and *Troilus and Cressida* – a tired composer's determined effort to break silence and keep his publisher happy.

The Concerto is superbly written for the instrument which is able to 'speak' more characteristically than in any cello piece since Bloch's *Schelomo*. The orchestral texture is glossy and opulent, complete with vibraphone. Walton may not 'look back in anger', but our ears can 'sink back in comfort'.

The first movement is perhaps the finest: here is Walton writing, for once, a slow movement without any underlying sense of anxiety. The scherzo recalls old favourites and synthesizes the emotions of the second act of *Troilus*. The finale is the least successful part, for the two solo variations show that unaccompanied Walton does not come off; he needs support for his melody. The coda is probably half a minute too long.

Piatigorsky's able tone was as fat as a house, and if his technique had a few faults in it they were as superficial as cracks in the plaster of a fine façade. Sargent accompanied as only he can when his sympathy is wholly engaged.

HS: Piatigorsky told me a year or two later that he had tried to persuade the composer to rewrite the finale with a loud ending (vanity cannot be ruled out; a loud finish elicits more applause). It was tried out but Walton rightly preferred his first thoughts.

Sir William Walton (1902-83) kick-started his career with the witty, brilliant and durable series of fireworks, the entertainment called *Façade* (twenty-one poems of Edith Sitwell spoken with the accompaniment of six instrumentalists). His mature oeuvre began with the Viola concerto. By the end of the '30s he was the white hope (Vaughan Williams being the older hope). But in the war Walton was busy writing brilliant scores for Laurence Olivier's Shakespeare films. At the end of the war he found that Benjamin Britten and Michael Tippett had become the hopes and that he, Walton, with no new works of esteem, was in danger of becoming a has-been. He retired to Italy with a bride and got busy (busy, that is, for a slow composer). Sets of variations on themes by his old friend Hindemith, and his rival Britten, notwithstanding, nothing Walton achieved postwar came up to scratch. The grand opera *Troilus and Cressida*, a chamber opera *The Bear*, a Cello Concerto, a second symphony and shorter works were all shadows of his former vitality. The same furrow was ploughed again and again. Agreeable but not important music.

Walton was a lucky man. He was taken up and encouraged at Oxford, the Sitwells made him their protégé and without their help his career might not have taken off. I was lucky, too, in being invited to stay with William and Susana, his bride from Argentina, on Ischia and had a chance to get to know him better than I did. He was a lively companion and a good host, thoughtful and at times thoroughly wicked with a black humour. In his interview he was frequently 'economical with the truth'.

BEECHAM AT HIS BEST:
25.3.57

I met a Cornish farmer last week at the Royal Festival Hall and for once he was not complaining about the weather although his farm, he said, was literally bogged down. Unable to sow, he had left a girl in charge of the cows and come up to town for some spiritual refreshment. 'Best musical weekend of the year' and although 'Thursday to Tuesday' would have been more accurate, he was right.

The weekend was truly festive: Beecham was at his best, two Klemperer concerts, Ralph Kirkpatrick giving an illuminating and invigorating harpsichord recital and a visit from the Concertgebouw Orchestra. And if my Cornish farmer had come a day earlier, he could have started his little festival with Lisa della Casa singing the Strauss *Four Last Songs* last Wednesday in the BBC Symphony Concert. The Swiss diva has a voice as glamorous as her looks and one has to close one's eyes to realize that she does not always support her glamour with musical penetration. On this occasion, she went through the motions very prettily and that was all; the accompaniment was careful at the expense of sonority.

Beecham visits the New World at the turn of each New Year, and we Londoners know that spring is here when Sir Thomas arrives home. Teasing the Americans seems to stimulate him, for he always comes back renewed in vigour and vigilance. Last Thursday he was, so to speak, a ball of fire, and the Royal Philharmonic Orchestra rose to great heights in Rimsky-Korsakov's *Scheherazade*. This was Technicolor, Vistavision, 3-D, wide screen playing; and the Sibelius Second Symphony was also given a vivid performance.

Klemperer and the Philharmonia Orchestra devoted one whole evening to Mozart and another to Beethoven. Klemperer's Beethoven is so utterly convincing – even the *Grosse Fuge* came off – that one might be forgiven for identifying the conductor for the composer. Here seems to be Beethoven himself: the stricken giant moving heaven and earth and the audience with musical will-power. And when Klemperer conducts Mozart, the impression remains: this is now Beethoven conducting the works of Mozart. This is Mozart seen through the eyes and ears of the composer who has experienced the *Eroica*, the Ninth and the *Missa Solemnis.*

The *Jupiter* can take this sort of treatment but the G minor does not fully reveal itself: the E flat partly succeeds, partly not. An evening devoted to these three last symphonies is quite an ordeal, but since the *Jupiter* naturally comes last, the result seemed justified. But the next morning one wakes up with a longing to hear Beecham do the same programme. Fortunately, he is conducting two of the late symphonies quite soon so there will be an opportunity to make odious comparisons.

Klemperer's Beethoven evening included the Seventh Symphony and the First Piano Concerto as well as the *Great Fugue*. The Fugue is said to be intractable, but when it as well played as on this occasion it is a revelation, a supreme example of unlimited vision brought into being by the most rigorous self-discipline. There is hardly a note in it that is not of vital thematic significance, so that the Fugue is a parallel with the greatest fugues in Bach: the Ricercare and Contrapuncti IX and XIII from *The Art of Fugue.*

Geza Anda's playing of the concerto was note-perfect but lacking in poetry, spontaneity and gaiety.

Eduard van Beinum has gained something in brilliance since I last heard him, although his orchestra remains just as wonderful an instrument as ever. Between them, Mendelssohn's *Italian* Symphony emerged new-minted, with virtuosity, impeccable balance and musical meaning. A Dutch novelty was a *Passacaille et Cortège* of Vermeulen (b.1888); this was said to be a sea-piece but it sounded more like ditchwater.

COMPLETE...FAULTLESS:
Fischer-Dieskau   10.4.57

Perfection in composers is not utterly impossible; after all, there are several centuries from which to choose a Monteverdi, a Bach, a Mozart, a Beethoven, a Schubert. Perfect performers, on the one hand have to be found at a given moment of time, but when they *are* to be heard there seems to be no sensible reason for withholding the adjective. The dictionary says 'complete, not deficient, faultless'; the definition fits the singing of Dietrich Fischer-Dieskau, so why not apply it?

This German singer has been to London during the last week: on Friday, with Walter Goehr, the London Symphony Orchestra and boys from Highgate School, he sang Bach's Cantata No. 56, 'Ich will dem Kreuzstab gerne tragen' and on Monday he gave a Schubert recital with Gerald Moore at the piano.

The Divine Authorities are usually cautious with their gifts. To one they may give a voice, to another musicianship, to a third good looks; to some they may, rather rarely, hand two of these gifts. But to Fischer-Dieskau was given all three, so that even now this young man is at the height of his powers and his profession. His singing is effortless, so that seen in the Royal Festival Hall, which is large and not flattering to the voice, he could afford to start the recital with 'Dem Unendlichen', which is virtually a vocal trombone solo. The sound of his voice filled the hall; following came the still quietness of 'Der Kreuzzug'. The groups were well chosen from amongst, on the whole, the lesser known Schubert: 'Totengräbers Heimweh', with its dynamic contrasts, the massive 'Prometheus', the horrifying ballad 'Der Zwerg' and the imaginative 'Meerestille'. However, there were old favourites among the last group and the generous ration of encores: I do not think I have heard 'Who is Sylvia?' more ardently or movingly sung. Gerald Moore started lumpily but recovered himself as the evening went on.

ZURICH MUSIC FESTIVAL:
Premiere of Schönberg's Moses und Aron 15.6.57

Every year there is a festival of the International Society of Contemporary Music and every year, apart from the five or six concerts of chamber, choral, orchestral and – a new feature this year – electronic music, there are 'sideshows'.

At Zurich this year the new music has not been up to much: of the concerts that I heard the only thing worth writing home about was the curious occurrence of an audience laughing a performance to a standstill. The piece in question was an *Epitaph* by Karl Heinz Fuessl, a young Austrian: a set of variations in the neo-Webern style, not too bad until the last one which proceeded by monotonous chords. The orchestra got the giggles, the audience caught them and, bingo, the damage was done.

Just for the record, perhaps I should mention that nearly all parties agreed on the worth of certain works. Praise fell on Matyas Seiber's *Concert Piece* for violin and piano, Roman Haubenstock-Romati's *Recitativo and Arias* for harpsichord and orchestra, and Hans Werner Henze's Five Neapolitan Songs.

Universal hate was reserved for a String Quartet by Billy Jim Layton and a piece called *Frequencies* by the Swedish Bo Nilsson.

The side-shows were two in number: a concert of music by Swiss composers whose quality reminded one of the dictum that if the Swiss had made the Alps they would have been a good deal flatter. The most important work of this programme was Frank Martin's *Etudes* for string orchestra (1956) but this turned out to be but his usual music 'writ small'.

No, the big event of the Festival was the first staging of Schönberg's opera *Moses und Aron* given in the Stadttheater, in the presence of a distinguished audience, which included the composer's widow and daughter as well as his pupils and disciples from all over the world. The composer himself fashioned the text, based on the Old Testament, in three acts. He finished the score of the first two acts between 1930 and 1932, often spoke of completing the work but never did so before his death in 1951.

In the first act comes the calling of Moses from the Burning Bush, the meeting of Moses and Aaron in the Wasteland; God's message is brought to the People and Aaron works his miracles, turning rod into serpent and Nile water into blood. Moses's inability to be a mouth-piece is signified by the fact that his is only a speaking (sprechstimme) rôle whereas the more eloquent and guileful Aaron is a dramatic tenor.

After a muttered interlude ('Where is Moses?') we see in the second act Aaron and the seventy Elders before the Mountain of Revelation. Aaron appeases the angry people by giving them the Golden Calf to worship. After scenes of orgy and killing, Moses returns from the Mountain with the laws written on two tablets, the final scene is the argument between Aaron (the Image) and Moses (the Word). The stage darkens as Moses, having broken the tablets, declaims: 'They have fashioned an image too, false, as an image must be. Thus I am defeated! Thus, all was but madness that I believed before, and can and must not be given voice. O word, O word, that I lack!'

Why, then, did not Schönberg set the third act wherein Aaron, released by Moses from the chains in which he has placed him, drops dead? There could be several answers. First, that all had been said in the first two acts. Secondly that Schönberg felt the problem of Moses and Aaron as two sides of his own nature and, possibly, with the technique of dodecaphony as the Image (or the Word). Thirdly, that the purely operatic problem, of ending what has been largely a 'chorus opera' with a single scene that is in effect an extended duet, was insoluble.

Scenically and dramatically the first two acts are well laid out and so the story does not fail to be effective and impressive. The production and decor at the Stadttheater were highly imaginative, and if the Golden Calf orgy seemed like a Swiss Folies Bergères one must say that such a scene would be difficult to film satisfactorily, let alone stage. (Schönberg asks, for example, for 'four Naked Virgins' but then, rather characteristically, adds a footnote 'Naked to the extent that the rules and necessities of the stage allow and require'.)

A diagonal platform protruded right across the orchestral pit and most of the decor was done by means of back-projection on to a cyclorama.

But what of the music? Music so difficult that its 92 minutes required 320 rehearsals for the choir and 70 for the orchestra, under the inspired direction of that single-minded conductor, Hans Rosbaud.

Well, to be autobiographical, I found that I was not moved by the music the first time and I liked it less the second and third times. Between the second and third performances, like Moses, I retired up the mountain with, as my tablets, the newly published vocal score of the opera (available in London at a mere four guineas).

Familiarity has bred the conviction that this is not music for me, even though I like some of Schönberg. One should beware of liking twelve-tone music simply because one can follow it.

Moses und Aron is rhythmically and texturally more interesting initially than many of Schönberg's works, but the constant busyness finally defeats its own ends. The result is thicker than Reger! At times it seems as if the composer is determined to cram as many rows into each bar as possible. Oh, the sound is so gritty, grey and grinding!

Maybe ears will become accustomed to such sounds in a few years time, but surely music which demands so much from performers and listeners will need to offer more emotional satisfaction than *Moses und Aron*? The Golden Calf episode, for example, does not sound either savage or exotic. The chorus that ends Act I is meant to be a rousing marching song: all well and good, the mind recognises what the composer is up to, notes that here is a broad chorus sung in canon and dodecaphony; does it rouse, does it uplift? No.

The parts I admired most were the muttered choral interlude, the painting of a wasteland jumping with horrid insects, one beautiful page in Act I Scene IV where Aaron tells the people that their spirit is broken (a curious Dallapiccola-like passage), and the final pages of the opera, where, at last, the texture simplifies to two lines (but this might be analogous to the lunatic who beats his head on a wall because it is so pleasant when he leaves off).

HS: The whole musical world and its Weib is here. And Felix Aprahamian and I are here in Zurich. We travelled together and we are staying at a hotel recommended by our mutual soprano friend, Adèle Leigh. Our wanderings round the town are complicated by the fact that Felix has utterly no sense of direction; and since he is unaware of the fact, we argue a lot if he wants to turn right when the blasted opera house is all but visible to the left. The press is well handled; there is even a list of journalists, where they come from, what journal they write for and where they are staying in Zurich. Our names being what they are, are at the top of the list. Journalists we don't even know keep coming up to us (especially the Swiss ones), asking us how we like our hotel. They don't actually nudge-nudge-wink-wink but there is obviously something funny about our hotel. To us it seems a perfectly ordinary, comfortable, middle-price hostelry. And then on the last day a couple of doors open that should not have and we suddenly realise that our hotel is a brothel, perhaps the only knocking-shop in Zurich.

Felix and I wonder about staying another night to verify what is going on but unfortunately our air tickets are concreted into the date of departure.

On that last evening we also find the only night club in Zurich which we visit with a few colleagues. The main event is a lady who does a strip tease act. After it is over Felix says we must all go round to the artist's room, just as we would if we were at the Wigmore Hall in London. So we stumble around and find the lady suitably undressed and somewhat astonished at our homage. 'Alors,' she says, 'c'est pas originale mais...'

One local musician that I met was the composer Robert Oboussier, born Antwerp 1900, follower of Busoni, pupil of Jarnach. He is amazed to find that I know and like his *Three Songs after Klopstock* and *Abbreviations* for harpsichord which I found on a German HMV disc, wild coloratura songs sung by the amazing soprano Erna Berger. Oboussier is in his late fifties and looks more like a banker than a musician, formal manners, formal clothes.

Shock horror: three days later to read in the papers that he had been brutally murdered by a sailor in Oboussier's own house in Zurich. It seems that he was found dead in the basement which had been kitted out as a torture chamber with pulleys, black leather, sound proof wall, nasty tools and so on. Very un-Swiss, *including* the sailor.

THE ALDEBURGH FESTIVAL:
Britten Rules the Staves   June 1957

The tenth Aldeburgh Festival has taken place this year in almost constant sunshine, tempered by a typical Suffolk sea-breeze. To compare Aldeburgh with Edinburgh would be to compare a Haydn String Quartet with Beethoven's Choral Symphony for, even with an influx of some 300 artists and visitors, Aldeburgh's population scarcely tops 3000.

You can walk anywhere in the town in ten minutes, you can soon get to know everybody – even the critics! – and if the face of the kind gentleman who shows you to your seat in the evening seems familiar it is because he has by day sold you your toothpaste. During the course of a visit you are bound to bump into the three artistic directors of the festival – Benjamin Britten, Imogen Holst and Peter Pears.

This year the composer Benjamin Britten was meagrely represented (by one gala performance of *Albert Herring* and a new suite of dances from old *Gloriana*), but Benjamin Britten the pianofortist was heard in a recital with Peter Pears devoted to Viennese song from Haydn and Mozart to Berg and Webern; Benjamin Britten the fortepianist played brilliantly in chamber music with the Amadeus Quartet; Benjamin Britten the harpsichordist was an imaginative continuo player in Bach's St John Passion; Benjamin Britten the conductor presided at the opera gala and directed a concert at which Yehudi Menuhin played Vivaldi's *The Seasons* and Mozart's *Haffner* Serenade.

This is not by any means to suggest that Mr Britten was hogging the show but to demonstrate that he worked like a Trojan and gave, as always, a stimulating and creative view of other composers' music. His playing in Schubert and Mahler songs was incomparably beautiful and quite unforgettable.

In one's youth one was told that there was another Bach Passion, besides the Matthew, but that it is a vastly inferior work. In fact, the St John Passion is in no way superseded by the great later work and is one of the great peaks in Bach's range. In her direction, Imogen Holst achieved a rare continuity, choosing unfailingly 'right' tempi and giving each part its own weight and place. Peter Pears was a sublime Evangelist and David Ward an eloquent Christus. Jennifer Vyvyan sang her second aria excellently but the performance suffered from David Kelly's rough bass solos and some even cruder tenor solos from Edgar Fleet and Philip Todd.

Julian Bream's lute was heard not only in this Passion but also memorably in Dowland's *Lachrymae*; this astonishingly gifted young artist was the hero of the concert in which, after the Dowland, he turned to the guitar and, after throwing off Villa-Lobos's (pretty dull) Concerto, played an exacting solo part in the new arrangement of the Courtly Dances from *Gloriana*. These dances were played in the opera by six players; in the orchestral suite the treatment was on the heavy side but this new arrangement, made for the combination of players available for this particular concert, comes off perfectly.

In the same concert Pamela Bowden's mellifluous alto voice was heard to good advantage in Haydn's *Ariadne* cantata and in the young German composer Hans Werner Henze's *Apollo und Hyacinth*, a non-tonal but poetic piece for voice, harpsichord and eight instruments.

Seven young composers had their works performed together in one morning concert. Most of them followed the neo-Webern-cum-Boulez path and I confess that I was unable to see any beautiful or interesting views from this path. Non-adherents included Malcolm Williamson who had written a pleasing little song on Blake's 'The Fly' and Alan Cohen who produced some engaging duet trifles for clarinet and trumpet.

The organisers of this festival have been wise in taking concerts out of Aldeburgh into some of the outstandingly beautiful churches in the vicinity. Yehudi Menuhin played a recital in Blythburgh (with its wonderful painted angel beams) and the Amadeus Quartet were on top form in a concert at Framlingham, playing Beethoven's Opus 132 with true insight.

It was at Framlingham that I heard the remark of the festival. A very charming editor of a magazine (it has quite a vogue in the bazaar, helps with good housekeeping and is womanly, but naturally I cannot say which magazine it is) said to me: 'Bartok 6 does make Schubert's Quintet sound rather like Daphne du Maurier, doesn't it?'

81

A LESSON FROM LOTTE LEHMANN:
October 1957

Last week I heard by far the most satisfactory performance I have ever experienced of the Flower Song from *Carmen*. There was no stage, there was no orchestra and oddest of all, no tenor. The singer was a woman of seventy-two and the occasion was a lesson.

It was one of the master-classes being given in the Wigmore Hall by that distinguished soprano, Lotte Lehmann. This great artist has now no soprano voice left but she has the gift of teaching and her classes have been inspiring, both for the audience and for those who were up on the platform having their lessons. There have been two series: one on lieder and one on opera.

The courses were arranged by the Opera School and the singers were auditioned preliminarily by a board of selectors chosen by the school. The singer, or singers, would come on to the platform, Mme Lehmann would explain the text of the song or the situation of the scene in the opera, and then the lesson would begin. The pupil would be put at ease to a greater or lesser extent by Mme Lehmann's reassuring personality, sometimes with the help of some often very funny and revealing anecdote from the past.

In a word, what Lotte Lehmann teaches singers is to think what they are singing about: the meaning of the words, the situation and the character; so often they are only thinking about how they are singing. Take the case of the Flower Song: the young tenor who sang is a talented boy; but he sang his song prettily, as if it were a set piece (which, in a way, of course it is, but it is so much more than that). Lotte Lehmann asked if she might have a shot at the song herself, singing it in German with a chest voice that cannot be said to have much tone to it.

Ivor Newton played as quietly as a mouse (he was a model of self-effacing efficiency throughout the series) and Mme Lehmann went through the song, beginning, not with calmness, as most singers, but with a fiercely pleading passion not far removed from anger. This really was a creditable Don José and the dramatic truth and beauty of the performance brought tears to more eyes than mine.

Of course, there were fierce arguments in the lobbies of the Wigmore Hall in the intervals. But it is something to get singers to think. Many of them thought that there was a tendency to overdo the actions in the operatic sessions. Maybe; but what had to be remembered was that we were eavesdropping at a lesson and also that a teacher often has to exaggerate by a hundred per cent in order to make the pupil respond by five per cent.

Myself, I think it is possible that, although the large audience learned a lot from these sessions, the singers themselves would learn far more with a much smaller audience; more time for each singer and a more intimate atmosphere than the Wigmore Hall.

What was encouraging was the high standard of those having lessons: some quite well-known of our younger singers took their turn and the unknown ones were also very good.

HS: Lotte Lehmann (1888-1976) on stage as the Marschallin in Richard Strauss's *Der Rosenkavalier* was apparently one of the Seven Wonders of the opera world. She captured every heart, including that of the composer, as far as a complete realisation of that character and that music was concerned. He said of her that he would sooner have Lehmann singing a few wrong notes than anyone else singing the right ones. She sang all three principal roles in his opera and also created three other roles in three other operas of his. But she was also a great Sieglinde in *Walküre* and equally successful in Mozart, Puccini and Beethoven. She was also a fine recitalist as her records show. Which all meant that she was, by her character, by her musicianship and her experience, ideally suited to teach and her masterclasses were some of the best, despite that she occasionally liked to show off just a little bit. She began her career in her native Germany but soon was in demand all over, especially in America where she settled, retired and died after a long and glorious career.

KLEMPERER TRIUMPHS WITH BEETHOVEN: 17.11.57

Last week Klemperer finished the Beethoven cycle which has occupied him, the Philharmonia Orchestra, the Royal Festival Hall's vast audience, and who knows how many more over the air. The last concert on Friday contained the Eighth and Ninth Symphonies. In the Eighth it was the weight of the orchestral texture which was so fascinating to hear; and so fascinating to compare with the weight of texture in the same work when, say, Beecham conducts it.

Beecham, of course, brings out the elegance and gaiety of the work; he might almost be said to be looking at it through Mozartian spectacles. With Klemperer, the specific gravity is heavier, the humour is gruffer; if there is elegance it is the elegance of a giant wearing court dress.

The performance of the Ninth Symphony was something to remember for ever; the race of musical gods appears to be dying out and it may be doubted whether we shall hear the like to this kind of performance when Klemperer is gone. When one of the greatest creations in music is played like this it is difficult to do more than say one's thanks. The detail was so clear that there were many things revealed for the first time, and yet it was the overall conception which made for the sublime experience.

So often when trying to grope for a reason for a conductor's greatness I find that one of the most important factors is the possession of the gift for finding the natural rhythm for a given piece of music and then being able to impart that rhythm to the performers. So many conductors have a superficial, unnatural sense of rhythm; it may seem to be accurate by the metronome but it is rhythm 'applied' and not 'felt'. But even this rhythmic gift is only part of the conductor's gifts. He must feel the music right and 'will' it across the orchestra. Certainly with Beethoven Klemperer approaches perfection, and that is enough.

Often a good performance of the Ninth tumbles to pieces when the finale starts. The vocal quartet was not perfect on this occasion but it was adequate, the debut of the Philharmonia Chorus was a stunning success. Wilhelm Pitz, the Bayreuth chorus-master, had worked a miracle with our local singers. Here was a choir which could enunciate words at top speed and provide good tone to the extent of meeting Beethoven's taxing demands. The top As rang out with joy and fervour, too; occasionally the notes went awry but they carried conviction and the movement crackled with excitement. There was none of the usual feeling that Beethoven had misjudged anything or was lapsing into vulgarity, only the subsequent feeling that the only misjudging or lapses have been on the part of former performers.

IN MEMORY OF BRAIN:
16.12.57

Dennis Brain and his Chamber Orchestra had arranged to give a concert for the Chelsea Music Club last week. It was decided that the orchestra should keep the date, before disbanding, and that the evening should be devoted to the memory of its founder. Three of Dennis's friends agreed to conduct: Norman Del Mar took on Mozart's Symphony No. 33 and Stravinsky's *Dumbarton Oaks* Concerto (which had long ago been scheduled for this programme), Peter Racine Fricker directed his own Concertante for cor anglais and strings (played by Leonard Brain); in the second half of the programme Benjamin Britten directed Purcell's Chaconne for Strings and a suite of songs from the same composer's *Orpheus Britannicus*. The evening ended with the last song from Britten's own *Serenade*. This sonnet of Keats is the number in which the horn player does not play, using the time to go off-stage to play the epilogue for unaccompanied horn. The effect in the hall on this occasion was sad and almost eerie, for in the silence one began to listen for the familiar and accustomed sound of Dennis Brain playing the horn-call.

The first half of the programme was gloomy and the playing utterly lifeless and dull (even *Dumbarton Oaks*), but as soon as Britten started to conduct the players responded and began to make music. Britten's orchestration of the Purcell songs is sometimes more Britten than Purcell, but as it is Britten at his most fascinating and sincere the result is pleasing. As an example one would cite the opening of 'So when the glittering Queen of Night'; the sound of muted cellos and basses playing in tenths in the key of B minor paints a bewitching nocturnal velvet sky. Peter Pears sang with all his accustomed mastery.

HS: Dennis crashed his car and was killed on his way home from playing in the Edinburgh Festival during the night of 1 September 1957. I think that part of the secret of his miraculous horn playing was the fact that, like Siegfried, Dennis knew no fear. And of course his immaculate musicianship which spread to his lesser-known ability at both the organ and the harpsichord. As a man (to be Irish) Dennis was a boy, a schoolboy game for any lark, with a passion for cars and a ready laugh whose loudness was in direct ratio to his non-comprehension of the joke. He was thirty-six when he died and had already got as far as he could in his profession. But we still mourn.

A YEAR OF MANY PLEASURES: 30.12.57

Carols are better sung than reported on, and there has surely been enough written about *Messiah,* so that there has been nothing new to comment on in London music this week except for Richard Arnell's new ballet, referred to in another column. The standby at this season of the year, of course, is the glance back and the prospect before us; what has a year's assiduous Metropolitan listening brought forth? There have been many pleasures – enough, indeed, to understand why Londoners are a little jaded and do not always support a worthy but well-advertised venture (like the Liverpool Philharmonic's recent London concert).

The year started with Britten's brilliant but still not fully appreciated score to Cranko's not brilliant *The Prince of the Pagodas.* There have been no other interesting ballet scores, but we look forward to the postponed Henze music for Ashton's new *Ondine,* scheduled for next spring. Bartok's magnificent *Bluebeard's Castle* had not been staged before in this country but this year we had two productions of it: Dr Chisholm's semi-professional attempt at the Rudolf Steiner Hall and Sadler's Wells's much better one.

A similar sudden outburst occurred in Berlioz operas: Carl Rosa's illuminating glimpse of *Benvenuto Cellini* and Covent Garden's grand Gielgud showing of *The Trojans.* Covent Garden also gallantly gave Michael Tippett's *Midsummer Marriage* a further two hearings to consolidate the work's tremendous musical value and to point anew to the unfortunate obscurity of the text. How much more worthwhile are ten bars of this opera than the whole of Gardner's *Moon and Sixpence,* although Sadler's Wells had lavished on it, through the great art of Peter Hall, perhaps the best piece of operatic production seen in this country, certainly in my experience.

My own favourite in the Wells repertoire, is Wolf-Ferrari's *School for Fathers, I Quattro Rusteghi,* a happy combination of Italian melody,

German musicality and British adaptation. At Glyndebourne the best value for (big) money came from Rossini's *Comte Ory*, a thoroughly integrated piece of confection. Television opera took a step forward when Rudolf Cartier showed us and his more operatically experienced colleagues how to tackle the problem with Menotti's rather unsavoury *Saint of Bleeker Street*. Joan Trimble's BBC-commissioned *Blind Rafferty* was not so well produced but it did point the way to a lyrical and likeable ballad opera style.

The London Philharmonic Orchestra finished off one carefully designed series of recent music, *Music of a Century* and started on another called *Grand Tour de la Musique*. Manuel Rosenthal gave, for the I.C.A., a fine Stravinsky concert on the occasion of the Master's seventy-fifth birthday; and the Master himself graced for a fortnight the Summer School of Music at Dartington, where a miniature festival of his works took place.

Other highlights were the new Cello Concerto of Walton, Peter Pears's moving Evangelist in the St John Passion at Aldeburgh and – perhaps the best single performance of the year – Klemperer's memorable Ninth Symphony which crowned his Beethoven series with the Philharmonia Orchestra in the Royal Festival Hall.

Souzay, Fischer-Dieskau, Michelangeli, Clara Haskil and de los Angeles (in *Madam Butterfly*) all lived up to expectation. A last-minute substitute, Gerda Lammers, made a sensation singing the title role in Kempe's well conducted *Elektra* at Covent Garden, Lotte Lehmann's master-classes at the Wigmore Hall were a revelation to singers and listeners.

My prize for the best young singer of the year would go to Joan Sutherland, for the most outstanding young conductor to Colin Davis; for the most talented unknown composer to Carlo Martelli (who has had several fine works performed by the Society of New Music: make a note of his name); and my prize for the finest work by a known but not senior composer to Franz Reizenstein for his cantata *Voices of Night*.

FLAWS IN A GENIUS:
A New Tippett Symphony   8.2.58

The most important event of the week was the first performance of Michael Tippett's Symphony No. 2, commissioned by the BBC and performed by its Symphony Orchestra at one of its Wednesday concerts at the Royal Festival Hall. Sir Adrian Boult aroused the sympathy and admiration of all when he stopped the orchestra after about two minutes of the first movement, took the blame for a slip which resulted in the horns and the strings being a bar apart and started again from the beginning. A lesser man would have hoped for the best, or stopped, glared hard at some unfortunate section of the orchestra and started again without apology. (I believe that Tovey, however, often provided a precedent for Boult's action.)

The new symphony is a work of tremendous power, human warmth and imaginative genius, like certain other pieces by Michael Tippett. Like them, though, and it is his opera *The Midsummer Marriage* and the Piano Concerto that I am thinking of, there are certain flaws which, I am afraid, prevent the work from making its full effect and thus coming to the wide audience it deserves.

In a nutshell, in many places in this new score, there is too much going on at the same time and the orchestral writing is so difficult as to make future performances rare. This is especially true of the first movement, which nevertheless – and one cannot stress this too much – is a movement of great stature and possessed of that poetic, imaginative vision which sets Tippett high above all his other British colleagues, even Britten. If only he had a tithe of Britten's infallible sense of clarity and effectiveness.

Tippett's second movement, a slow one, is the most successful; it is a movement that proceeds by magic, colour and song rather than by development. It will remind the listener of *The Midsummer Marriage* (so does much of the symphony) and yet he will be conscious of the fact that Tippett has moved on from the opera and that many of the sounds are new.

The scherzo is a gay dance in an unequal rhythm whose harmonic rate of change is slow enough for the ear to be enchanted without being baffled. The finale is loosely put together, after the manner of an Elizabethan 'fancy', its centre is a thrilling but brief chaconne and the succeeding section, an imaginatively scored accompaniment to a tune that comes out of the skies and descends deep into the earth, seems altogether too slack a means of returning to the pounding Cs on the double basses that are the beginning and end of this new symphony.

BRITTEN'S NEW WORKS:
20.6.58

This year's Festival at Aldeburgh, the little seaside Suffolk town where Benjamin Britten lives, has many attractions among the various exhibitions, lectures, concerts and operas. But the most notable events have been the performances of two new works by Britten himself. On Tuesday we had Opus 8, six *Songs from the Chinese*, set for voice and guitar, and on Thursday Opus 59, a new children's opera called *Noye's Fludde*.

The two works have much in common yet are as different as chalk from cheese. The six settings of Arthur Waley's translations are highly sophisticated music, written for two virtuosi to perform – no amateurs could get near the notes. The two virtuosi in question, Peter Pears and Julian Bream, romped through the difficulties with scarcely a twitch of the eyebrows, putting over the songs in masterly fashion. With the fewest possible notes, Britten evokes the scenes that the poems describe: the dust of the big chariot, the old lute, the autumn wind, the herd-boy, depression and gaiety.

He writes with his customary sympathy and sets his extraordinary imagination to the possibilities of the guitar, making the instrument turn old technique to new account and inventing new sounds for it that suit it perfectly.

There is beauty here in abundance in these songs that are tinged with an autumnal quality inherent in the words. The concert took place in the drawing room of Great Glemham House, a good setting for such intimate music.

So much for Opus 58, a work for two virtuosi. Opus 59 is at the other end of the scale; for this new opera can be performed almost entirely by amateurs, as on this occasion. The performance took place in the rather square Parish Church of Orford (a sizeable mediaeval town when the church was built but now a village about five miles south of Aldeburgh). *Noye's Fludde* is a setting of the Chester Miracle Play. In Britten's oeuvre it follows the style of the cantata *Saint Nicolas*.

Performers included 150 children and a handful of grown-ups. Seventy-five of the children were either Noah's family or the animals who entered the ark that the family had built so speedily upon the stage. The other children were employed in the orchestra; for Britten has written special parts for strings, percussion, recorders, and buglers. There were tots playing on tiny violins, others on half-sized cellos, with parts that did not exceed open notes or passages in the easiest position; the recorders were given wonderfully imaginative music representing the storm, the buglers stuck to simple fanfares in B flat, which made a hair-raising effect in the final joyous hymn in G major, while the percussion instruments included such simplicities as hand-bells (their use to describe the rainbow is so telling as to amount to a stroke of genius) and teacups of various pitch suspended from a length of string (the composer himself chose and tested these instruments in the local stores).

The professional forces consisted of five string players, recorder, percussion, piano duet, and organ. The conductor, Charles Mackerras, kept his vast numbers well in order.

The language of the old play is most affecting, and the drama is played out with us, the congregation, joining in three times with appropriate hymns. Colin Graham's staging and production matches the simplicity and ingenuity of the composer, and the total result is both enchanting and exceedingly moving.

Owen Brannigan is a lovable Noah, Trevor Anthony is the Voice of God, and Gladys Parr is just right as the gossiping, tippling, unworthy Mrs Noah. One or two of the children are inaudible, even in the front row, but they have such charm that they can get away with anything. The scores of children have been called from schools over most of the county, and their colourings and features are so similar as to give the impression of one big family. And a happy family at that, all enjoying themselves as hugely as the audience, so imaginatively, melodiously and dramatically has Benjamin Britten done his work in this new forty-five-minute opera which many schools all over the country will do well to perform.

CALLAS TRIUMPHS DESPITE VOCAL DEFECTS: 23.6.58

La Traviata at Covent Garden was a triumph for Maria Callas: tonight's performance was a return of the one-big-star system.

With just about as much support as Garbo had in the film *Camille*, Callas scores almost as big a success in the opera built on the same story.

Callas's success was the more remarkable because, as radio listeners may have judged, the diva was not in great form vocally. There were those at Covent Garden who were complaining that, with closed eyes, this performance was often almost unbearable because of Callas's spreading top notes and her mouthful-of-plums chest voice; they were quite right, too.

But to *see* this performance was to witness a histrionic triumph and to be very much moved by it. Callas completely identified herself with the heroine.

The over-all conception of the part was a striking success and there were about 100 details to aid it.

To see her in the first act, listening to Alfredo and gradually taking notice of his ardent advances; to see her in the second act, listening to Germont Senior, gradually realising what the old man was trying to get her to do – this was the work of a great actress.

Add to this Callas's suitable slimness, her extraordinary looks, her fine sense of musicianship and the occasional superb phrase, brilliant fioritura or bewitching coloratura – and there was a Violetta to remember all one's days.

Just as Garbo was not helped much by her fellow-artists but was given an able director, so Callas was given – or chose herself – two principals vastly inferior to herself, but had the benefit of an extremely able conductor.

Nicola Rescigno has been associated with Callas in America, and he clearly knows her requirements. The way he swiftly adjusted the tempo of '*Sempre Libera*' in the first act was a splendid piece of fielding.

Immediately the prelude got under way the orchestral playing took on an Italian warmth, attack and flavour. Strange to say, there was a voice across the footlights ad libbing in the prelude; presumably this was the prima donna warming up.

Cesare Valetti seems to have established himself firmly with the American public, but his vocal ability was on this occasion not particularly distinguished, although it was certainly adequate, and his acting of the part of Alfredo was weak. Mario Zanasi, as Germont Senior, has also entrenched himself in America, but the same limitations were noticeable.

The rest of the cast and the chorus were from the Covent Garden Company singing in Italian. Sophie Fedorovitch's costumes and sets still delight the eye and enhance an otherwise nondescript production.

HS: I met Callas once and was struck by her beauty. I had been interviewing Giuseppe di Stefano at the Savoy Hotel. I found him a cocky swine despite my admiration for some of his singing on records; the early Sicilian songs and the *Tosca*, one of the finest recordings of any opera, Callas and Gobbi at their best and de Sabata's conducting is out of this world. Anyway, after we finished the interview he asked if I would like to meet Callas and we went down to the lobby and there was the goddess. I can't remember what she said because I was in awe and just thrilled to meet her; what I do recall is how badly di Stefano behaved, treating her like a possession. I would like to have hit him. She was much more beautiful than any photograph I ever saw of her.

Story: Once in recording *Tosca* de Sabata snapped, 'Callas, follow me,' and she replied sweetly, 'No, Maestro, you follow me. You can see me; I can't see you.' (So short-sighted.)

History: I mentioned a return of the one-big-star system. When Covent Garden re-opened after World War II it was building up a company and did it pretty successfully although the hard-working but riddled with inferiority complex music director Karl Rankl was not ideal in his job. A national company was built up and a number of excellent singers were heard regularly: Adèle Leigh, Amy Shuard, Sylvia Fisher, Constance Shacklock, Edith Coates, Walter Midgley, Michael Langton, Richard Lewis, Edgar Evans, Otakar Kraus, Frederick Dalberg, and many others. They performed best when a guest star appeared like Erich Kleiber to conduct them. Otherwise they did their best under Rankl, Warwick Braithwaite, Peter Gellhorn, Reginald Goodall and John Pritchard. The company also did well by the British operas that were put on: *Troilus and Cressida* (Walton), *The Olympians* (Bliss), *The Midsummer Marriage* (Tippett), and several Britten operas. But eventually the Board gave in to those who clamoured for international stars and operas were given in the original tongue. It was a case of local roundabouts and foreign swings.

OPERA AT ITS BEST:
Don Carlos at Covent Garden 12.10.58

To mark the centenary of the opening of the present Royal Opera House in Covent Garden a new production of Verdi's *Don Carlos* was given on Friday night.

A magnificent cast has been assembled to give the work in Italian, with Luchino Visconti and Carlo-Maria Giulini, the most renowned producer and conductor in Italy today. No expense has been spared to make this new offering a celebration worthy of the occasion.

On many similar occasions when such an effort is made, with all the stops pulled out, the result falls short of expectation. But this presentation of *Don Carlos* exceeds hope, and is nothing short of magnificent. There have been, since the Opera House reopened after the last war, comparable musical experiences – notably Kleiber's *Rosenkavalier*, *Wozzeck*, and *Elektra*, Beecham's *Meistersinger*, Kubelik's *Jenufa* and Kempe's *Ring*, but of no opera has there been any complete performance as good as this *Don Carlos*.

Here everything combines to give the work in all its glory: singing, orchestral playing, musical direction, acting, décor – this is opera at its best. 'Integration' is the word that comes to mind to describe the rare harmony between first-rate talents that have combined to give here the most complicated of art-forms a near-perfect representation.

Never have I seen such good use made of the big Covent Garden stage; each of the seven sets is a beautiful sight in itself and completely right in the context. Visconti has not only produced the opera, but also designed, with the help of two assistants, these sets and the fine costumes. He is perhaps better known as one of the foremost Italian film directors, but he shows himself now as a masterly operatic producer.

The opera – written in 1866, preceding *Aida* – is a long one, for Verdi sets himself the task of working out the many conflicts in Schiller's drama of the court of Philip II of Spain: Catholic Spain opposed to Protestant Flanders, the liberal Rodrigo to autocratic State, King to Grand Inquisitor, and also the frustrated love between Don Carlos and the Queen, his intended bride who becomes his stepmother instead, owing to a change of State plans.

Verdi succeeds in his task and creates six substantial parts for singers; six genuine operatic characters of considerable depth. The score has many fine things in it, but the quality is not even; individual numbers do not always sustain otherwise excellent scenes and the promise of the opening scene in the forest of Fontainebleau is not made good until after the big auto-da-fé scene in the third act. In the opening scene of Act IV occurs the extraordinary scene between King and Grand Inquisitor, two basses, followed by several numbers, including a quartet, that are amongst Verdi's very finest creations.

The singing reached a high level; Boris Christoff, as the King, gave a performance that combined dramatic power with musical refinement; Gre Brouwenstijn, as the Queen, sang with more warmth and beauty of tone than hitherto; Tito Gobbi was in excellent voice and made a convincing Rodrigo; Jon Vickers both sang and acted with more subtlety than would have been suspected from his past performances; and Marco Stefanoni was suitably dark-voiced for the Inquisitor. Fedora Barbieri had the misfortune to catch a frog in her throat in 'Don Fatale', impeding a performance that was anyhow not in the same class as her colleagues.

But the performance was dominated by the conducting of Giulini. Here was the complete realisation of the score in what was easily the finest Verdi that London has heard for many a long year.

HS: Even forty years later I still think that this *Don Carlos* was the best thing I ever saw on the operatic stage, the most completely integrated performance including all aspects: conducting, singing, acting, production, sets. Part of the secret of its success was, I believe, due to the fact that designer/producer Visconti and conductor Giulini attended every stage rehearsal. Giulini at this stage of his career was at his most dedicated and passionate. Alas! The clock ran down later on and his tempi got slower and slower, the passion

94

dimmed and the textures became glutinous. There were six performances of this *Don Carlos* and I actually paid to attend four of them!

Runners-up in the best opera performance stakes would be Felsenstein's production in East Berlin of *The Magic Flute*, Kubelik's *Katya Kabanova*, Peter Stein's production of *Otello* with Welsh National and Glyndebourne's *Porgy and Bess* with Trevor Nunn-Simon Rattle.

BRNO MEMORIES OF JANACEK:
Prolific Czech Composer   31.10.58

It is becoming more and more obvious that Janacek is one of the most important composers of this century. He was born as far back as 1854, but he matured so late that there is scarcely any work of greatness before the opera *Jenufa*, completed in 1903. In spite of a local success in Brno, it was not until 1916 that *Jenufa* was produced in Prague. A triumph in the capital made Janacek an international figure overnight.

Once he realised that the world wanted his music Janacek turned out works at a remarkable rate, especially for such an old man. Until his death in 1928 he remained in vigorous good health, producing during these twelve years four operatic masterpieces and two near misses, two string quartets, a mass, several tone-poems and the magnificent Sinfonietta, a violin sonata, two works for piano concertante, a wind sextet, the dramatic cycle *Diary of One Who Disappeared* and several other lesser works.

Janacek is an especially important composer for Czechoslovakia for his influence came at a time when his country was trying to throw off the excess of German domination as regards language and culture. Even more than Smetana, Janacek's music springs from the soil and language of his native land. In this respect he is as important a composer as Mussorgsky or Bartok or Vaughan Williams. But the parallel with Mussorgsky is the strongest for they were both Slav in type, although, curiously enough, Janacek had no liking for the Russian's music and did not even become acquainted with *Boris Godunov* until 1909, a fact which gives the lie to any charge of Janacek copying Mussorgsky.

Janacek's is some of the most original music in history. Its main characteristics are its Moravian flavour, both in rhythm and in its melodic dependence on the language, its starkness combined with a surging warmth and sympathy for people of every kind, complete absence of sentimentality, brevity – none of his operas plays for more than two hours – and a captivating rustic eccentricity.

To commemorate the thirtieth anniversary of his death a festival of his music was organised in Brno. During the course of three weeks all his major works were performed and most of the minor ones, and in the middle week the League of Czechoslovak Composers arranged a congress which was attended by 135 delegates from 17 countries. Some of the papers read brought forth some interesting data, but on the whole it was more instructive and worthwhile to concentrate on the music itself and on the 'side-shows' arranged for the congress. These included four exhibitions of photographs, documents, scores, manuscripts, stage set models and gramophone records.

For a Britisher there was one glorious howler in the title on one record label: the piano pieces about rustic life entitled *By an Overgrown Path* have been translated, presumably with a Czech-American dictionary in hand, as *By Weedy Sidewalk*. Then there were get-togethers with pupils, friends, colleagues and relatives of Janacek: and there was a visit to Huckvaldy – near the Polish border – to visit the little village, set in ravishingly beautiful wooded hills, where the composer was born and lived later on.

But it is time to mention some of the music, especially those works which have not been performed in this country yet. First of all there was the complete cycle of operas. *Sarka* (1888) is a heroic legend with a score that contains elements of Dvorak and Wagner, but only the beginnings of Janacek's own style. The one-act *The Beginning of a Romance* (1891) is a very ordinary Smetana-and-water operetta with a triangular plot of a village-girl-pursued-by-the-wicked-lord-and-yokel type. *Jenufa* (1903) is well known, and the world premiere of *Osud* or *Fate* (1904) was reviewed at some length in *The Scotsman* last Wednesday.

The double-bill of *Mr Broucek's Excursion to the Moon* and *Mr Broucek's Excursion to the Fifteenth Century* is an experiment in comic opera which does not quite come off. Mr Broucek himself is a beer-swilling bourgeois and meant to be an object of scorn but, to western eyes at any rate, he earns considerable sympathy as he encounters the arty, airy-fairy aesthetes on the Moon, and the Hussites who try to make him go to war in medieval Bohemia.

This Czech counter-part of *The Yankee at the court of King Arthur* dispels the Mooners by breathing garlic-sausage fumes in their faces and fortunately wakes up before the Hussites wreak their wrath on him. There are some stirring Hussite choruses and some touching love music in the prologue of the Moon episode, but in general one has the feeling that comedy was not Janacek's strong suit and that the opera was too long on the stocks (1908-17).

Next came *Kat'a Kabanova* (1921) and the British delegation were proud to find the Brno production certainly no better than the Sadler's Wells one and Kubelik's conducting in London greatly superior to that of Jilik. *The Cunning Little Vixen* (1923) attempts the dangerous mixing of animals and human beings, but the magic evocation of nature in the music carries all before it.

The Makropoulos Affair (1923) is a setting of Karel Capek's play about an opera singer who has lived for 300 years; apart from the last scene, where the singer is given a finale in the Strauss manner, the opera seems too bound to realism to admit of Janacek's feeling for lyricism and humanity.

It has to be admitted that none of the conducting of the operas and only one operatic production at Brno rose above the level of sincere competence. The exception was Milos Wasserbauer's outstanding production from Frankfurt of *The House of the Dead*. In this opera, completed in his last year of life, Janacek compiled his own libretto out of parts of Dostoievsky's autobiographical novel. The result is grim, episodic and contains four lengthy narratives. It is a scheme which might be guessed to be doomed to failure but Janacek's score is a masterpiece and comes off magnificently. One comes out of the theatre feeling purged and profoundly moved.

There is only space to mention one facet of the many concerts at Brno: the impressively high quality of all the choral singing. Several choirs combined for the exciting performance of the Slavonic Mass and there was also a whole concert of Janacek's music for male voices given by the Moravian Teachers' Choir, conducted by Jan Soupal. I have never heard such a magnificent body of voices as this last named, a choir of unparalleled sonority, musicality and virtuosity.

Every time they come to Llangollen they win the prize and it is high time that they were invited to Edinburgh. They scorn the usual virtuoso choir's tricks and, moreover, the Moravians' repertoire is full of real music and not just encore snippets. The wild beauty and haunting tenderness of their Janacek programme would surely win all hearts.

TRIUMPHANT DEBUT BY COLIN DAVIS: 28.11.58

Colin Davis, assistant conductor of the BBC Scottish Orchestra, conducted his first professional opera on the stage at Sadler's Wells on Wednesday night and it was a triumph. The audience gave him a warm reception and the critics in London have welcomed him as an outstanding Mozartian. It is difficult to avoid saying 'I told you so' for this column has repeatedly acclaimed his work in conducting concert performances of operas by Mozart, Verdi and Beethoven in Oxford and Cambridge with the Chelsea Opera Group.

Sadler's Wells will be well advised to snap up Mr Davis when his contract with the BBC expires next year for they badly need a conductor with a sense of style and the authority to achieve a lively and well-balanced performance. The debut at the Wells was made with *The Seraglio*; the music emerged warm, flexible, meaningful and with, above all, an excellent pace and rhythm. The singing, alas, was not in the same class, although it was clearly not for want of rehearsal.

Jennifer Vyvyan sang the fabulously difficult part of Constanze and her musicianship and feeling for the role were immeasurable. Much of her singing was meltingly beautiful except – and it is a notable exception – that she developed a disturbing quick vibrato on nearly all high notes from F upwards. In the interval rumour had it that she has been troubled with asthma recently – that would no doubt account for this unexpected flaw; and we sincerely hope that it is a temporary one.

The other lady, Blonde, was sung by June Bronhill like a parody of a soubrette with a voice like a squeaking mouse. When the two girls sang high together the noise was like one of those Goon Show sequences with a speeded up tape.

William McAlpine seemed inhibited. He sang all the notes that Belmonte has to sing very well indeed, but one wanted to put a squib in his pocket, it was so dull. Kevin Miller's Pedrillo was badly sung and his speaking was a silly imitation of a university accent.

There only remains the Osmin of William Clarkson. He was quite unsuited to the part by temperament – there is not an ounce of honest rage in him – yet by applying his usual commonsense to the task he succeeded tolerably well. The staging and settings were quite acceptable.

Aida at the Garden this week brought Rudolf Kempe as a new conductor in this rather ineffective production. Kempe made a very good job of it and showed that he can be exciting when he is not too self-consciously holding back climaxes. It is not easy to approve of his habit of keeping *The Valkyries* down in order to make *The Twilight of the Gods* more telling, and certainly Verdi needs a fortissimo when he marks one – and Mr Kempe obeyed him to the letter.

Lately I have been wondering if the Chorus, for so many years the most stable excellence in the Opera House, is not getting rather lack-lustre. A bit more ginger is wanted. The greatest pleasure of the evening came from the singing of Jon Vickers as Radames and Regina Resnik as Amneris; John Shaw's Amonasro grows apace and Amy Schuard was almost mellifluous in the second and third acts.

The numbers 385, 622, 550 and 551 indicate no mysteries of American football but are the catalogue designations of the works of Mozart that Sir Thomas Beecham conducted in the Festival Hall: the *Haffner* and the last two symphonies together with the Clarinet Concerto. One came out ecstatic but almost exhausted by so much beauty. Some of Sir Thomas's tempi were on the fast side but they were powerless to rob the music of its validity.

I should like to tell a story that shows a side of Beecham which may not be familiar to all my readers. I rang Mr Brownfoot, Sir Thomas's faithful librarian for many years, to make sure about the first of the two encores played – it was the March, K.249, with Beecham's own fairly discreetly added clarinets and trombones – and happened to ask him if he had been marking the parts of the G minor Symphony at the time.

The G minor Symphony, No 50, was played after the interval, complete with Sir Thomas's latest emendations. Now this work has been played by this conductor perhaps more frequently than any other Mozart symphony. And yet here he is, at the age of seventy-nine, having new thoughts about the work (and I know from experience that this remarking of old parts is a constant process). This is absolutely typical of Beecham. It is no whim of an old man but the continual searching for truth that is the hallmark of an artist ever young in spirit.

HS: Good old Scotsman! Mozart reaches his fifty.

MOZART FOR THE GODS.
Clara Haskil Works the Old Enchantment. 10.4.59

Listening to music day in, day out, one begins to notice curious predilections. For example, after some years the prospect of hearing the symphonies and piano concertos of Beethoven is no longer appetising.

Faced, however, with Haydn symphonies or Mozart's concertos and symphonies, the eyes light up, the heart sings and one feels like Bertie Wooster on a spring morning, choosing the nattiest of bow-ties and feeling supremely equal to the task of looking the old eggs and b. fair and square in the face.

But, when it comes to the actual performances of Mozart's piano concertos, the vernal optimism is usually rudely shattered. For, once the performer has set fingers to the ivories, a cloud appears on the horizon – just as surely as in the Wooster household on a spring morning Jeeves will so strongly disapprove of a chap's neckwear as to hand in his notice or there will be a shattering letter from an Aunt Agatha propped up against the toast-rack.

Only once, in some twenty years of concert-going, have I heard a Mozart concerto played in the way that the imagination tells me they must be played. The pianist was Clara Haskil then: and now she has come again to London and again worked the old enchantment. The result was a performance of the D minor Concerto K. 466 fit for the gods. The only disappointment was that there were so few people in the audience to hear this great playing.

The concert was one of a series that Klemperer should have conducted. When Haskil last played the D minor he was the conductor, and Haskil was not quite at her best. Perhaps she found his personality too strong and Beethovenian. The other night, however, there was the most perfect accord between soloist and conductor, and the conductor gave the pianist the fullest possible support: the tuttis were drenched with the restrained passion that abides in the work, and the actual accompanying passages were balanced nicely and sensitively. This concert was a great opportunity for Colin Davis and he took it well.

To perform Mozart so well at his age gives one some slight consolation when the old age of performers such as Beecham, Klemperer and Haskil is considered. For if Davis is good now, how much better will he be in fifteen years time, when he has acquired more experience, wisdom and wit. The Serenata Notturna was rather dull, its intimate gaiety eluding both conductor and audience in the Royal Festival Hall. But the concerto fired successfully. And the 39th Symphony in E flat, after the interval, was a warm and satisfying revealment of this great work. Really, for such a young conductor, Davis scales the Mozartean heights in a remarkable way. No wonder that even the hard-boiled Philharmonia Orchestra paid him the double compliment of playing well and then applauding him at the end.

HS: Clara Haskil was not as old as she looked, sixty-four on this occasion, but, alas, she had only one year to live before her sudden death. Bad health had dogged her even from the time of her debut in her native Bucharest at the age of nine. She was taken up by Cortot and played later with Ysaye, Casals, and Enescu, with whom she shared Romanian citizenship and a curved spine. In later life she made some records but not all of them reveal her unique gifts, although her Mozart sonatas with Arthur Grumiaux are rewarding. Her playing of the last Schubert B flat Sonata is a cherished memory of all who heard her play it in the Royal Festival Hall. Manoug Parikian told me a story which indicates her self-criticism: on a tour with the Philharmonia Orchestra and Karajan, Haskil played Mozart each time more beautifully than the last. The orchestra bought her a huge bunch of flowers which Manoug was deputed to take to her dressing room after the last concert (in Lucerne, I think). He found her in tears, miserable because she had – she thought – let the orchestra down with her wretched playing.

BEECHAM IS EIGHTY TODAY: 29.4.59

Another world-famous conductor once tried to sneer at Beecham as an 'amateur'; and, in a way, Beecham is an amateur. In fact, he is the apotheosis of the amateur for he had no proper musical training and bought his way into conducting. And amateur basically means 'lover'.

And then, what happens at rehearsals? Apparently the man doesn't know how to rehearse. He plays through the works; if something goes wrong, he may stop and go over it again, but he will very rarely take it to bits to see what is wrong.

He never gives instructions of a technical nature to the players; nor does he, on the other hand, talk about the music in non-technical language. What does he do? Plays through the music and cracks a few jokes; that is all that goes on, so far as appearances are concerned.

But it's all very sound, really; the players adore Beecham, and they will tell you about him from their side of the platform. First of all, he lets you play the work through without stopping you all the time so that you have a chance to get the measure of the work. So many conductors point out the mistakes you know you made the first time through. Beecham gives you time to phrase. Beecham assumes that you are master of your instrument, gives you confidence.

Beecham doesn't talk much; when he does, he relaxes you. Most of the hard work is done behind the scenes; he knows the score by heart, has penetrated the essence of the work, found out where the melody lies – whether it is in the top or in the bass; Beecham always goes for the melodic line – and has marked the parts with scrupulous care.

With some conductors, the final rehearsal exhausts the music and the players: with Beecham, there is always something extra for the concert. You know the notes but you have to keep an eye on him, for he acts on something which can only be called inspiration.

This rhythm will be a little more tense, that dying phrase will take a shade longer, there will be something you don't quite expect, but it will immediately seem just right.

You may have played Mozart's G minor with him a hundred times, but tonight it is somehow new and fresh, just as it was the other times. Nothing is ever allowed to become routine. That is why Beecham spoils British players. They measure other conductors by his freshness and the apparent ease with which he achieves success.

What is the secret of this success? Inspiration, knowledge, love and hard work. For two or three seasons recently Beecham has begun to use scores quite a bit, but this last season they were banished again.

Was it coincidence that this last season was better? I don't think so. I know that Sir Thomas felt the loss of his second wife keenly (perhaps the only person who did!) but I also suspect that for some years her ill-health must have been a drag on his energies.

On his eightieth birthday today, many of us may recall the pleasure of Beecham's past and the unremitting service that he has rendered to the world of music for over fifty years. But Sir Thomas himself is busy planning for the future, and I have a serious suggestion to make about this.

We all know that sometimes Sir Thomas has – ahem! – been short of money and has even, quite recently, spent a whole financial year out of the country. Now, if and when Sir Thomas makes his departure from us – pray heaven, not for many a year – we shall surely want to make some suitable and appropriately expensive memorial.

My suggestion is: why not anticipate matters and stump up the money right now? Express our gratitude to the great man now, give him a large cheque, and let him spend it the way he has spent most of his own huge personal fortune, in entertaining us.

In this way we could all have a magnificent spree: festivals of Mozart, Berlioz, Handel, Sibelius, Delius, Strauss, Haydn…

LOTTE LEHMANN NOW RUNS MASTER CLASS: 29.5.59

When Lotte Lehmann retired from singing ten years ago, she looked forward to taking it easy, tending her garden in Santa Barbara and having a perpetual holiday. But, as she said, she soon got bored with it. The Academy of the West – a musical institution in her town – implored her to come to teach, to lecture, or even just to read a chapter of her autobiography.

After some persuasion, for she had always refused to teach, modestly thinking her own approach to art too intuitive, she devised what she prefers to be thought of as a demonstration class.

It is, in fact, what is generally known as a master class, with students being taught in front of one another; but with Madame Lehmann the audience has been admitted too, so that the students have the ordeal of performing and being corrected in public, but with the advantage of audience response. (And, says Madame Lehmann, when they perform in public next they are a little bit used to it and enjoy not being interrupted by me all the time.)

The idea caught on and Lotte Lehmann is now in the middle of her second course in London at the Wigmore Hall. This time, the students – and young professionals from the Wells and the Garden have wisely come along as students – are of a higher standard.

Madame Lehmann says that what she looks for in a student is imagination. A pupil can be intelligent, musical, good-looking and clever on the stage up to a point; but without true imagination that pupil will never go to the top. Students come to these classes, many from reputable teachers in London, but very many of them do not think about what they are singing. The words are the essence, Lehmann teaches, not pegs on which to hang vocalises.

On this trip Lehmann has changed the repertoire somewhat; there has been more Strauss and Wagner. Her handling of the slow, almost static tempo of, say, the Bridal Duet from *Lohengrin* has been most illuminating. At Lehmann's classes one learns many fundamental points about the relationship between words and music, between movement and words, between art and life.

Seeing her on the platform and meeting her off it, you cannot but be infected with her enthusiasm and be utterly charmed by her personality. She has the knack of putting you at your ease – a valuable asset whether you are a trembling beginner on the platform or a diffident reporter behind the scenes.

'Ach, no,' to a photographer. 'Please not my profile with all those chins; take it better full face because I am seventy-one, ja, but still terribly vain.'

When I commiserated with her because one of the singers at the last class had been wooden, she recalled that she herself was an incredibly slow starter. 'I was fired by my teacher, told to give up for just twenty-four hours. Later, when I first went on stage, I was terrible; if I had to move from the table to the chair, it was a three-act tragedy for me.'

Madame Lehmann talked about Richard Strauss: 'In private life he was a little disappointing; at his house the dominating personality was his wife (Pauline) whom he adored; she nagged him and he loved it. But when he sat down at the piano, he came into his own'; and Puccini, 'He was such a gentleman, so elegant, so Italian'; and Klemperer, 'He was the first to show me that I could perhaps be an artist'; and Elisabeth Schumann, 'You know in that recording of *Rosenkavalier* with Schumann and me, in the last scene, in the duet between Sophie and Oktavian, the Marschallin has just two words to sing, 'Ja, ja,' and I was not in the studio that day and so Elisabeth imitated me. If you listen carefully you can hear it.'

Then she mentioned something I did not dare bring up: the occasion in 1937 at Covent Garden, when she burst into tears in the first act of *Rosenkavalier* and could not go on. Many theories were advanced as to the reason why, but Madame Lehmann was silent; and with good reason, for her husband was very ill in Germany at the time and on the stage at Covent Garden were many singers from Nazi Germany.

Was she going to hear *Rosenkavalier* at Covent Garden or Glyndebourne this week? 'Ach, you know, I cannot hear it any more now.' And I understood, for she has, in her time, sung Sophie, Oktavian and the Marschallin. Would she be going to *Parsifal* then? 'My dear, life is too short to go to *Parsifal*.'

The Wigmore Hall classes end in June; then Madame Lehmann goes to Vienna, to Bad Gastein, to Pontresina, then back home to America. But she is coming back to Britain soon and she will always be welcome here, this great singer, great teacher, great person.

THE END OF AN ERA AT GLYNDEBOURNE:
Ebert and Christie Retire: 5.6.59

Glyndebourne started in 1934 under the direction of Fritz Busch and Carl Ebert at the opera house built by the inspired Audrey

Mildmay and John Christie. Busch and Mildmay are, alas, dead; at the end of this season Carl Ebert is retiring from the post of Artistic Director; and John Christie has already handed over the leadership of the executive side of things to his son, George.

It is the end of an era. And in fervently thanking these four great sons of art, for one can scarcely separate the deeds of those present from the deeds of those that are gone, we also and equally fervently hope that next season will mark the beginning of a new and equally successful era.

But it is also time to take stock. Time to think of building for the future; time to think of building, not only those extra technical aids, dressing rooms, rehearsal stages and the other accoutrements that Mr Christie rightly takes such a joy and pride in, but also the building up of an operatic directorate comparable with the great team of Ebert and Busch, such as it was in the days before the war.

For, after the war, Busch was a shadow of his former self, and Ebert would have touched greater heights if only he had had, during his time, an opposite number on the musical staff against whom to pit his wits, and from whom to draw fire.

At the end of the first evening of the new season – which opened with a new production of *Der Rosenkavalier* – Mr Christie presented Carl Ebert with a rosebowl commemorating his great achievement at Glyndebourne. He recalled the early days in 1934 – seven people got out of the special train the first night, one more the next night – went on to refer to Busch as 'an honest and capable conductor' (goodness, was he no more than that in his hey-day?) and continued by saying that the secret of Glyndebourne's success was 'to do it better than the other man'.

This is a dangerous way to talk, for although many of the Mozart productions were peerless, and some of the Rossini and Verdi have been magnificent, not everything has been of this standard; for often in recent years the musical direction has not been good enough, there has been no one to keep Ebert from stepping over the traces on some occasions and the casting has often just failed.

Take the first two productions this year; one hoped that Ebert's own new production would be something that would put Covent Garden's *Don Carlos* in the shade. But Ebert's *Rosenkavalier*, in spite of many felicitous touches, did not even put Covent Garden's own

Rosenkavalier completely out of court, even though it was done the night before Glyndebourne opened.

Covent Garden had only members of the company in the cast and gave an honest and satisfactory performance; Constance Shacklock has never sung Oktavian better; James Pease has gotten himself less American as Ochs; while Una Hale gave the performance of her life as a very promising Marschallin. Then too, Rudolf Kempe's direction had more sweep, more detail, more glamour and more wit than Leopold Ludwig's down in Sussex. But then, of course, the acoustics at Glyndebourne are fearfully dry and add no bloom to the orchestral playing, so that an opera like *Rosenkavalier* is at a severe disadvantage tonally.

The chorus and orchestra in *Idomeneo*, under John Pritchard, were first-rate vintage Glyndebourne, but the solo singing was substandard. Richard Lewis, in the title-role, had a cold, William McAlpine's Idamante needed guts, Sylvia Stahlman, as Ilia, had the right ideas but not the technique to carry them out, while Angela Vercelli only came to life in her final aria. Good production and musical direction carried the day, with Mozart's not inconsiderable help, but…

A brief look at the Glyndebourne cast of *Rosenkavalier*. Régine Crespin looked too old and too big a Marschallin, but her voice had some of the magic her personality lacked. Elisabeth Söderström was a quite adorable Oktavian; if only her voice were richer and deeper this would be a perfect performance. Annaliese Rothenberger was an excellent Sophie. Oscar Czerwenka was a youngish, likeable Ochs, very bumpkinish and with a fruity accent – not the whole part, but very acceptable, especially from so young a singer. The second act was finely played, except that the Italians were neither well performed nor imaginatively produced.

Footnote:- I hope the above remarks will not seem too unfestive. We all know Glyndebourne's golden worth, and it is love of good things that makes us want Glyndebourne to go on and do better. Finding a new Busch and a new Ebert is no easy task, of course; how about alternations of Rennert with Schmidt-Isserstedt and Giulini with Visconti?

MEDEA *TAILORED FOR THE DIVA:*
22.6.59

For a few days Callas in *Medea* achieved the feat of ousting *My Fair Lady* from pride of place in the Personal Column of *The Times*. Expectations ran high, tickets became as rare as gold dust, Mr Onassis brought a party, the Begum Khan arrived dignified and dripping with diamonds, Mr and Mrs Eddie Fisher dripping with publicity; every other person in the stalls was a throat specialist or a lawyer, ready to offer their services.

Cherubini's opera *Medea* would be termed a museum-piece if it were not that the best known opera singer in the world chooses now to appear in it. Composed just before the close of the eighteenth century, it tends mostly to sound like Beethoven on an off-day, with occasional recollections of Gluck and premonitions of Berlioz.

The continual tension leads one to expect a great moment which never materialises. The libretto follows the classical story ending; the chorus has a good part but otherwise Medea herself is the only solid character. Her familiar, Neris, has one fine aria with pathetic bassoon obbligato, but Jason is almost as much of a paste-board figure as Purcell's Aeneas; Glauce, his intended, has one decent aria at the beginning of the opera but her father, Creon, is only a stock bass figure.

Mind you, this is a version of *Medea* tailored for the diva. The original contained as much dialogue as *Fidelio*; the (orchestral) recitatives used nowadays were composed by one Ferdinand Lachner.

The opera stands or falls, then, according to the soprano who take the title role. Could Maria Callas carry the opera on her shoulders in a part that contains much effective writing for a dramatic soprano with a big range but no coloratura? Well, Callas is certainly capable of doing so, as her gramophone record of the works proves, but at Covent Garden on this occasion she was not in her best voice and she made very few sounds which could be remotely described as beautiful. Her acting was fine, suggesting briefly the woman demented by jealousy and hurt pride, a perfect plum, as it were, of a neurotic..

But the beauty of the part, her aria in Act 3 when clasping her two children to her, for example, went almost for nothing without the sustained vocal line it requires.

Fiorenza Cossotto, as Neris, revealed a fine voice – reminiscent of Jurinac in some lower notes – and Jon Vickers made the best of Jason. The orchestra was occasionally caught on the wrong foot in spite of the sympathetic direction of Nicola Rescigno. Joan Carlyle and Nicolai Zaccaria filled in the parts of Glauce and Creon satisfactorily.

The sets of John Tsarouchis were noble and effective; the costumes were presumably designed so as not to interfere with the triumphal progress of Maria Callas. Her costumes were full of drapes, her handling of which occupied a good deal of her time.

The production was by Alexis Minotis from Athens. There was some tiresome drill for the chorus ladies, but the drama was suitably if uninspiringly, played out.

If the evening was a disappointment for many of us, the fans gave the diva her customary ovation. It is impossible, indeed, not to applaud this remarkable artist, even when she is not at her best.

STOKOWSKI'S MOST EXCITING CONCERT:
Glasgow Herald 6.7.59

Leopold Stokowski came on to the Royal Festival Hall platform last week looking remarkably like the character that had a conversation with Mickey Mouse in Walt Disney's *Fantasia* but looking quite unlike a conductor whose birth date is given in the books as 1882 but is universally considered to be at least ten years older. The hands, the white hair, the photogenic features, and the attractive stickless technique are still in evidence.

Give this man a programme of well-mauled classics and he will maul them as much, if not more, than the next conductor. But let him choose a programme of relatively unfamiliar music which does not bore him and see what magic he can produce.

Last week Stokowski chose for his concert Gabrieli's *Sonata Pian' e Forte*, Tchaikovsky's *Hamlet*, Respighi's *Pines of Rome* and the Fifth Symphony of Shostakovich, and the result was one of London's most exciting concerts for years.

Stokowski, like most great conductors, can create his own sound with any orchestra – a sound of extraordinary voluptuous sonority – and he can make the players follow him with those beautiful hands of his. In the slow parts of Respighi's *Pini* he was shaping the tunes with the sinuous rubato they require. The London Symphony Orchestra followed every minute direction he gave; moreover, they played with an intensity and fullness of sound that has rarely been heard from them in the last ten years.

Hamlet was given a performance of such dramatic strength as to give the work a unity of line it seldom achieves. Shostakovich's excellent symphony was made to sound like a masterpiece. An audience that was not a capacity one – the programme was not pot-boiling enough for that – gave the conductor an ovation he fully deserved, and it was one that the orchestra both joined and shared.

BERNSTEIN RUINS CLASSICS: 19.10.59

Impossible not to feel a certain Anglo-Saxon resistance to Mr Leonard Bernstein: here is this little man, scarcely forty – and he is a celebrated composer of serious music, a brilliant pianist well able to throw off a Mozart or a Ravel piano concerto, a virtuoso conductor and the first American to be appointed musical director of the New York Philharmonic, a TV idol and, if you please, the world-famous composer of *West Side Story.*

Having all-rounders at cricket is one thing, but Bernstein goes too far, what?

The New York Philharmonic's tour began this summer in Athens and finally came to rest in London's Festival Hall on Saturday, having duly wowed most of the countries in Europe, especially Russia. The house was sold out, despite the presence on the programme of two modern American works: it is a great point in Mr Bernstein's favour that he nearly always features contemporary music and that his popularity enables him to get away with it.

Even more important is that he plays contemporary music superbly well. Samuel Barber's *Second Essay* is a well-argued piece, but not really anything special and certainly not as good as Bernstein made it sound.

Charles Ives's *The Unanswered Question* is a typical work of that pioneer, in that it was written way back in 1908 but sounds as if it might have been premièred at Darmstadt or Donaueschingen last week. Against a series of very quiet diatonic string chords a solo trumpet and a quartet of flutes pose the questions in other keys and other rhythms that the Druidic strings have no reply to, except to continue with their serene chords. The work is a miniature, but a vastly impressive one.

At this point Mr Bernstein's stock was high, and the piano was brought on for the Mozart Piano Concerto in G, K. 453, which Mr Bernstein was to play – Kapellmeister-wise – directing from the piano. As the tutti began, one noticed with pleasure that the strings were phrasing in an eighteenth-century style that one had always thought impossible with an Eastern-seaboard oomph orchestra like the great bands of Boston, Philadelphia and New York.

But, alas, disenchantment set in. Mr Bernstein calculated the style nicely but there was too much calculation and a total lack of heart. The soft pedal was used too often and the sound was like crystallised fruit; the slow movement was taken so slowly that it fell to bits. One longed for Mr Bernstein to have a biff at it in a more manly style, risk a wrong note or two but stop giving it the *Eighteenth-Century Drawing-Room* routine.

The interpretation of Brahms's First Symphony was so appalling that your critic left after the slow movement. Everything was over-dramatised, the rhythm dragged out, the points underlined with a heavy hand, and the shape and life of the music disappeared into a glutinous mess of beautiful but sickly playing.

Mr Bernstein is a phenomenal musician and personality: the New York Phil is a wonderful orchestra. We wish that together they had given us more contemporary music – perhaps the Shostakovich Symphony, whose performance so delighted the Russians, perhaps a larger work of Charles Ives.

During the Brahms, I would have welcomed a selection from *West Side Story*.

PART Two – (A Miscellany)

ARTHUR M. ABELL:
7.6.91

On my birthday in Aldeburgh I picked up a very curious little book called *Talks with Great Composers* by Arthur M. Abell. Let me quote from his Foreword: 'During my long residence in Europe, from 1890 to 1918, it was my privilege at various times to discuss the subject of Inspiration with Brahms, Strauss, Puccini, Humperdinck, Bruch and Grieg... . The discussion with Brahms which occurred in the late Fall of 1896 was made possible only by the intercession of Joseph Joachim. Acting upon Joachim's advice, I secured through the American Embassy in Vienna the services of an expert bi-lingual stenographer who made a verbatim record of that three-hour conversation... . Why then are these revelations of six so famous composers now published for the first time?...and the answer is that it was Brahms' peremptory demand that his disclosures not be published until fifty years after his death.'

Who was Abell? He seems to have been a music critic. The blurb quotes several reputable musical journals who took him seriously. He was a friend of Olin Downes and I have seen a photograph of the two together. Sir Thomas Beecham is also quoted: 'Yours is one of the most interesting books I have ever read. In fact I was so fascinated with it that I read it twice.' He did not publish the book until 1955, under the aegis of New York's Philosophical Society, the author's reason for the delay was that in 1947 the world seemed in such a mess, unlikely to be interested in spiritual matters.

So, after all that, do we believe Abell? Did he touch things up long after the conversations? But I must quote a few passages to show you what the book is like. The most interesting, the longest part of the book concerns Brahms. Now Brahms of course was agnostic or atheist; but all sources agree that his knowledge of the Bible was profound. Brahms said: 'The powers from which all truly great composers drew their inspirations is the same power than enabled Jesus to work his miracles. We call it God, Omnipotence, Divinity, the Creator, etc. Schubert called it "die Allmacht" but what's in a name? It is the power that created our earth and the whole universe, including you and me, and that great God-intoxicated Nazarene taught us that we can appropriate it for our own upbuilding right here and now and also earn Eternal Life.' He also quoted John 14:10 and 12: 'the Father that dwelleth in Me, He doeth the works' and 'He that believeth Me, the works that I do shall he do also, and greater works than these shall he do.' Brahms said of composing: 'I am in a trance-like condition – hovering between being asleep and awake; I am still conscious but right on the border of losing consciousness, and it is at such moments that inspired ideas come. All true inspiration emanates from God, and he can reveal Himself to us only through that spark of divinity within – through what modern psychologists call the subconscious mind.' Brahms also quoted Mozart who once explained composing: 'The process with me is like a vivid dream.' Another quotation that Brahms made was of Laotze, five hundred years before Christ, who said, 'We cannot define Spirit, but we can appropriate it.' When Abell quoted Addison

"Tis the Divinity that stirs within us:
'Tis heaven itself points a hereafter,
And intimates eternity to man.'

Brahms went to the piano and struck a series of C major chords fortissimo by way of approval.

(Here I must add that I have searched in the letters and biogs of Brahms and nowhere can I find reference to Arthur Abell. It is the same with the other composers, some of which I now quote. Not that that proves anything one way or the other. Se non é vero, é jolly ben trovato.)

Abell met Richard Strauss in Weimar two years after the composition of *Don Juan*, the year 1890, the composer was twenty-six. After discussing American orchestras and conductors, Strauss said: 'Composing is a procedure not so readily explained. When the inspiration comes, it is something of so subtle, tenuous, will-o-the-wisp nature (*Feinheit wie ein Irrlicht*) that it almost defies definition. When in my most inspired moods, I have definite compelling visions, involving a higher selfhood. I feel at such moments that I am tapping the source of Infinite and Eternal energy from which you and I and all things proceed. Religion calls it God.' And Abell adds (rather reassuringly for the sake of possible credence), 'I thanked Strauss for having the patience to allow me

116

plenty of time to write down his own words in German concerning inspiration. In interviewing great men I have always made it a rule immediately to put on paper their actual words so as to have a verbatim account of what they said.

'Later in 1909 after the *Elektra* première at Dresden Strauss said to me: 'You have known me for nineteen years and you are well aware of my enthusiasm for music as expression but there is a limit, and I feel that I have reached that limit with *Elektra*. If I were to go further in trying to stir up human emotions by orchestral and vocal violence, it would no longer be music. My next opera will be written in a much simpler style.'

After the next opera (*Rosenkavalier*) Strauss talked again about what he called Cosmic Force: 'I know that I can appropriate it to some extent and that after all is the main consideration for us mortals. I can tell you, however, from my own experience, that an ardent desire and fixed purpose brings results. Determined concentrated thought is a tremendous force and this Divine Power is responsive to it. I am convinced that this is a law and that it holds good in any line of human endeavour.' To Abell's asking how many composers contact this Power today in his opinion, Strauss replied, 'Less than five per cent in my opinion.' (Brahms put it lower, answering the same question, two per cent.)

Puccini: 'The great secret of all creative geniuses is that they possess the power to appropriate the beauty, the wealth, the grandeur and the sublimity contained within their own souls, which are parts of Omnipotence, and to communicate those riches to others. The conscious, purposeful appropriation of one's soul's forces is the supreme secret.' 'I said to my friend, Pietro Mascagni, after I had finished the score of *Madam Butterfly* last October: "The music of this opera was dictated to me by God; I was merely instrumental in putting it on paper and communicating it to the public...God does not do for man what he can do for himself. We mortals here on this earth are partners of the Creator but few there be who realise it. For instance, God makes the tree grow, but man, if he wants to build a house, must cut it down and saw it up into boards. It is the same with a composer. He must acquire by laborious study and application the technical mastery of his craft: but he will never write anything of lasting value unless he has Divine aid also." '

Puccini told Abell how he needed peace of mind and quiet to work in, detesting interruptions. He described how he managed to get rid of a local priest who at one time kept calling, fearing for the salvation of his distinguished parishioner. Puccini told him that if the priest interrupted him once more he would renounce the Catholic faith and become a Protestant. That did the trick.

Grieg: 'We composers are projectors of the infinite into the finite.' Humperdinck explained to Abell that he had asked Wagner about inspiration and some things he said were: 'There is this universal vibrating energy that binds the soul of man to the Almighty Central Power from which emanates the life principle to which we all owe our existence. This energy links us to the Supreme Force of the universe, of which we are all a part. If it were not so, we could not bring ourselves into communication with it. The one who can do so is inspired... . Many things militate against us – heredity, environment, opportunity, early education, etc. For instance, an atheistic upbringing is fatal. No atheist has ever created anything of great and lasting value.'

Max Bruch: 'My most beautiful melodies have come to me in dreams.'

So much for Abell. More recent composers have said much the same thing: Stravinsky: 'I am the vessel through which *Sacre du printemps* passed.'

Benjamin Britten once told me that in certain circumstances he felt as if he were connected to some Inspirational grid.

Michael Tippett: 'I feel curiously objective about composition. I am the person to whom the inspiration comes but I know that I am not its originator.' (TV programme, made by Mischa Scorer, 1990.)

PERCY GRAINGER:
2.7.59

I saw that Percy Grainger was going to be in England and Cecil Sharp House put me in touch with the composer who agreed to do an interview with me for the BBC Transcription Service (the producer was Laurie Constable). I remember the composer in some kind of dark blazer, grey flannels, brown shoes, nothing smart or even very prepossessing. It was my first encounter – I was knocked sideways by the god-like head, on a small man's body. His wife Ella came too and she sat near the wide table across which we conversed.

A strange thing happened: at that period London suffered from power cuts and, sure enough, the lights went out shortly after we had started to record, leaving just enough daylight from one small high window for me to see Percy's eyes. Now, normally, I would have made an apology but for some reason I said nothing but continued to look into those blue pools. And he said nothing and continued to look into my eyes. After three or four minutes (so the controlroom boys told me later) the lights came on again and we continued the interview without any reference to the interruption. But now in some curious way I felt that I had known PG for ages, even that we were friends. The impression seemed mutual. Mind you, I had told him before the interview how much I adored *Lincolnshire Posy*, had brought along a full score for him to autograph and had explained that we were using the first sixteen bars of 'Lisbon' as the signature tune for a whole series of music magazine programmes (the series is still going and we're still using 'Lisbon'). And, with hindsight, I guess it was lucky that my eyes are also blue!

Percy's speaking voice was clear though throaty, free of any kind of accent, not particularly sonorous, veering somewhat towards monotone. When amused, humour would enter the speaking voice in a delightful way, as in the interview when he spoke ironically of it being better to collect Mr Dean's song even if it killed him, or in the gently bantering initial explanation of why he had never used sonata form.

Interview

Well, I started composing seriously when I was fourteen or fifteen and I never brought my compositions out until 1911, that's 1895 till 1911. I remember when 'Handel in the Strand' was first published I said to Willy Strecker, my publisher: could 'Handel in the Strand' ever be worth the paper it was printed on. He said: not from a publishing standpoint because there are too few organisations with three strings and one piano, but when radio came in, it became one of the best sellers, of course. I mean, one of *my* best-sellers.

You were lucky to have a nice, honest publisher like Willy Strecker.

Yes, but I also had an honest system. I paid half the cost of production.

Did you?

Always have.

How did you come to write what you call mock folksongs, like 'Mock Morris'?

'Country Gardens' is a variant of 'The Vicar of Bray'. [Sings snatch of the latter, then the former.] That's a variant isn't it?

Yes, so you deliberately constructed it that way?

No, it was collected by Cecil Sharp as a folk thing. And he sent me the first volume of his 'Morris Dances' saying: I think these two tunes would stand arranging well – that was 'Shepherd's Hey' and 'Country Gardens' – but when I saw them I thought that 'Shepherd's Hey' was just a variant of 'The Keel Row', [same again: PG sings illustrations of both].

You've turned them into original tunes.

No, I never altered the tune at all, and I never use a folk song in a composition of my own. When I arrange a folksong I try to be the servant of the tune.

You've never gone in for sonata...?

I've never touched it.

Why?

Well, the Italians were on our side in the First World War, were they?

Yes.

Yes, well that spoils the story.

Well, I'll say no then...

My story was that I wouldn't write anything that had an Italian title. No...my whole attitude has nothing to do with the date of the war. My attitude is simply this: all my life I've found that the best art comes from the North. When I was about ten I came in contact with the Icelandic Sagas. And I've never found anything to equal them: in psychology, in touchingness...and altogether. So, when I was ten years old and gave concerts in Melbourne, a committee was formed to send me to Europe and raise some money. They only raised £50 but it was very much better than nothing. The question was: where should we go to? England, France, Italy, Austria or Germany? Well, I was thinking only of the sagas, so I said: oh, Germany would be the best I think because Germany is closer to Icelandic than any of the other languages. And that was my only thought. So, when I composed I was not going to have any suggestion of the Mediterranean in my music if I could help it.

When did you start collecting folksongs?

Miss Lucy Broadwood was the secretary of the Folksong Society and she had a programme in 1904 which I heard, and although her harmonizations were very simple, I thought they were very touching and I said to her: I should like to collect. They were organizing a festival in Brigg, Lincolnshire, and I went up there, and Miss Broadwood was collecting; and I collected. And the next year I bought a phonograph and I went up with the phonograph. You went into a village like Brigg and you met the schoolmaster and the squire and the doctor and the postmaster and so on. And he'd say: what are you doing? Oh, I hope to collect some folksongs. Oh, you won't get any here, this is a most unmusical place – and by that evening you might have fifty or seventy songs. For example 'Lisbon' was sung by an old man in the workhouse and as he sang he commenced to cry and the matron of the workhouse said to me: I don't think we should do any more just now, he hasn't sung those things for years and years and it makes him think of his youth and it works him up, it might kill him. So, there's nothing to be said to that, of course, so I just left it uncollected or, rather, badly collected. A year or so later I came back with a phonograph and I went to see him and I said: Well, here I am Mr Dean, with a phonograph to take down your singing. And he said, oh, I cannot sing my head's too baad, ahm too weak and so on. And I said: never mind, you don't really need to sing, Mr Dean, but I'd like you to hear some of the other people here who have made records. So he listened about one verse and a half, and he said: I'll sing for you, y'ung man. That's how they were.

And did it kill him?

No, I thought that really it was better to kill him and get the tune than to have him die without being collected. What use was that?

You're a real collector! Did you collect 'Brigg Fair' at Brigg?

Yes.

121

And then you showed it to Delius?

I published my c(h)oral version and when I met Delius he said: but our harmonies are absolutely identical. And he said: do you mind if I use 'Brigg Fair' for a rhapsody? And I said: no, of course I'd be very proud, and happy.

Could I ask you now about Grieg? I believe you met him first in 1906 but could you please say how and where?

I met him at Lady Speyer's. The Speyers were then financing the Queen's Hall Orchestra and Grieg was engaged to give two concerts; and Grieg was staying with the Speyers and was very ill, it was only a year before he died, and Lady Speyer asked him if there was anybody he'd like to meet in London. And he said: oh, I'm so weak and ill. I would much rather if I could just go to the rehearsals and nothing else. Then he said: no, there is one I would like to meet, this young Australian composer I'd like to meet, and he mentioned my name. And Lady Speyer said: oh, you should hear Percy play your music. And he said in a rather weary voice to me very politely – he was always sweet and kind to everybody – what pieces of mine do you play? And I said: well, chiefly the Folksongs opus 66 and the Norwegian Peasant Dances opus 72. And he said: I've never heard them. So, of course, that pleases a composer to hear something he hasn't yet heard. And my knowledge of English folksong, if I may say so, made it quite easy to play Norwegian ones because they're very similar...in some ways.

And you studied the Concerto with him?

We rehearsed the Concerto, he was to conduct it at Leeds. And he conducted and I played the solo part, and some of the orchestral parts and so on. We just rehearsed it.

Do you remember any particular things he said about the Concerto?

Well, he said about all the playing of his music in general: the thing I would have liked if I'd had better health, if I'd been stronger, I would have liked to be a strong player. I like loudness and I like accents. But my health has never permitted me to play like that. But you have strength and that's what I value in your music (correcting himself) in your playing.

What about Grieg as a conductor?

He brought out the contrasts tremendously, particularly the accents. In almost every piece that I heard him rehearse, he rehearsed the accents quite specially, and talked about them: and so on, an accent doesn't consist of a louder note, it consists of a louder note which immediately falls back into piano and that is a disease that most groups of people have in an accent: they play the beginning of the accent but they don't do the downhill part of it.

These are the same Speyers that 'Salome' is dedicated to?

Is it really? I met Strauss at the Speyers too. He was charming. I met there Grieg and Strauss and Debussy at the Speyers. And Debussy was like a little spitting wild animal. Lady Speyer invited some friends to tea and he said: Tea! I won't be in the same room with anybody. Bring me in my tea here, where I can drink it alone.

And did he play?

No.

And did you play with Grieg in Norway?

That was in Hop, a few miles from Bergen.

He was very much the grand seigneur in Norway, wasn't he?

No, I wouldn't say that. He was very disillusioned and, what shall I say? he was a very undignified man. I mean this was a typical thing: we went up a hill where there was a restaurant up at the top, and Grieg was quite happy. And there was a German-American came over to speak to him, and he said in a drunken voice: (imitates) we're proud of you and we think of you always and all that; and Grieg said to me: There, that's it, if I get any praise from anybody, they're always drunk. And then another morning he'd be peering down at the earth and he'd say: no, I can't understand it. I can't understand the ants. I can't understand what they're trying to do.

Why was he disillusioned? He had fame and...

Because his three best works: (again the gurgling laugh) the Folksongs opus 66, 'Lost in the Hills' for baritone, two horns and strings, the Symphonic Dances and the Album for male chorus opus 30, they were never done in his time in Norway.

Piece for two horns and strings did you say?

'Lost in the Hills', literally 'Taken by the Hills'. They believe that the hills opened up and closed on people. It begins: [PG plays first bar on the piano].

Sounds like VW.

Yes, that was done in Copenhagen when Grieg was a young man.

And Grieg felt bitter that these pieces weren't played?

He felt very bitter about everything. I don't mean bitter in a bad sense, but he felt very pained about everything. But of course that's true of all Norwegian poetry. It's one long...

Moan?

Moan, a hero's moan. Not a weakling's moan. The sadness of a hero.

HOFFNUNG:
26.9.59

I can remember thinking about Maurice Bowra whose autobiography I had been reading on my holiday with small Angela Richards and long Cecily Fortescue. We had got to Geneva on the way home and as I approached the news stand I recalled his habit of entering the Common Room, picking up the newspaper and asking nobody in particular, 'Any amusing deaths?'

I picked up a paper, to read in *The Times* with horror that Gerard Hoffnung had died at the age of thirty-four. Apparently he had complained to Annetta but his wife was used to that, once a week or more, and had thought little of it until Gerard was violently sick for no reason or stomach upset. It went on and on until she called an ambulance and he died on the way to hospital, ill only a matter of hours, death totally unexpected; cerebral haemorrhage.

His friends were shattered, left with our memories of this quite exceptional human being and cartoonist. It proved that his prodigious amount of work during his last eight or so years would be enough to sustain his reputation, his name entered the language. The cartoon books sold well, records of broadcasts, the Hoffnung Festivals ditto; later cards, jig-saw puzzles, table mats *et al* kept the name alive, and made some income for Annetta, having to provide for herself and their two young children: Emily (later sculptor) and Ben (later percussionist). What everybody remembered in particular was the bricklayer story which he told (and recorded) as part of a speech (turn) at the Oxford Union in December 1958.

It was Donald Swann who had introduced me, by proxy, as it were, suggesting I go to a certain gallery near Piccadilly where this unknown artist, born in Germany but brought up here, was exhibiting. I went and was the only visitor. Hoff sat at the receipt of

1   *John Amis aged three.*

2 Above: the autho
with Donald Swann

3 Left: the autho
with Manoug
Parikian and John
Warrack

4 Left: George Enescu,
Master Musician at
Bryanston.

5 Bottom left: Olive Zorian.

6 Bottom right: Noel
Mewton-Wood.

7 *John Amis by Hoffnung.*

8 *John Amis with Hoffnung.*

9 *Top left: With Alfred Brendel atop a tor.*

10 *Top right: Harrison Birtwistle.*

11 *Below: John Amis and Michael Tippett.*

12 *Top left: Benjamin*
Britten, George
Malcolm with the boys
chorus in A Boy was
Born, *Dartington*

13 *Bottom left:*
William Glock

14 *Bottom right:*
George Mackay Brown,
Orkney poet

15 Above: From a cruise ship, Kizhi.

16 Bottom left: Sandor Vegh, Master Musician.

17 Bottom right: Opera producer Peter Sellars.

18 Above: Joh
Amis as Empero
Pauline Tinsley a
Turando

19 Lef
Schönberg's il
fitting memoria
stone, Vienna

20 *Right: George Malcolm takes flight.*

21 *Bottom left: Constant Lambert.*

22 *Bottom right: John Amis with his father.*

From a drawing by Gavin Gordon

CONSTANT LAMBERT

conducts

THE B.B.C. ORCHESTRA

in a concert tonight at 9.0.

For programme

23 *John Amis in Snape.*

24 *Early morning: the view from the author's window.*

25 *John Amis with Frank Muir appearing in* My Music.

26. The Apostolic Constitution *Munificentissimus Deus*

custom but I didn't recognize that until half way round the exhibition where my laughter was immediately echoed by the (as I thought) *elderly* party with bald head and tweed suit who had taken my dosh. I went back to the money table and accused him of being the artist. He admitted as much and before we knew it we were deep in conversation and the beginning of a life-long, if brief, friendship. It turned out that we both loved the same kind of (usually loud) twentieth century music: *Sacre du Printemps* (which he always pronounced as Germans do, with the accent on 'temps', Walton, Roussel. I impressed him by knowing and even being able to whistle the rather obscure *Colas Breugnon* overture of Kabalevsky which he adored. Whistling, vocalizing and making mouth noises became a feature of phone calls, usually at inconvenient times, recalling some new enthusiasm. Others present too having thought we were bonkers (in the old sense) and we were: bonkers about music. Hoff was unstoppable, you couldn't somehow say 'no' to him or terminate a conversation for the inadequate excuse that you had to go to work or had guests waiting.

It was the same when visiting him in his Hampstead Garden Suburb house which contained delightful Berlin furniture brought over by his refugee parents. There is a charming Baltic beach snap of the infant Gerard and his seaside pal, André Prewine (later to become Andrew Preview in the Morecombe and Wise show; A.P. also played piano and conducted a bit, even made a career for himself), before both their families decided to emigrate, one to UK, the other to USA.

No, an evening with Hoffnung was a Hoffnung evening. You had to submit to Gerard's will. And you had a damn good time, too. Music played on the gramophone, music played by Hoff on one of his many ocarinas or later his tuba. There were the latest drawings to see, sometimes those of his colleagues Ronald Searle or the wonderful André François (I remember a splendid old stiff collar he sent Gerard as a Christmas greeting). Then there was the supper cooked by his housekeeper Marie who looked not only like a troll but also one of Hoff's cartoon characters. It was usually hare, with red cabbage and dumplings, followed by a mouth-watering fruit tart or perhaps a disgustingly delicious suet pudd. Gerard never talked about his good works, such as prison visiting or the efforts he made to rehabilitate ex-prisoners (often resulting in petty thefts by itchy fingers). He used to go to the Friends' Meetings saying that the silence was productive of cartoon ideas. It must have been an effort for him not to laugh because he was an inveterate and infectious giggler. Hoff was larger than life even to the point of embarrassing you because you could not match his generous impulses. He ate inhibitions for breakfast. He didn't care much for booze: 'rotting grapes' he would say when wine was mentioned or consumed.

Food was important to him; and 'big' ideas or plans could not be revealed except over a hearty meal. I remember that the idea to start the Hoffnung Festivals was first revealed over a blow-out of a Chinese lunch at Ley-Ons. I said I thought it was a barmy idea so let's do it. And we did; and I organized it; although I nearly threw my hand in because he was so single-minded that he nagged about everything. We used a monstrously large bass drum in one number which Boosey & Hawkes kindly lent us from its Edgware Museum. It had been made for a prewar Verdi Requiem conducted by Toscanini. Gerard was worried it was too large to get into the Royal Festival Hall.

'But, Gerard, the drum has been measured. Festival Hall have said they can get it in, the transport people say it's OK; Boosey & Hawkes say they can handle its exit; it will get in!' Of course it didn't; they had to remove a big door on South Bank to get it in. Gerard was usually right, dammit. However it all came right on the night. Huge success. And the rest you know.

Another memorable meal was one he and I had at the great German restaurant, Schmidt's, in Charlotte Street (why, oh why, did it defunct itself?). Anyway our main course arrived and the waiter asked Hoff if everything was all right. 'No,' said Gerard, 'it isn't; I don't think this is the proper cut of meat for a Kassler Rippchen.' (Rib cut and cooked in a special way.) A flurry of waiters. Gerard and I were eventually asked to step into the kitchen where the chef was waiting for us, ominously fingering an evil-looking cleaver. 'Was gibt?' he asked menacingly and a loud and furious argument ensued during which I tried to prevent Gerard putting his hands down on any table in case the chef used the cleaver. Eventually, the chef gave in and admitted that perhaps it wasn't the right cut of meat. That was typical of Hoffnung; he was prepared to speak out and be counted.

Marie the housekeeper was quite jealous of her position (as far as I recall her English was less than minimal). Nevertheless she was eventually ousted (and I am sure financially taken care of, if heart-broken) when Gerard married Annetta in 1952. We used to say that Annetta was the only possible wife, being prepared by her profession to take on Gerard: she was a children's nurse. It was a hazard because at twenty-eight he was a staunch bachelor, a child of nature. But he was prepared to take on new disciplines.

If Annetta was hardly a discipline, learning to read music was, but he did it – and to count bars and fit into an ensemble. And how rewarded he was by being able to play in the Morley College Symphony Orchestra conducted by our mutual friend Lawrence Leonard. One of the greatest moments in our lives was when the orchestra first rehearsed a piece G.H. had commissioned from Malcolm Arnold called *A Grand Grand Overture*. The second subject/ tune, brought back writ large at the end is one of Malcolm's best tunes, heart-warming (at the concert Dennis Brain put down his horn and played the organ part). The Arnold was one of many commissioned works, most of them excellent and a few of them too long. Malcolm himself wrote *The United Nations* with half-a-dozen military bands marching through the auditorium playing national themes, the result being a cataclysmic explosion followed by a string quartet reiterating pathetically the optimistic U.N. march. Another gem by the same composer was his *Leonora No. 4*, a satirical Beethovenian hodge-podge culminating in a whistle setting off the familiar rushing strings episode.

I suggested that for the '58 Festival we should have a tilt at contemporary music (I had recently been to a concert at which a cellist had sat down and *not* played his instrument for fifteen minutes – I think the so-called work was called *Paradigm III*). Gerard said he had heard two analysts on Cologne radio dissecting for fifty minutes a piece which had then taken all of three minutes in performance. I wrote a script to be spoken by Gerard and myself dressed as two German musicologists and Humphrey Searle sportingly composed a piece exactly following the analysis I wrote. Many people have asked for the script, so I print it here. (Karajan and Henze said it was their favourite record.) But before the script here is a commissioning letter:

Letter from G. Hoffnung

5 Thornton Way
London N.W.11

29 March 1958

My dearest Kohlroulade,

This is just a little note from your old mate to confirm that you are to write a libretto for 'three (or two) German Professors and Orchestra' for us.

I have been wrestling with the budget for the past month and if I take the money bag between my teeth and shake it violently I can offer you £24.19s.6d for two professors and £25 for three professors, and I do hope you will be able to do it – bearing in mind the great difficulties about paying out fees that are restricting me from paying you £565. In fact, I think the thing to do is remember that old saying 'every penny makes the water warmer'.

Now, my little palatschinken, the next thing is for the two of us to have a salami pudding with chocolate sauce, with a glass of camembert, and discuss something... So I will phone you quite soon and make a date.

All my love to you and your Wanst!
Rumbletummy

※

Punkt Kontrapunkt

Amis: Herr Doktor Domgraf Fassbender and meinselb have the honour that we are inwited by your Britisch Council to introduce to your Englisch audience the first hearing in London of the masterpiece of Bruno Heinz Jaja, Punkt Contrapunkt.

Hoff: Musik began when Arnold Schönberg has inwented the tone-row. Before 12 tone composing, was chaos absolut. Haydn, Mozart, Beethoven – all has been superficial, Schlagers, or, like you say, flagellated cream.

Amis: Whipped! Whipped! Whipped cream! Now to perform the music of Jaja in England brings a problem already, for here you are not ganz organiziert, you have not the electronic maschine werks.

Hoff: In Chermany we make it other; in Chermany every selbst respecting young composer carries no more the pen or the forking-tune but the mathematical sliprule and the spanner.

Amis: Musik paper is altmodish, graph paper is essential and every good Cherman composer is ready to put his spanner in the works, nein? (both laugh) Ja, ja, we make the Englisch yoke, ja?

Hoff: In Chermany we like the good Englisch yokes: 'If Britten can make it, Booseys can Hawke it.'

Amis: Ja, und in Mainz we say: 'If Michael writes rubbish, Schotts can Tippett.'

Hoff: (Tee-hee kind of laugh)

Amis: Aber, enough of yokes; we must to serious matters. We must tell the nature of the basic tone rows and their permutations in Jaja's *Punkt Contrapunkt*. First of all: this is absolut strict in form, ganz organiziert...

Hoff: Each note is dependent on the next. Each note is like a little polished diamond, like what Igor Stravinsky has said...

Amis: But of course Stravinsky has only said this after, Gott sei Dank, he has stopped composing his old tonal Kitsch. Jaja, unlike Stravinsky, has never been guilty of composing harmony in all his life, Jaja is pure, absolut twelve-tone...

Hoff: Never tempted, like some of the French composers, to write with thirteen tones. This, says Jaja, is the baker's dozen – the Nadir of Boulanger.

Amis: Also, now we have functional analysis: the basic row of twelve tones of *Punkt Contrapunkt* is like this: (MUSIC No.1)

Amis: And the inversion of the basic row is so: (MUSIC No. 2)

Hoff: You notice, I am sure, that the length, the intensity and the oktave pitch of each note is werked out according to the same mathematical series...

Amis: Now comes the basic row in the looking-glass or, as we call it in German, the Spiegel...

Hoff: Spiegel? (MUSIC No. 3)

Hoff: And now, the inversion of the mirror...

Amis: Sometimes called the crab through the looking glass. (MUSIC No. 4)

Amis: Also, with these four versions of the tone-row is Punkt Contrapunkt built up. First the quasi exposition...

Hoff: And the quasi development...

Amis: And then what seems like a quasi recapitulation...

Hoff: Then comes the Hohepunkt, so quasi lyrical as to be quasi emotional: three bars of silence.

Amis: The first is in 7/8, the third is in 7/8; but the second bar of silence is in 3/4 and this gives to the whole work a quasi Viennese flavour.

Hoff: But what makes this middle bar so important is that the silence makes a crescendo because it is the only moment in the whole piece when every instrument in the orchestra has the mute off.

Amis: But there is yet more of a climax: the fourth desk of Bratschen, wiolas, you call them, has a bottom B flat in this bar marked 'tremolando ma quasi pensato...'

Hoff: They must not play this note, only think it.

Amis: In fact, they can only think it, because this bottom B flat is not on the instrument exactly.

Hoff: After this silence the work is played backwards and upside-down for Jaja has made an exact hippodrome...

Amis: Dummkopf, nicht hippodrome aber palindrome... palindrome...

Hoff: Why do you underbreak me always?

Amis: Hippodrome! Just like a pupil of Pfitzner to make such a mistake...

Hoff: From you who studied with Max Reger...

Amis: Schinkensalat!

Hoff: Kalbsroulade!

Amis: Kasslerrippchen!

Hoff: Windbeutel!

(At this point Del Mar taps his baton on the desk; Hoff and Amis remember where they are and bow to each other with bad grace. MUSIC No. 5 the whole piece.)

HS: Experts in the same subject have little love for each other; as soon as I can I correct his English.

Fritz Spiegl had put on funny concerts in Liverpool and considered that Gerard had somewhat stolen his thunder by doing so in London so that there was a certain frostiness...hence the obscure reference to Spiegel/mirror. Nevertheless, the good Fritz, flautist, musicologist, printer and author, took part in the first Hoffnung festival conducting a (choral) *Geographical Fugue* by Ernst Toch.

BEECHAM'S RE-BURIAL
29.4.91

One of the hardest bits of writing I ever had to do was speaking a eulogy over Sir Thomas's grave when he was re-buried at Limpsfield Parish Church. The re-burial occurred because the big Woking cemetery of his first interment was being ploughed up. The noise of traffic and rain was so heavy at Limpsfield that no one could hear my eulogy so I thought I would print it here.

Eulogy

Nearly fifty-six years ago Sir Thomas Beecham stood by a graveside here and spoke eloquently of his friend Frederick Delius. Now he himself is to be reburied in the same churchyard. Those of you here know of Beecham's achievements, his performances are some of your most treasured memories, some of us knew the man, some had the experience of making music with him. We none of us *need* to be reminded of his greatness. Yet I feel we cannot let this act of re-interment happen without expressing why we revere and honour this musician, and without marvelling once again at the remembrance of performances of such understanding, wit, elegance and passion.

Asked once how he produced that unique magic in his conducting of the music of Delius, Sir Thomas replied: 'Because I've taken the trouble to find out what the scores are about.' 'Do you mean that you asked Delius about them?' 'Oh, good God, no; he couldn't tell me anything about them. I occasionally asked him, Frederick, what do you want done here? He said, "I can't remember anything about it, do what you like with it." So I did. And I have applied that principle to the work of every other composer.'

Beecham did know what the music was about, and, because of his intensity, industry and imagination, there was magic in his performances in a vast repertoire from Handel to Offenbach, from Haydn to Wagner, anything French, anything Russian, an air de ballet or a Strauss waltz. He savoured details but never at the expense of the whole. His music-making was never ponderous, his rhythm was utterly natural, like his phrasing; he sought clarity from his players so that he could illuminate the music he conducted. He had mind, he had charm, he had panache, he knew how to excite the passions. He never distorted, he avoided routine like the plague, he was the music while it played.

He was human; occasionally he could conduct very badly a work new to him (which he never conducted again). Paradoxically he seemed to study most the scores he had most often performed; he would bow and rebow, sometimes even in the afternoon before an evening concert, parts of a work like the Mozart G minor Symphony. All this in the quest for greater insight and for spontaneity. Not for him the butterfly pinned down in a glass case; it must be alive and breathing.

Admittedly what remains of Beecham, besides memories, is pinned down, on gramophone records, second best in that respect but, I submit, infinitely better than most of what we hear today. How he would hate what Nathan Milstein calls musical fast food, today's tonal hamburgers! And isn't it interesting how, as more and more Beecham performances are being reissued on compact discs, younger generations are discovering that we olduns were not talking out of our hats when we raved about Sir Thomas? Critics are even finding out that his interpretations of Handel and the Viennese classics have a spirit in common with the latest musicological dicta. I suppose all they are saying is that there is nothing like discovering *what the music is about.*

Of course with Beecham there was more to it than performing, and raising standards of playing. We owe him much for his entrepreneurial deeds. He brought the Russian ballet to England, Chaliapin and the great Strauss operas. He tried out hundreds of operas and symphonic works to satisfy his curiosity and, incidentally, to educate the public. He made Covent Garden glow and glitter, engaging the world's finest singers and conductors. He created orchestras and helped other organisations with his generosity, services and public spirit. He did much for Britain's musical prestige by conducting all over the world.

His rapport with orchestral musicians was such that they paid him their ultimate compliment: 'He lets us play.' Beecham was in command yet they felt that they were autonomous, those great soloists in his orchestras: Goossens, Kell, Riddle, Brain, Jackson, McDonagh, Brymer, Brooke. With Tommy it was never orchestral drill, always music-making.

We owe much to Shirley, Lady Beecham. As wife and secretary, she devoted herself to him in his last years. Since his death she has helped keep his name, his memory and his work alive. By founding the Sir Thomas Beecham Archive in support of the Music Scholarship Fund she has ensured that her husband's name will be carried into the next century through the generosity of Beecham supporters.

In spite of his flamboyant public persona I found that Sir Thomas was an intensely private person. His wit was often self-protective. He was a patriot. He wasn't by any means a saint but he was a genius, one of this century's most remarkable musicians, and certainly the finest conductor this country has produced.

Beloved, never forgotten Beecham, may your remains find peace and rest here forever!

EROS:
20.10.93

One question that came up tonight in the BBC Music Quiz show *My Music* was: can/is music erotic? Interesting question, and it was interesting that Frank Muir and Denis Norden both quoted as their supreme erotic piece of music a song/number called 'The Island'. Intrigued, I got hold of the record; it has a nice gooey, electronic accompaniment but the *music* is by no means erotic. The *words* are, though. The girl sings of approaching the Island, getting near and, wham, she has landed on it. But it is clear that Island for her means Orgasm.

So, what about *Tristan, The Poem of Ecstasy*, the *Rosenkavalier* Prelude, the interlude in Walton's *Troilus and Cressida, Rape of Lucretia* et al. Erotic? I can get a kind of mental orgasm sometimes in *Tristan* or Rachmaninov or Szymanowski First Violin Concerto or Delius *Song of the High Hills*. I think music can sometimes suggest but on the whole can only heighten feelings already there in your mind.

I interviewed Leopold Stokowski once and he turned the tables on me and asked what kind of bad effect music could possibly have? I said that I thought if you were evil anyway, music might heighten that evil and give you delusions of malheur. Like Hitler listening to Wagner. He thought I might just have a point but hesitated to put any blame for Hitler on Wagner.

Incidentally LS turned up forty-five minutes early for his interview. The day was one when a heatwave was at its zenith but the conductor wore thick Donegal tweeds and green leather gloves. He was on his way to conduct a supreme Mahler 2. Now there's a mental orgasm for you: finale when soprano and mezzo lines close and then divide just before fig. 33 (at the words 'wird rief, dir geben). They occur again very near the end, at fig. 49 'zu Gott wird es dich tragen'. But the only liquid is tears.

STRAVINSKY:
1.8.90

Stravinsky's first return to Europe after WW2 was in Paris in 1952. Librettist Jean Cocteau had got into the performing act, declaiming the part of the Orator in *Oedipus Rex* (including, Hi recall, an aspirated aitch at the words 'Il tombe de *h*aut') and had arranged some inept, poncey choreography. In the interval I met dear old critic Fred Goldbeck, looking like J. Worthington Foulfellow as usual: 'You know Stravinsky? No? well come backstage and I'll introduce you.' Oh, my Lord, pitta-patta, what does one say to GOD? During Creon's boring aria and the dotted rhythm bit which Stravinsky dubbed 'enter the girls, kicking' I desperately tried to think what liturgies I could utter in the 'présence divine' and made my mind up...to get the hell out quickly after the concert in case I met Freddie.

So I legged it up the Champs Elysées as quickly as I could. A narrow escape because at that time Stravinsky was God for me of twentieth-century music. Nowadays I think I would say Debussy for all that *Pelléas* and *L'Après-midi* date from the 1890s. I used to think that Constant Lambert, for all his pith and wit, had got it wrong about Igor. Now, although I still find IS stimulating and moments in *Symphonie des Psaulmes, Oedipus Rex* Gloria, top and tail, lots of *Apollon Musagètes* supreme not to mention *Scènes de ballet,* all the symphonies and the early ballets, yet the nervous dislocations of the beat, the vogueish quality and the lack of a Stravinsky *melodic* style do often mitigate his claim to supremity. With every new work he must have wondered how to épater not only the bourgeois but the haut monde (with *h*aspirate) as well, not forgetting the petite soeur des riches (Nadia Boulanger).

But GOD entered my life in person in 1967 when he accepted William Glock's invitation to come to Dartington to the Summer School complete with Vera, wife, and Robert Craft, secretary, friend, assistant conductor, v.snooty twitchy, intellectual snob companion, who could be quite nice sometimes. The party had a house to themselves in Warren Lane and David Drew's wife, Judy, cooked for them. Craft conducted the choir that week (Bach Cantata No. 131) and the great man came to rehearsals (complete with beret), even signed one or two autographs gratis. After the evening concerts the Party came upstairs to the Elmhirsts' drawing room for a drink or two, just a few of us including, I remember, the composer, Priaulx Rainier. His speaking voice was low, heavily accented and utterly enchanting. His manners were impeccable. This was before the *Diaries and Notebooks* had come out and of course we were dying for anecdotes. He told us of a visit one day chez Debussy where they played, one piano four hands, their latest ballets. He did not like *Sacre*, said I.S., but then I did not like *Jeux*. Snap! After one, maybe two such stories, Vera (who no doubt had heard the anecdotes scores of times) stood up and said, 'Igor, we go to bed.' We hated her.

Dear Colin Mason, who died young, wrote, could he do an interview for his Guardian newspaper? He was asked to send his questions in advance. He sent them, a couple of dozen at least. I.S. countered that the answers would constitute a small book; and for that his price would be X dollars (payable in cash, in advance).

Stravinsky liked cash in advance. William Glock had once seen him prewar in the Artist's Room of the Wigmore Hall counting banknotes '...ninety-eight, ninety-nine, hundred', put them carefully in his wallet and only then go on stage to play his Concerto for Two Pianos with son Soulima (who also came to Dartington a few years after Papa). Part of the reason why Igor, Vera and Bob came to Dartington was because W.G. was also Controller of Music, BBC and therefore in a position to employ I.S. to conduct for many dollars, payable in advance but nowadays by certified cheque. One time the cheque failed to materialize. Since the concert was being broadcast IS went on stage but with bad grace, refusing to speak to William that evening and for the rest of his stay.

Eye gore, curiously, was how Nadia Boulanger used to say his name sometimes, although more often she referred to him more reverentially as *Mister* Stravinsky. How illuminatingly she analysed his works at Bryanston (Summer School). I never forgot how she went through his *Orpheus*, referring back to other works and comparing that latest work with other composers' masterworks, illustrating by heart, of course. It was her analysis that stood me in good stead when I submitted my first script to the BBC for a talk about *Orpheus* to herald its first British performance. With her pince-nez and her elderly aunt appearance she was formidable with her exquisitely cut severe Lanvin clothes. With her utter devotion to Eye gore she was a counterpart to Imogen Holst in her adoration of Benjamin Britten. 'Oh,' Nadia once said, 'if he would wash the floor I am sure he would wash it very well. If he would send a package he would tie the string so well, put the stamp just where it must be.'

GEORGES ENESCU:
1.12.59

Back to Bryanston 1949; at one concert Monique Haas played Enescu's Sonata No. 1 and he himself played an impromptu recital of Bach which was ghastly: out of tune, something (we gathered) to do with his hearing. So when he came again in 1953 we thought we couldn't stand a whole evening of his violin playing but, because we thought he might be hurt not to be asked to play at all, we asked him to play just a single piece and he said it would be the C major unaccompanied Sonata of Bach. He did and it proved to be a monumental experience, the very heavens seemed to open and touch both Bach and this dear old man, now engaged on an act of revelation. He came off to cheers, once the audience had recovered a little; he looked at me and, with a twinkle in the eye, said, 'Shall I play a small encore?' He went back and played...the Bach Chaconne. It was magnificent until about half way through and the heavens abruptly closed and there was this old man scratching his fiddle wildly out of tune. It was pathetic. Heaven and then hell.

The Boyd Neel Orchestra and Maurice Clare again played within an inch of their lives for the Maître. Enescu also gave a course in interpretation which included several lengthy discourses, especially about Bach. He continually illustrated his talk by singing, whistling and tootling accompanied by his magical playing on the piano, occasionally waving a hand as if conducting, occasionally reinforcing a melodic strand by playing it on the leyboard. Somehow the Amadeus Quartet played better than anybody had experienced previously. It was the same at rehearsals with the Boyd Neel; he rarely said anything, made few movements, never histrionic ones and somehow his thoughts were committed to Maurice and the musicians who played as never before. What came out was the very essence of music.

I don't believe Enescu ever thought of himself. Except once when I asked him if I would get anything for himself. He said no, no, nothing. And then he said rather coyly, he would love a spoonful of jam; he got it of course. I was impressed because I had not seen anyone before eat jam *by itself*. (Since that time I have seen it many times... in the mirror.) August 19 was the Master's birthday and we anticipated his seventy-first birthday by giving him some presents, including a score of Purcell's cantata *Welcome to all the pleasures* which we then performed in his honour. He hadn't known the Purcell before this and he was suitably pleased to hear it.

The day after Enescu was ensconsed in The King's Arms in Blandford, William Glock and I went to his room to fix a schedule. It was impossible to get a plan from him. In answer to our asking did he want to teach in the morning or the afternoon he said 'Imagine the scene: Brahms and the players for the first run-through of his Clarinet Quintet in the middle of the room, and myself, a little boy of ten, in a corner of the room.' In the end we rang through to the manager of the hotel and said we would be calling for the master next day at half past nine. That did the trick and he was always ready and prepared.

After his visits to Bryanston Enescu came no more to the Summer School – he died in '55. But Olive and I saw him in Paris a few times, visiting his apartment where he lived with the dotty Princess. Her rooms were all highly decorated, furbelows with knobs on; his room was like a monk's: just a bed, a chair and a crucifix. He had one joke which pleased him: Bucharest, he would say, c'est la boue qui reste: Bucharest, it's the mud that remains. One afternoon when he was ill in London, Olive was invited to bring her scores of the Beethoven string quartets, and he went through every movement, giving her the tempi as he had learned them from Hellmesberger who had played them for Beethoven. So by shaking hands with Enescu one was shaking hands with Beethoven at only two removes.

Arthur Rubinstein once told me a story about Enescu. One day Enescu was packing in his Paris flat, preparing for a European tour. Knock at the door. Which reveals the patron from Bucharest who had made it possible for Enescu to come to Paris many years previously. 'Georges, there is something you can do for me. I have a son who plays the violin. Will you teach him?' 'Well, you know, I am very busy, a tour imminent, and on my return I must finish my opera *Oedipe-roi*.' 'But Georges, remember it was a great favour I did you.' Eventually, Enescu agrees to take the boy on.

A year or two passes. Another knock at the door, the patron again. 'Georges, I am disappointed with you.' 'Why?' 'I know it is the custom, after a year or two's study, for a teacher like yourself to put on a recital for a student, such as my son.' 'Ah, but you see, he is not ready for it yet.' 'But Georges, his aunts say that the boy plays marvellously, almost as good as Heifetz. It was, after all, a great service I did you.' Eventually Enescu gives in and hires the Salle Gaveau. Three weeks later another knock at the door: 'Georges, the tickets are going awfully badly.' 'Well, what do you expect, there are in Paris many concerts, the profession is over-crowded, your son's name is not known.' 'Georges, if you would play the piano for my son's recital, I am sure that...' 'No I can't play for him; I am a violinist, a conductor and a composer. All right, I can play the piano but I am no pianist.' 'Georges, do I have to remind you...?' So Enescu gives in and his name is announced to play at the recital for this violinist who is untalented.

The evening arrives and so, backstage, does Enescu. He says to one of the attendants 'Oh, you will turn pages for me, won't you?' The man explains that unfortunately he has not got his spectacles with him, cannot see without them. 'Your colleague, then?' 'Alas, he does not read music.' 'Well then', says Enescu 'since I must have a page-turner go out into the hall and the foyer, find one of my students, there's bound to be one or two there.' The attendant comes back after a few minutes and says he can't find any students, in fact the only person he can recognize is Maître Alfred Cortot, the famous pianist. 'Oh, then ask him, he's an old friend I haven't seen for sometime, we can chat at the piano between numbers and in the intermission.' Cortot obliges and the recital duly takes place.

After the customary day or two a review of the concert appears in 'Figaro', beginning: 'Last Tuesday, a curious recital took place. The man turning pages should have been playing the piano; the man playing the piano should have been playing the violin and the man playing the violin should have been turning the pages.'

THE MARCHIONESS:
8.4.90

Last year I was in correspondence with the conductor June Gordon, she was a pupil of Boult's at the RCM, married to a Scotsman who unexpectedly (cf. *Kind Hearts and Coronets*) became Marquess of Aberdeen and Temair. I had heard about her activities at the family seat, Haddo House, some twenty miles north-west of Aberdeen, but had never been there, so I asked her about recent and forthcoming events. I knew that she had conducted the three Elgar oratorios and that Vaughan Williams, Britten and Tippett had been there directing their own works, *Spring Symphony* and *A Child of our Time*. What I had not realised was that the Haddo House Choral Society actually staged operas: *Oberon, Nabucco, Macbeth, Pearl Fishers, Hugh the Drover* and, last year, *Gloriana* with Sarah Walker. What had started out in the late '40s as a carol concert for the estate folk had blossomed out in a big way. The venue is an all-purpose wooden hall built on Canadian lines as a community hall some ninety years ago; it can seat 400, an orchestra of 70 and has a stage that accommodates quite a large chorus, excellent acoustics, good to sing in. Every spring there is a choral concert and an opera in April.

When June Gordon wrote to me last year she was still trying to cast *Turandot*. I replied not too seriously that if she was still stuck for an Emperor I would have a go; after all, Hugues Cuénod made his debut at the Met in the role in his eighties...and the score calls for 'an old man with a decrepit voice'. June called my bluff and so at the end of March I presented myself with considerable apprehension at Haddo. I have often done speaking parts – *Façade*, *King David*, *Oxford Elegy* and sung small parts in choral works; but staged opera was something new, even though my part is less than fifty bars long and mostly accompanied by percussion. 'Should I put on an 'old voice'? I consulted singer friend Linda Hirst. 'No,' she counselled, 'just sing with your usual voice and...' (charming smile) 'it'll probably come out right.'

The orchestra at Haddo is professional, the chorus amateur, likewise smaller parts (like mine), but the principals included John Graham-Hall as Ping, Graeme Matheson-Bruce as Calaf and Pauline Tinsley in the title-role. Tinsley lifted us all onto another plane, beautiful sounds in all parts of that wide-ranging voice of hers, never scooping, always dramatic and musically true, utterly reliable, a great artist. We only had four days all together so that it was just as well that the production was straightforward. We had costumes from an old Covent Garden production designed by Cecil Beaton. I was delighted to hide behind a magnificent outfit; and of course the old Emp. doesn't move about much, sits centre stage and pontificates. I remembered my lines and actually got my one difficult entry right on the third and final night! In fact, as my colleagues remarked, the show was incredibly hitch-free, helped by thorough preparation; true, one standard-bearer fainted but was unobtrusively removed from the scene.

I wondered if it wouldn't be a good thing for all critics to have some practical experience of being onstage, to feel the terror, to know about the split-second pitfalls that can turn into pratfalls, to learn what happens if somebody comes in late, making you look silly coming in right and vice versa, to decide what to do when you don't get an important lead, wondering what happens if your beard starts coming unstuck or your costume is so heavy it pulls you back when you are trying to go forward.

June Gordon does a wonderful job at Haddo and although I missed her May concert when she conducted R.V.W.'s *Sea Symphony*, Britten's *Serenade* and a new Scots work by John McLeod, I might go and sing in the chorus for a *Matthew Passion* in November to be given in celebration of the ninetieth birthday of Sir Keith Falkner. Haddo is a handsome house, designed by the elder Adam, 1732, in that part of East Scotland that Frank Muir characterised as 'kempt'.

Of course it is great to hear the world's finest performances in the recognised concert halls and opera houses in the capitals, but I am so pleased at Haddo to have found another happy hunting ground where music is made by a mixture of professionals, students and amateurs.

GLYNDEBOURNE:
5.6.90

I came back from my Russian cruise two days early so that I woke up on Friday morning feeling that I had somehow won a day and that something special had better be done with it. I saw that *Kat'a Kabanova* was to be performed that evening so I rang up Glyndebourne and asked if I could have a press ticket. Yes. Short opera so caught the 3.47 for a 6.30 curtain up. Vivid performance of *Kat'a*, result shattering as always. Kreizberg brought the music to the boil, straightforward production (although just back from Russia I observe that the church in scene 1 had a cross atop it which surely means that it is a catholic building and not, as it equally surely ought to be, Greek Orthodox), Amanda Roocroft was vocally and histrionically just right (a relief to hear her back on form) and Helga Dernesch gratefully seized Janacek's gift of a part to former soprano divas who can act as the black-hearted (mezzo) Kabanicha; Tichon feebler than his part warrants though. Am constantly amazed how compressed Janacek can be: you learn all about Katya, her situation, her relatives, the whole set-up, you know them well and the first act ends dramatically; then you notice from your watch that the

141

whole thing has lasted twenty-seven minutes (Wagner with that amount of plot would be into his third evening by now).

The food has been good at Glyndebourne for some years; I hadn't booked a place but I had an excellent cold buffet (really decent ham and beef), a half of fine Santenay, summer pud and coffee for £47. Plus John Schlesinger at the next table (I still miss his lovely sister Susan – who committed suicide at least twenty years ago, a love death).

My association with Glyndebourne goes back to the '40s when the house reopened after the war in 1946 with Britten's *The Rape of Lucretia*, a canny choice after the success of *Peter Grimes* the year before but a curious choice considering John Christie's hatred of anything modern. The *Rape* was successful and was followed a year later by *Albert Herring* proving once again Britten's incredible ability to compose an opera within the span of a year (o.k. what about Mozart and Rossini completing operas in much shorter times? Yes, agreed, but the work involved then was less arduous, textures much simpler, and there were often many and literal repeats – I have seen at Bologna the manuscript of *The Barber of Seville* which shows Rossini's extraordinary skill in laziness, repeat signs and arrows to shorten the actual writing all over the score). So, in 1947 *Herring* ran at Glyndebourne in tandem with Gluck's *Orfeo* starring the young Kathleen Ferrier, radiant and unforgettable in the title role, not helped by Fritz Stiedry's inelegant, Prussian conducting. My wife Olive had always raved about Glyndebourne because the Mozart productions she had seen prewar had been the summit of excellence. After the performance of *Orfeo* we went round to see Kath and, with tears in our eyes, tried to thank her. Reverting to broad Lancashire she asked, 'Was it all right, luvs?'

Christie hated both the Britten operas and their composer too. It was quite mutual. Ben also hated the acoustics of the Sussex theatre, referring to it as 'Mr Christie's horrid little opera box'. It is true that the sound was quite dead and the lack of resonance became even more marked when the auditorium was enlarged. Christie likewise hated the Henze-Auden *Elegy for Young Lovers* and might have approved of Hugues Cuénod's revision of its title as 'Allergy for Old Buggers'. The story goes that when Auden arrived in Sussex to attend rehearsals there was actually one going on so the poet went in unannounced. The only listener in the stalls was Mr Christie so at a suitable pause Auden thought he would introduce himself. 'Good afternoon, Mr Christie, I've just arrived, I'm Wystan Auden.' 'Who?' 'I'm W. H. Auden, I wrote the libretto of this opera.' 'Well, you shouldn't have.'

In 1946 Britten asked me if I would get together the thirteen-piece chamber orchestra for *Lucretia*. I did so and included in it some members of the as yet unformed Amadeus Quartet. Some players stayed many years, like John Francis, flute, Steve Waters, clarinet, and the Wilson brothers, bassoon and percussion, also Neil Sanders, and became the nucleus of the English Opera Group Orchestra (which a few operas on, by *Turn of the Screw* time, was led by my wife Olive Zorian). I was fairly green about contracts and I was held in some contempt by Rudolf Byng, the general manager of Glyndebourne, and he soon swept me aside. But it was nice to have been in at the start of postwar G-bourne; or Glyndeburn, as Beecham always called it; Christie and Beecham didn't get on either. Two prima donnae. And Beecham never liked any outfit he wasn't boss of anyway. The amazing thing was that, as far as I know, Christie and Carl Ebert got on. But that was because Christie worshipped Ebert; and because Ebert owed his post Nazi-Germany career to Christie.

In later years when Glyndebourne reopened properly with Ebert in charge of productions, Fritz Busch as musical director and Jani Strasser in charge of vocal studies, I was down at the opera house quite a bit. I had formed a friendship with Byng's assistant, Moran Caplat, who later took over from Byng. The L.P.O. had been in the Sussex pit before the war and when Glyndebourne proper started up again. But things were not always satisfactory because the orchestra was not always at its best. I was also by that time the London music critic of *The Scotsman* so I managed to see all the productions for many years. In those days they actually managed the considerable feat of having the first nights of three new productions on consecutive evenings, which worked out very nicely for the critics because we would mostly take hotel or guesthouse accommodation and stay in Sussex for three days.

One thing I couldn't quite understand was this adoration of Carl Ebert. When he did a production of an opera that was new, or fairly new, to him, like *Idomeneo* the result was fabulous and revelatory, especially when backed up by Fritz Busch. But when it was yet another production of a more familiar Mozart opera, the result was fussy and mannered. But then one evening Anton Walbrook was ill and the non-singing role of Selim Pasha in *Entführung* was taken by Ebert. It was one of the greatest stage performances I have seen in my life; you could not take your eyes off him. Mostly he stood perfectly still but that was enough to rivet attention; and his gestures and movements were even more riveting. And they say he could and did put on such performances throughout rehearsals, acting everybody's part, switching languages to suit the multilingual cast. And of course he was very handsome, too, with all that white hair.

A short visit to the buses: the scene is after the first night of *Lucretia*. It is not long after the war, not many cars about so that even that distinguished guest Francis Poulenc has come by train and is now seated in the coach waiting to return to Lewes and thence to Victoria. It so happens that Poulenc came and sat by me; I didn't dare talk to the great man, especially as I knew from having shoved him on at the National Gallery Concerts that he spoke no English although he seemed to understand it perfectly. Et alors, two ladies in front of us are discussing the performance. The younger one says, 'How did you like the opera by Britten, dear?' 'No, darling, that was Mozart.' 'But, dear, it was a new opera by Benjamin Britten.' 'No, darling, that was Mozart. This is Glyndebourne, they only ever perform Mozart.' (As an old *Punch* might add: French composer goes away wondering if he heard aright. Actually Poulenc was grinning hugely, looking more like Fernandel than ever.)

Before the production of *Pelléas* took place some years later there was an educational weekend of lectures and I did the one on the Debussy. To make the family connections clear I had a blackboard set up and chalked up a family tree which had at the base, Pelléas equals Mélisande with underneath a line towards their progeny which Mél holds in her arms before snuffing it in Act V. This progeny has no name but is known to be a poor weak thing, a 'puny brat' in the libretto. So on the blackboard in place of a name I wrote 'puny brat'. After my talk a lady came up and asked if 'puny brat' (pronouncing it as if it were a French word) was a common name.

144

Another lecture giver was Anthony Besch. Poor Anthony, he was dying to be given a production at Glyndebourne but all they gave him, after slaving away for years as Ebert's assistant, was the curtain-raiser *Schauspieldirektor*. He obviously wasn't Christie's favourite boy because Mr C went round all the lecturers, saying kind words. But when he got to Besch he said, in a withering way, 'Very clever, Anthony, very clever.'

Glyndebourne on a wet day could be very lowering to the spirit, no wonder people took to Pimms. Sunny evenings were another matter: Guardian critic Philip Hope-Wallace and I used to race, one each side of the pond, to take possession for a picnic of a stone bench just by the escaping trickle of water from the pond. Philip was my favourite to talk to of the critics, because unlike most of the others music was only one of the arts that interested him, he was also a theatre critic and knowledgeable in all the other arts including painting and literature. He was an educated man and a tolerant one; he had high standards but was also humane. When the singer Tom Hemsley's false nose came off in *Savitri* and he managed to retrieve it before it fell to the ground Philip wrote: 'If ever Mr Hemsley thinks of another profession he could be a first-rate slip catcher.' P.H-W. was a tall man with a large head set somewhat on the skew; he was known either as Humpty-Dumpty or Phyllis Hope-Wallop.

Memorable performances at Glynders? Well, for years Sena Jurinac was the star and darling of the regulars. As Fiordiligi in *Cosi* and the Composer in *Ariadne* above all but in any of the many parts she took and Ilia in *Idomeneo*. Her name does not now resound as it should because she did not record very much or very well but her presence on the stage was overwhelming and overjoying; strong men were at her feet, powerful women too. She herself was from Jugoslavia (Christie had a little conceit of putting singers' nationalities in: Geraint Evans was always Welsh and Sena Bosnian which latter has sad overtones now); she was married to Sesto Bruscantini, excellent baritone, and Sena's exit from Sussex had to do with her divorce from Sesto. The following season Sena's roles were taken over by a Swedish singer whom we all hated in advance. But the Swede was Elisabeth Söderström so that meant that she soon took over our hearts as well as Sena's roles. Richard Lewis was marvellous in the title-role in *Idomeneo* and good in any role: his singing in any foreign language was always easy to understand! Another tenor, who varied from day to day but when on form was the best in his 'fach', was Juan Oncina, Spanish light lyric tenor and coloraturist extraordinary, unbeatable in Rossini. Outstanding in the smaller tenor parts was the Swiss Hugues Cuénod, unforgettable as M. Triquet and Basilio. He had a way of splaying out his long legs as Basilio that made us laugh before he sang a note. One morning Hugues cooked me a boiled egg at Gerry Almond's guest house at Ringmer and his stance at the stove was identical with his Basilio. Though Swiss Hugues had a Scottish grandmother and had a most elegant tartan dinner jacket. He also had the most elegant manners, never looking, for instance, over the shoulder of my tiny girl-friend Angela, as most men did, to see who was in the offing. And the classic example of that over-the-shoulder look occurred when dear Charlotte Bonham-Carter asked a friend about his wife's health and she obviously switched off while he replied, 'Well, I'm sorry to say she died last month.' Charlotte missed that, turning back to him to say, 'Splendid, simply splendid.'

ALDEBURGH:
10–24.6.98

To Aldeburgh for my annual visit to the Festival. I thought I had been to every year except just after my marriage broke up; since Olive Zorian, my wife, had such connections with the place, as leader of the English Opera Group, leader of the Zorian String Quartet, and violinist with Julian Bream's Consort I thought it was her place rather than mine. But when I came to examine the early programmes it seems that I must have missed the opening year, 1948. The first concert I can actively recall is one when a Dutch choir was the backing group for a Bach Passion. In that year jet planes were unknown to most Londoners but those in the audience that day became forcibly aware of them. It happened almost as if on cue in that part of the Passion which depicts the rending of the temple. A jet flew low over the church. The politest way to describe the effect on many of the audience was when one of them said it reminded him of what happens to men who hang themselves.

Totting up the days and the months I must have spent over a year in Aldeburgh, some of the happiest days in my life (though that would also be true of Dartington where I ran the music summer school for thirty-four years). Aldeburgh is sometimes compared to Bayreuth but the chief difference is that the German town always performs the same old ten Wagner operas whereas, although Aldeburgh performs many Britten works and saw the première of a good few, yet the Festival performs much else. Until Britten's stroke and death he was the life and soul of the place, together with his tenor companion Peter Pears. Britten chose most of the programmes and performers and appeared as the most musical and inspiring conductor and pianist. He really lived up to that saying for he 'was the music while it played'. He positively illuminated any music he took part in. And to be in Aldeburgh in his presence, especially for the premières of those works that poured from his pen year after year, made for a well-being that made one glad to be alive.

After he died things dipped and the joint directorship of Oliver Knussen and Steuart Bedford, ending in 1998, has proved a mixed blessing. They are both excellent conductors especially in Britten but too often whole programmes have been grey and seemingly loveless. Instead of looking through the advance information to see if there was any event one could skip, one looked with desperation to see if there were anything one wanted to hear, very often not much. Especially to be avoided were the visits of American composers and performers that one felt were quid pro quos, returning hospitality. Exceptions were during the years when Murray Perahia shared the directorship and gave wonderful concerts, often with performing friends from over the pond. True, Ollie Knussen brought us Takemitsu and Schnittke but also, alack, he brought us Peter Lieberson, Leon Kirchner and Paul Niekrug (all of whom were given hefty commissions and, no doubt, performing fees, travel expenses and payments for the expense of performing material). When I was a member of the Aldeburgh Council I asked questions about these matters and also about the amounts of money handed out by the Britten Trustees and to the upkeep of the Red House, where Britten and Pears lived. Because of these questions and others relating to finance and programmes I was kicked upstairs to be a Vice-President of the Aldeburgh Foundation.

This year I have taken my usual cottage in Crabbe Street which is, as it were, the backside of the Aldeburgh Bookshop; it consists of rooms on three floors: the entrance is a foot or two below sea level into the kitchen; half a floor up is the sitting room, half a floor further up is the bedroom and through the bedroom is the only room not facing the sea and that is the bathroom which is in the High Street, facing the half-timbered Cinema, and in the bathroom is a quaint old-fashioned iron bath tub, free standing and narrow with lion claw legs. Cosy.

The first festival event I attended was in the half-timbered flick house and was the 1935 Hollywood *A Midsummer Night's Dream.* I was expecting something corny and over the top but it seemed to me a masterfilm, really conjuring up an atmosphere of dream and magic, a remarkable use of the medium. Amazingly it was the first and last sound film of the great German stage director, Max Reinhardt. Bronislava Nijinska is credited with the choreography but it is said that the studio altered her work; it looks as if Berkeley Busby had a hand in it, but if so Busby at his best. James Cagney of course is small and wiry but he is a superb Bottom whilst Mickey Rooney is just the best Puck I have ever seen, almost unbelievably bounding with energy and amused malice. Olivia de Havilland is adorable as Hermia, Victor Jory commanding and evil as Oberon, and Dick Powell, yes, Dick Powell makes a good Lysander and speaks his lines well. Only Hugh Herbert is boring with his trademark giggle; Joe E. Brown clowns his way through Flute like a true Shakespeare comic. Reinhardt rescued the composer Erich Korngold from Nazi Austria to eke out Mendelssohn for the music which he does tactfully and efficiently; there is no grinding of styles when Korngold takes over, for the last act rustics' play for instance; and somebody ensured that the braying Ophicleide is clearly heard on the sound track.

The effect of magic was caught better in the film than in the production offered in the opera presented this year. Opera being so expensive these days the only way Aldeburgh can present it is by students of the Britten-Pears School. As a student production it worked well: as a festival production of a great opera it was

148

inadequate. The singing was accurate enough and that's a tricky assignment in itself to be sure but the piece calls for more than that; in a word, for experience. But it was a good reminder of the piece. It was played in the Jubilee Hall where the work first saw the light of evening in 1960. The Jubilee referred to is that of Queen Victoria when the little Suffolk town put up an all-purpose hall, little suspecting that it would see the birth of one of the greatest operas of all time, a worthy successor to the Shakespearean masterpieces of Verdi. Even enlarged and rejigged the hall has a tiny stage, little or no space behind it and less than three hundred seats in front of it, with room for an orchestra of twenty-seven. Britten wrote the piece in nine months. Now just to put down the notes on paper in that time is quite a feat but where did he find time to think out all the complexities, the way the work is organized with such subtlety: the different musics for the lovers, the royals, the rude mechanicals and the fairies, the way Britten takes into account the four chords that begin Mendelssohn's *Midsummer Night's Dream* overture and builds most of the second act on variations of his own set of four chords, his flirtation with serial techniques, the amazing use of his little orchestra? The second act is the best act, a miracle of beauty from which I would single out the sensual clarinet theme in the 'love duet' of Titania and Bottom, and the exquisite bursts of sound that accompany the trumpet runs as Puck leads the lovers a dance. Breathtaking beauty.

The best thing about this production was the orchestral playing under the distinguished direction of Michael Rosewall. Oberon was a black, burly, sinister figure in the Saturday afternoon show with his mate a sure-voiced Japanese Titania with a mask-like face. Would Britten have been amused or bemused? What is certain is that he would not have liked a Puck with breasts although he might have admired everything else about the performance of Dawn Hartley.

Nessun dorma al Aldeburgo so it was hurry, hurry to Snape Maltings for a so-called Carnival Night given by the BBC Symphony Orchestra under the expert direction of Oliver Knussen. It began with his own *Flourish with Fireworks* which paid homage (and royalties?) to Stravinsky's early composition, a wedding pres. to the Rimsky-Korsakov family, followed by a vivid performance of Copland's *El salon Mexico* which lacked only a horse whinny in the

149

cheeky E flat clarinet solo in the middle; but since Oliver did not ask for it at rehearsal, I wonder if it is in the score. Must look. There followed one of what I call Ollie's follies, Piano Concerto No. 1 by Peter Lieberson, one of those dull as ditchwater American composers who get asked over to Aldeburgh, who writes such boring music I wonder why they get asked. Aren't there enough boring British composers who could be given a go? Or enough not boring composers, like Simon Holt, or Judith Weir or Thomas Adès. (But the last is sure to get a good share of performances from now on as he has just been named as festival director.)

The next night we had medieval vocal music. When Imogen Holst, way back, conducted Pérotin's *Viderunt Omnes* she conjectured some instrumental accompaniment for the voices and very entertaining it was, bells and so forth. Last night it was *a cappella*, probably more pure but once you've got the idea of four beats in a bar with triplets in each beat boredom sets in for me.

In fact, what with finding so much contemporary music boring and medieval music likewise I begin to wonder if I haven't been listening wrong all these years. When my memory isn't called into play, or when it gets quickly dulled by repetition, when there is no melody that delights, no rhythm that intrigues nor any harmony that tickles, when my emotions are not stirred...then music bores me. The later Schönberg (not Webern), and atonal or minimal music up to and including, oh boy yes including, Maxwell Davies, Birtwistle, Glass (not Adams) and Reich, it goes in one ear and out the other. I call it lack of imagination on the part of those composers. But perhaps it is my ears that are at fault. Awful thought.

Only today have I discovered in the programme book why Crag Path is so named. It runs as a footpath from the Brudenell Hotel on the south end of Aldeburgh down a quarter of a mile to the Moot Hall more or less the length of the little town. Crag is an old word, not meaning rocky eminence as elsewhere, but a 'fossiliferous shelly sand'; this coralline crag is apparently unique to south-east Suffolk (not many people know that!). The streets mostly lie parallel to the shore line and 'tis said that there are one or two such streets now under the sea. It's a funny old town with the accent on the old; people come here to retire, boat or play golf. But there are now two or three good restaurants, a good bookshop and the aforementioned half-timbered flick house. There are scarcely two houses alike, mostly Victorian, few of them handsome but the general effect is pleasing and the atmosphere makes for instant nostalgia. And, of course, Benjamin Britten lived here and was visible in the little town, shopping very occasionally, more usually speeding round in one of his high-powered cars, a sporty black Jensen or in a Rolls, driven by George Behrend (who wrote learned books about trains and was sometimes known as 'Doch-doch').

I have slept around in Aldeburgh: of the hotels mostly in the Wentworth at the north end where I remember meals with the Del Mars (Norman winningly asking the almost Dickensian old waiter 'would it be terribly greedy to have a fifth Aldeburgh dab?') and Joan Cross (by turns hilarious and wittily demolishing); I also recall staying there in winter once when making a film for BBC-TV about Britten's *Owen Wingrave* and went once into the dining room to be greeted with joy and dismay by members of the xxxxx String Quartet, with joy because we were old friends, dismay because three-quarters of them had girl friends with them rather than their spouses. Brudenell's down at the south end where the sea comes nearest to Crag Path, bit Trust-House-Forte without much character; the White Lion where E. M. Forster often stayed and used to hold court on the wooden bench just outside the hotel opposite the Moot Hall; inland was Uplands, lovely silver on the dining room tables, run by eccentric Connie Wynn who lived in the garden in a railway carriage and used to enter the dining room with a parrot on her shoulder and bawl for ten minutes to guests sitting at the *far* end of the room; I recall one such interminable noisy chat with Sir Robert and Dorothy Mayer. Then there was a pretty house near the Suffolk Hotel, clapboard from the first floor up where I and my wife shared the place with Norman and Pauline Del Mar and the pianist Noël Mewton-Wood (Roberto Gerhard Piano Concerto, that year). Then one year I had digs at 44 or 45 Crag Path where my extremely ancient, Eton-cropped landlady had a hammer and sickle above her bed, quite a cough-drop she was. And there were many years digging with the Hammelmanns in an exquisite house (Regency Cottage) between 44 and the Brudenell: Hanns, blond German, utterly charming with Elspeth his lovely top-drawer over apologetic wife, and his radio collaborator Michael Rose who became my best chum.

151

They made Third Programme marvels called *Birth of an Opera* put together with letters, autobiographies and music. I came in as a paying guest and was allowed to bring in friends who stayed, such as Julian Bream and Irene Worth.

Once in Canada Julian was asked by a local tenor who had been approached by Aldeburgh to come and sing but was worried, is Canada still as prim? about the sexual goings-on. 'My advice to you, young man,' said Julian, 'is when working at Aldeburgh at all times to keep your back to the sea...and...watch out for the early morning bathers.'

A year or two back Ian Bostridge the tenor raised hopes with a penetrating performance of Britten's *Sonnets of John Donne* so expectation was high for his recital this year, especially since I had heard him do a beautiful Evangelist in Bach's St John Passion. But alas, something seems to have happened to his style of singing. The line has gone: the top part of the voice is in good order but the tone in the middle came and went in a way that mashed up the music in a disastrous way (*Dichterliebe*, half a doz. Wolf Eichendorff settings and Britten's *Winter Words*) and the lower part of the voice is very weak indeed. And he didn't help himself by moving not only his head but walking around, turning his back and sometimes confiding his thoughts to the piano. (I remember Hans Hotter telling me that it took him twenty years to stand still when singing lieder; at the beginning of his career Fischer-Dieskau stood stock still but for the last five years or so he moved around, to bad effect). And yet this handsome and wholly delightful looking tenor has recently scooped up many prizes in the gramophone business. Maybe he stands still when at the microphone; moving around does nothing to make his delivery clearer; mind you, he is on the whole a good and thoughtful musician. Yet he messed around with note values and tempos in the Britten. He seems to want to act out lieder. But the acting should all be done with the voice. That's what all the greats have done, from Dieskau to Pears to Sinatra.

It is strange and wonderful how many good string quartets there are these days, compared with thirty years ago, the adjectives applying especially since the genre does not pay well. But of course the repertoire contains a higher proportion of masterpieces than any other form of music, so it must be very satisfying even if not lucrative.

Present at many festival events has been Marion. I knew her first as a beautiful teenager, daughter of Erwin Stein, mouthpiece of the second Viennese school, friend of Schönberg and Berg; later, at Boosey and Hawkes responsible for seeing through the press the works of Benjamin Britten whom he loved like a son, like the genius he was. Erwin was diminutive, almost a caricature of a German professor musician with strong accent (Austrian in fact, not German), several pairs of glasses though never the right pair on his nose. He was trenchant about all music that he did not approve of. I reminded Marion (who married first George, Earl of Harewood, and second Jeremy Thorpe) of Erwin praising a work on his terms by saying of it: 'Of course it is bad, my dear, but not *so* bad.' And another time: 'Yes, I heard the piece but I tell you, it's not as good as it sounds.'

BENJAMIN BRITTEN:
17.6.91

'Damn braces: bless relaxes' Journalists and writers take William Blake to heart/desk top. Beaverbrook once berated Kenneth Tynan about the copy he had delivered for the *Evening Standard* because it was neither particularly for or against the show he had written about: either one or the other, boy. And so it is with Britten: the good is often interred but the evil is always left uppermost and showing (for the Sunday newspaper extracts).

Let me say then that Benjamin Britten was a wonderful companion, one of the most attractive persons I have met. A beguiling speaking voice that unfortunately loses its charm on recordings where the upper class modesty is noticeable in that he says all the time 'one' instead of 'I'. But he was middle, not upper class and he dressed like a prep schoolmaster, nothing flashy (exotic ties were left to Peter Pears). He knew who he was but was modest: 'Oh, I'm so glad you enjoyed it.' But you didn't mess about with Ben. I think he had one skin less than most of us. If he thought you were going to be hostile, he snapped first. As time went on, he got the power bug; and was cowardly in not telling people they were dismissed. He could sulk and take offence. Once at a rehearsal two double-bass players with umpteen bars tacet laughed at a cartoon in the paper. Ben thought they were laughing at him, therefore wouldn't conduct the LSO for two years.

He and Peter came to Morley College for a house concert, invited by Michael Tippett. They clicked and since I was a sort of unofficial secretary (no sex) to Michael, they extended their friendship to me and when Michael was put in the Scrubs for three months Ben thought I might be missing his company and asked me for dinner in his shared house with the Steins in St John's Wood. Two evenings we spent à deux. One day we listened to the British broadcast première of the Sixth Symphony of Shostakovich. In the first movement there are two passages where the violas trill for ever, seemingly marking time. BB commented on this as though DSCH were trying to make his piece longer to get more Performing Rights money. But of course the Soviet did not belong to this group. In an interview with me later BB said he preferred DSCH's chamber music to his symphonies; in Russia DSCH had played BB his No. 10 and the Englishman had been 'knocked sideways' by it. DSCH and his wife stayed at Aldeburgh. PP said DSCH was awfully good at playing the game Happy Families and had won. I think BB must have *let* him win; and it shows BB being a good guest because he hated not winning, as I had found when I played tennis at Dartington with Ben as my partner, against Peter and Leonard Elmhirst, squire of Dartington. Ben had a dirty cunning serve; he placed the ball as carefully as he placed a note.

Peter Shaffer was the first to comment how incredibly clever a composer Ben was. He knew exactly what he was doing all the time: when he put down a note he *heard* it, knew how the note was produced, how the player could play the passage, where the chorus could get its note from, all the practical details were in his head. Before he wrote Julian Bream's guitar piece, the *Nocturnal*, he borrowed a guitar and a manual and was therefore able to invent new sounds and even told Julian how to play certain innovatory passages. This after Julian had explained that certain things could not be played in the work. As indeed they had not been until BB told JB how.

Once, and only once, did he foozle, writing a low G for the piccolo in *Billy Budd* that is not on the instrument. He even used to point it out in an amused way.

154

But what a genius! Not only the technical mastery that enabled him to compose something like the opera *A Midsummer Night's Dream* in seven months, but also directing the Britten cottage composing industry that had to go into production full tilt, with an amanuensis (Imogen Holst at that period) and copyists at hand day and night. It must have been very similar to Handel's establishment in Brook Street when he was going hell for leather with an oratorio or an opera.

And besides the actual setting down of notes, what about the controlling brain that could think up and dare to carry out such feats as *Billy Budd* ('an all male opera, he must be mad' we all said when he announced the project), 'a requiem combining the church liturgy and poems of Wilfred Owen involving a Russian, a German and an English soloist, children's choir, full choir and two separate orchestras, you must be off your nut' – yet he did it, and made it work). The sheer imagination, seeing the possibilities of poems and stories and instruments and voices, not destroying poems but going to the heart of them, adding new dimensions to them, making us appreciate the originals even more, whereas so often poems are destroyed by being set to music.

Oh, all right, Ben *was* a monster in some ways as well as being a devilishly enchanting man. But he had a right to be one, didn't he?

Ben's friendship with Michael Tippett was an on/off affair (on both sides).

Fortunately their talents were patently diverse, a fact recognized by both of them. Ben couldn't stand clumsy technique (for that reason Ben didn't like Janacek). He once said to me that he thought Michael would have succeeded even if he had not chosen to compose; and said he sometimes wished Michael hadn't (chosen music).

I was more wary of Peter than Ben. Peter could be just as bitchy and egged Ben on. Both of them could drop a singer if a couple of performances had been below par. Even a singer who had been in such favour as Jennifer Vyvyan for whose voice and personality Ben had written the Governess in *Turn of the Screw* and Titania in the *Dream*. And what happened? She sang below her best in a couple of things and the 'boys' cut her in the street, several times. She was dreadfully hurt. And this happened many times. Such people

155

became 'corpses'. Ben recognized this and even told Ronald Duncan once, 'You'll be one of my corpses one day, Ronnie.' And he was.

Even after Ben died Peter could 'corpse' someone. One of the managers of the festival was sacked by Peter Pears for, amongst other things no doubt, programming a Brahms Symphony (No. 2 I think). 'You know Ben hated Brahms!'

Ben never looked you in the eye, always an inch or two lower. His digestion worked best with nursery food; it wasn't happy with alcohol but he drank quite a lot, needed it desperately when conducting. There was always a brandy bottle in the pit not far from his conductor's score. When playing the piano, drinking would have gone to his fingers so his nerves suffered more. Was it fear of failure that made him so apprehensive or, more likely, fear of not doing justice to the composers? These composers that he loved the most, Dowland, Purcell, Mozart were like living beings to him and it was dangerous to criticize any of them or even make jokes about them. Ben would *loathe* you, his favourite verb of unendearment.

BB HELPERS

Devoted workers, behind and sometimes in front of the scene at Aldeburgh, where Britten would never have met his deadlines without helpers to rule the barlines, often write out in full score what BB had just completed in pencil, making vocal scores for soloists to learn their parts from, choral scores, band parts, proof-reading and so on. It was a real cottage industry up there at Crag House on the front and then later at the Red House.

Arthur Oldham was one of the first, helping with *Peter Grimes*. He was given both lessons and house-room. Ben never taught from his own scores, only other composers', an example of his modesty. Arthur wanted to be a composer and was encouraged, even to the extent of having his works at Aldeburgh not only performed but staged. One day, however, things changed abruptly and he was told that he was persona non grata; he had flown too near the sun, told his works aped Ben's. Of course he aped Ben, could scarcely help being influenced by such a strong and overwhelming musical personality. But the shock of the reversal of help and affection had the effect of bringing on a nervous breakdown. I saw him sometime later at the BBC in one of those horrible beige overall coats; Arthur was sweeping the studios, collecting the fag ends. On his uppers. Composing any more was out of the question. But Arthur had guts; he became a choir-trainer, one of the very best we ever had. Under his direction the Edinburgh Festival Chorus did wonderful work, earning the thanks of world-famous conductors, the critics and the public alike. I wonder if Britten ever conducted a choir Arthur had trained and, if so what happened when they met. I must ask Arthur one day. After Edinburgh Arthur was very successful at the Paris Opéra.

Imogen Holst was chief helper No. 2; I believe she has chronicled her work in her books. Imo was fairly potty about Ben. She could gush a bit, could Imo, and I think it eventually drove *him* potty. He couldn't even attend to the fireplace without Imo rushing forward to put another piece of coal on. Her finest hour was *A Midsummer Night's Dream* when she r-r-r-ushed through to give Osian Ellis the next pages of the harp part, condensed from two parts into one when the engaged second harp couldn't cope and fled.

Then came the adorable and retiring Viola Tunnard, marvellous pianist and musician as well as amanuensis. When needed she played 4 hands with Martin Penny in works like the Rossini *Petite Messe Solonelle* and with Ben in the Percy Grainger disc. Viola was also a notable accompanist, used very frequently at one time for recitals with Janet Baker. For years, too, she played for Joyce Grenfell, went on ENSA tours round the world. Viola was modest to a fault, would avoid taking a bow (after playing like an angel), many a time I have seen her grovelling under the piano pretending to pick up music while her fellow artist would be receiving the applause and trying desperately to get Viola to share it with her. If you caught a glimpse of her at a concert hall, and she of you, Viola would most likely disappear behind the nearest pillar. It wasn't that she didn't want to see you because if you tracked her down she was genuinely pleased, truly affectionate. She got a fatal muscular paralysis and was looked after devotedly by Jean Cowan in a little house in Aldeburgh between houses in Crag Street, just opposite where Ben lived and wrote, amongst other works, the *Spring Symphony*. She was ill a long time: Peter and Ben went to see her *once*, I am told. Ben hated hospitals and ill persons.

After Viola came Rosamund Strode, one time soprano soloist and headgirl in Imogen Holst's Purcell Singers, small excellent professional choir. Rosamund followed Imo's lead in wearing echt-Dartington clothing, home-spun etc. After Ben's death Ros became a keeper of the archives and a reliable archivist. If you can write a programme note or a lecture about the Aldeburgh Festival without corrections from Rosamund you must have got up very early in the morning.

Colin Matthews was the last of the BB helpers' brigade and he has done sterling work in tidying up, editing and possibly even composing the odd note or two; invaluable industry in giving a helping hand beyond the grave. Whether all the posthumous BB stuff is as valuable to the musical world as it has been to Faber's Music Department is a moot point.

AMISCELLANY:
29.6.90

The 15.40 from Euston is called the Cambrian Coast Express but Dawdler would be more accurate; it suffers dismemberment both at Wolverhampton and Shrewsbury and takes fifty-five minutes to do the thirty miles on to Newtown, where I am picked up and taken to Greygynog where the Festival 1990 is taking place for a week. Greg (for short) is a handsome half-timbered white building with a concert hall seating 200. Elgar, Holst and RVW attended concerts here and Boult, Walford Davies, Britten and Pears have made music. Two spinster sisters, the Misses Davies bought the place, instituted a book press, organised music parties and were among the earliest collectors of French art in the UK: Renoir's *La Parisienne*, Monet, Cézanne, Pissarro; there are two fine Rodin portrait busts still here, one of Victor Hugo, the other of Mahler. Last time the collection was insured it was for £39 million. The house is now administered by the University of Wales and is in use for courses, conferences and other events.

The tenor Anthony Rolfe-Johnson started a festival here in '88 and I am on my way there to speak *Façade* with the Northern Chamber Orchestra under Steuart Bedford. I arrive half-way through a concert with Stephen Roberts singing *Leider eines fahrenden Gesellen* by Mahler (why didn't they have the Rodin on show in the concert, I wonder?) in the boiled down Schönberg arrangement, very suitable in this hall. The first thing I heard, however, was the last bars of a piece I couldn't place at all – which turned out to be Organ Concerto No. 2 by Rheinberger (John Birch), a perfect piece of quiz fodder.

Saturday

As usual, slightly anxious about the amplification of *Façade*. The 'electrics' ruin a lot of performances, no matter how much one alerts the organisers. Best ever in my experience was a marquee at the old Bracknell Festival when the conductor arrived so late that we had no rehearsal or mike balance. Worst (also with the divine Eleanor Bron) was at the Bath Festival when the composer was present and commented, 'Couldn't hear a bloody word.' I asked him about the metronome marks which are on the fast side: 'Depends how I'm feeling,' he said. 'When I'm fed up with Edith's words I take it fast; usually I'm not, so I take it slower.' He also said that Constant Lambert was the best reciter, like a talking percussion instrument. On the other hand I can remember that CL used to take off John Ireland and E. J. Dent at some points and nearly always (what a comfort!) lost himself several times, substituting 'something something something' for the authorized version. Is it generally known that CL composed the majority of 'Four in the Morning'? The average age of the band at Greygynog seems to be about seventeen but they are more than up to it – Steuart takes immense trouble. In 'Popular Song' I can't help noticing that a lady in the front six feet away from me is fainting. I can see only the whites of her eyes. Her friend put her arm round her. I wonder whether to indicate to them that there are just a couple of numbers to go but decide that if I put two fingers up it might be misconstrued. She manages to survive and comes round afterwards to chat about it.

Taking to the road – railroad in my case as I don't drive – for things like *Façade* (by a fluke I have three in this one week) I find it fascinating to share the life of travelling musicians because I think we all find on the way interesting objects like the Rodin/Mahler or

People/friends. After one of the Waltons I talk to a cellist I haven't met for years, especially about her last husband but one who was a famous instrumentalist who committed suicide not long ago; apparently the poor fellow bought a dog leash and made more than one shot at it before it worked. This puts me in mind of Robert Tear's autobiography that I was reading en route. In between the musical bits Bob asks why we all make such a palaver about the one thing in our lives which is certain, which is leaving it. Why don't we look it in the face, call it by its real name, then we wouldn't be so frightened of it? And do we want to stay living so long that we become a nuisance to ourselves and others? Would it be better to emulate those Central African tribes who, when the old become ill or senile, give 'em a good meal and roll them into the mud?

Another fascinating thing you see when you travel is unusual plumbing. At Greg there is a wonderful old 'bog' kept for inspection only, with lovely porcelain, a long wooden bench and a splendid plunger to pull – there are one or two like it in the ENO's Coliseum, if you know where to look (that's enough about chamber music – ED).

TIPPETT'S NEW YEAR:
1.7.90

UK première of Tippett's New Year at Glyndebourne. Stunning production by Peter Hall. LPO/Andrew Davis on top of it all, and performances deep in the bones by those who were in the Houston première. But then Philip Langridge wasn't in that première and he is stunning too. Agreeable score, quite touching Things to Come Mills and Boon story, familiar late Tippett gung-ho noises and many new ones too. Amazing how Tippett's ear changed. It was none too reliable or inventive in the '40s, the music strong on form and line almost at the expense of texture. And then suddenly, as he once put it, 'the dam burst', everything proliferated in The Midsummer Marriage. Then 'all change again': the old forms give way to blocks, mosaics, juxtapositions, all managed, tuned and tweeted by new colours and combos: the Concerto for Orchestra is, for me, the finest example – whoever heard of a duet for harp and tuba? or piano and xylophone in skittering tandem?

160

The end of the new opera is a cop-out, verbally OK with a Mandela-type message, but musically it's as if Michael were waving his hands saying I'm eighty-five and I can't write any more just now so get on with it. I wondered how many times I will want to hear the music of this opera on the Virgin recording because the textures and trouvailles scarcely sustain the evening. (Subsequently I heard the concert suite première on Radio 3 from Cheltenham – BBCSO/Davis A. – and found that even that palls after five minutes or so.) However we have all been wrong about Tippett in the past, mostly under-praising. One thing should be mentioned though: the apt and brilliant use of electronic music for the comings and goings of the space ship; I always hoped someone would provide a sequel to the only other good use of electronics, that is, Stockhausen's *Gesang der Jünglinge*; it's taken a long time.

MT was at Glyndebourne, not alas in his custard-coloured shoes, but in fine health and naughty fettle. He told me there's a fifth quartet in the offing. And after that? A fifth piano sonata? even perhaps a fifth da-da-daDUM? He says he's preparing for his ninetieth birthday, so watch out!

Reading the Wimbledon reports in the quality newspapers in which the players praised or criticized their own performances I wondered how long it would be before Zubin Tilson Rattle would say:

'As soon as Radu Benedetti Richter served with his opening G major chords I knew I had to gain control when I brought the orchestra in. So I upped the tempo without losing the initiative or the sympathy of the crowd. He tried to put pressure on me but I dug in deep and held my own. At the end of the cadenza he tried to throw me with a passing shot on the trills but I fought him all the way. In the slow movement he nearly outplayed me with his original pedallings but I managed to wrongfoot him by lobbing the unisons at him early before he had finished his follow through. In the finale I faltered momentarily when he caught me with his first upward runs but the second time I was able to smash his chromatics before he got to the top. I feel I owe my performance yesterday to my change of coach last year, having plenty of rehearsal time and, above all, to my re-marriage in the spring which gave me peace of mind and time to focus my concentration and strategy. If Richter wants a replay next year I feel I shall be more than ready for him.'

LUNCH WITH MICHAEL TIPPETT: 18.9.97

During the '40s we were very close (see his letters from Wormwood Scrubs when he was jugged as a C.O. in 1944) and I became a sort of unpaid secretary because he was living at Limpsfield Chart and needed a runner in town. 'Unpaid' yes, but rewarded with meals, holidays, weekends and I was his companion at rehearsals of new works, premieres and so forth. I am seventeen years younger and although sometimes we slept in the same bed we were, as the gossip column put it, 'just good friends'. He taught me such a lot about music, and life in general. When I first met him he was quite unknown so that I saw the burgeoning of his career and took tremendous personal pride in the gradual recognition of his music. It is such a pity that the word 'gay' has become debased, for gaiety was the quality that describes him. He was in his late thirties when I met first him and in no way discouraged about his career, he had absolute confidence that things would come out right.

At ninety-two Michael, now a knight and O.M., is living, not with his long-term 'partner', but in a house, part of a group of newish but pleasant dwellings on the banks of a backwater of the Thames in Old Isleworth, not far from the Old Church. Bill Bowen, the partner in question, had warned me that M had had a stroke during the last year and I should be prepared for deterioration. The shock is indeed distressingly great. The old Michael has gone, leaving a wraith with sunken face and fairly useless limbs. A couple looks after him; she, a Thai-lady who cooks, he, who reminds me of the 'Bruder' who shifted Delius around when he was blind and paralysed. As with Delius, Michael, as he actually mumbled (teeth trouble) still has his marbles – 'I can still tick people off' (glint in the eye as of old). He messes his pap food but at lunch I find that there is one angle of profile where the Michael of old lurks but it is sad to find this bright-eyed Celt reduced to being a complete invalid.

I didn't check his current account of memory but certainly his deposit account was sure. We talked mainly of friends and events of fifty years ago and he recalled more details of certain happenings than I did. Naughtily I tell him a story of the pitch deafness of a certain knighted British composer which provokes his comment, 'Well, I've always thought X was a bit of a phoney.' M.T's eyes have been bad for years so he can't read but likes being read to, TV is an almost total wash-out. He is hoping to go to Sweden for an enormous Tippett retrospective in November. As I talk to him I remember hearing about a certain African tribe that gives old people a good meal and then sinks them in bubbling consuming mud. Wouldn't it be a quick way of sparing this wonderful old genius any further indignity...and his heirs any further expense? Poor Michael asks me to come back but I'm not sure I have the heart to. There is no pathos apparent, no asking for pity, as indeed I guessed there would not be. Bliss was it (no pun intended) to be around when Tippett and Britten were producing one masterpiece after another. And to have known them.

When Meirion Bowen telephoned to say that Michael Tippett had died, I wept. And was surprised to do so, but then we had been close yonks ago, in the '40s and early '50s. I was captivated by this extraordinary man, so ebullient, so confident in his own powers although he had, at thirty-five in 1940 when we first met, had little or no success. I joined his choir at Morley College and became a sort of dogsbody runaround help. He taught me much about life and music. He paid for meals and holidays: we went once to Mevagissey with Tony Hopkins and his future wife Alison, once to the Scilly Isles with Priaulx Rainier, South African composeress that we were both fond of, and once somewhere else in Cornwall but I've forgotten where, it must have been near Mevagissey because we several times met John Layard the psycho-analyst who wrote a fascinating book about 'The Stone Men of Malecula'. Through Michael I met that fascinating old queer don, A. L. Rowse and also Walter Goehr and, not least, Benjamin Britten and Peter Pears.

Michael's letters from prison are full of references to me and how close we were. While he was in jug I went to visit him, once with Peter and Ben who gave a recital on a Sunday afternoon to the prisoners (pin-drop silence, almost uncanny). I had got in as turneroverer for Ben but we managed to bamboozle the Chaplain into thinking that the turning over was so complicated that we needed an extra pair of hands. On asking where he could find anybody in the audience of screws who could read music I suggest that 154302 Tippett, M. could do the job. We got an extra chair and the two of us turned alternate pages. Ben's dismay at Michael's imprisonment was touching. He had got out of difficulties himself at a tribunal and therefore felt much worse about Michael's incarceration than Michael himself.

Michael was wonderfully the same with everybody, from duchess to dustman. He was fresh, lively, stimulating and free from evil. The only time I knew him to be nasty was towards Alan Rawsthorne at the Summer School. They had been at the Royal College together. In his old age Michael could be teasing almost towards bitchiness. I was turned out of favour when John Minchinson became unpaid secretary. He must have been better than me because he got the dedication of the Second Symphony (mind, he shared Michael's bed more actively than I did). It was twenty years later that I saw a bit of Michael when he was joint Festival Composer (with Elgar) at Malvern. We did two chat shows in public and I had meals and concerts together with him. On the fourth day I said to Michael that I had to return to London and that it was nice to see him. 'Well, goodbye Johnnie, and it's nice to see you too...occasionally.'

AMISCELLANY
17.10.91

Having had an itch on my left bollock for the last few weeks I go to my clever, attractive Portugese-Goan doctor, Marisa Viegas, to see if I have cancer. No. What I have is an itch in my left bollock. Not contagious. And I have leave to fondle my balls with some ointment until the rash and itch have disappeared and then continue for ten days *after that*.

June Mendoza arrives to spend several hours painting in to my portrait some scores in the left hand side which she thinks looks otherwise a bit bare; got to be done this weekend as she wants to enter the pic in an exhibition at Coutts. Go to Covent Garden to see acts two and three of *Götterdämmerung* from a box over the orchestra, which plays magnificently under Haitink. Horns play continuously in act two it seems, and very well too. How few strings there are, looks like 88553, can it be or did I miss some? Sounds good, though. But Götz Friedrich's production is feeble beyond description. Suffice it to say that for the Rhinemaidens they threw a dark cloth over the floor, switched on the mottle light stop and the three ladies mimed swimming half-and-who-shall-blame-them-heartedly? Either do it properly (Peter Hall's production at Bayreuth), symbolically, or don't do it at all; this was laziness, contempt for the public. Hunding/ John Tomlinson fine, Gwynneth Jones held her top notes but the rest was scooping and swooping; Reiner Goldberg substituted for Réné Kollo (who sounded clapped out in concert performance act II *Walküre* the previous week with Tennstedt) as Siegfried. Not bad but really when the punters are paying a hundred quid for a stall should they not put on another opera rather than have this woefully inadequate singing? If first horn, oboe or cello swooped and scooped about like this, they'd be sacked, not even engaged in the first place but Wagnerian singers seem licensed. Needless to say the audience cheered the singers as well as Haitink and the orchestra.

18.10.91

To Birmingham for the National Indoor Arena's first artistic manifestation, *Aida*. David, Lord Willoughby de Broke, calls off at the last moment so I go by train and stay with Harlan and Delia Walker. I come prepared to scoff at my first British arena opera, all the critics have panned previous efforts at Wembley and Earls Court. But I quite enjoy it; it's a 12,000-seater and the walkaround ring with foodstalls and no seats is depressing but the arena has red seats. The enormous set, pyramid steps and large blocks, occupies one end. Mario Rossi's production really is spectacular, colour spectrum ranges from sun yellow to sunset russet, gold and silver lamé abounds with four or five hundred Brummagem soldiers marching around, grouping and regrouping, a cage of Abyssinian prisoners appearing almost magically at one point. The only contrasting colour is the slate blue dress of Aida herself, Grace Bumbry, she semaphores which is about all she can do (and ever does) and she belts out the top notes except two of the high Cs which get to a B, squeal and die out; below that she often wobbles; Amneris also sings flat but it can't be easy in such a vast space; the Radames, Carlo Cossuta improves in voice as his army career deteriorates; Ingmar Wixell, Amonasro, is a sorry shadow of his former self. I see Paul Griffiths of *The Times* (beginning to behave like a middle-aged eccentric, slinking about furtively), Hugh Canning of *Sunday* ditto, Geoffrey Norris of *Daily Telegraph* and Max Loppert of the *Nancy Times* – I suspect they will all pan it, the critics dislike any popular art efforts, just as they are always down on anyone whose fame or publicity gets too hypeish (Galway, Callas, Fischer-Dieskau, for example, or the Lloyd Webbers; curiously enough Rattle hasn't had any stick yet; he will, Oscar, he will).

Supper. Harlan has sweetly kept a '75 Lynch Bages and some foie gras for such an occasion. Poor Delia is in pain from a very nasty broken leg and the *Catch 22* situation doesn't help: painkillers impede recovery.

19.10.91

With Harlan to Barber Institute, well kept, welcoming gallery, one, at most two, of a painter, some good pictures by painters unheard of (by me) and some marvellous pics by painters one has heard of, like a stunning Rubens *Landscape*. They also have 243 drawings mostly of musicians active in the '30s and '40s by Edmond X. Kapp but, none being on show, I happened to bump into Richard Verdi, the director, who directed not an underling but a middle-ling to show me some; they are very good some of them, particularly the earlier ones (except that there's a good one of Fistoulari). I wrote later today to thank Mr V., pushing myself forward as a useful person to write the catalogue if the Barber does, as he said, put on an X. Kapp Ex. Next year.

QEH for concert performance of Bliss opera *The Olympians*; some good bits but it won't wash, not enough characterization in the music, libretto by Priestley feeble, things go on. Madeleine's aria act two still the best piece, ravishing; but it was only competently sung, not ravishing the senses. The best singing came from Jupiter who looked like an orang-utan. An Egyptian ex BBC engineer/knob twiddler called Peter Sidhom, now doing things I discover for WNO, ENO and an audition for Covent Garden. Adrian de Peyer/Bacchus nice comprimario stuff – which reminded me that I do not intend to read his lecture on the *Passagio* because, as I wrote to him, after those years of singing and trying without success to understand Lucie Manen or the Husler-Rodd books on singing, I now have a complete block to reading a word about the subject. Life is too short…Lady Bliss gave me a kiss, still very pleased with the programme I did about Arthur (Bliss) and his music on Radio 3 in August.

WARLOCK IN RUTLAND: 21.10.91

Round the corner to catch coach at 8.30 with members of the Warlock Society, myself a new member; we are off to Langham, one of six places in England of like name; this one used to be in the smallest county, Rutland, but is now in Leicestershire. We get off smartly after one telephone call to a member who turns up, naturally, while Dr de Mowbray is trying to contact him. Off to the House of Usher, the soubriquet of the house in Muswell Hill, where my 'father', the doyen of the critical brigade, resides in that house so packed with books and music that it very nearly did fall, a new loft groaned its disapproval. 'My father' is Felix Aprahamian; we have this routine which consists, in company, of which of us can get in first introducing the other, 'This is my father,' to which the riposte is 'An ungrateful bastard.' We trundle up the main road to Ruddles of Rutland. Ruddles act as sponsors to some publications of the Warlock Society and host this annual outing to their brewery. On arrival we descend to vaults turned taphouse (private) where the taps are turned on for Ruddles County (wow, that's strong stuff, good too, almost enough to convert this lager-lout!). There follows a tour of the brewery; how pleasant to find vats that don't need invoices; of course as usual the fascinating part is seeing all the bottles being filled and capped (*Modern Times* all over again); no, that's not quite true, the best things was smelling and handling the raw hops and finding the scent of the contents of three of those more-than-mansize sacks had a different fragrance. Then more of the product so that I can't quite remember at which point we saw a small film plugging the product and then we had lunch which was local stilton, salad, jugs of beer (Ruddles almost rhymes with fuddled) and Melton Mowbray pie. I take a picture of Dr de Mowbray eating an eponymous pie. Tony Ruddles signs our copies of the Warlock song-books that his firm has sponsored and then we attempt to sing some of 'our' product, rather belch canto in our somewhat ruddled state. Especially ruddled in my case, sightreading the solo tenor part in *The Lady's Birthday*; we fling ourselves into *One More River* and act out *Fill the Cup, Phillip*; all these flagged vigorously by our chairman with electronic keyboard accompaniment by our secretary and our treasurer. (It pays to take office!)

The conversation has been good, committee men and others spilling out Warlockiana, only three or four ladies present but I suppose that is a suitable percentage, not that I am suggesting that Warlock was homophonic.

The thought strikes me that it might be a good wheeze (maybe it's been tried) to write to the powerful parliamentarian Heseltine to ask him to be an honorary member of the Society; it might tickle him, even unlock his purse. After lunch a few of us look at the local church which has some curious architectural features: what I believe are known as 'ballflowers' except that these, unusually, are more human than flowery, more like little circular gargoyles, whole patterns of them dotted about on the outside walls.

HS. Philip Heseltine, born in the Savoy Hotel 1894, went to Eton, took pseudonym Peter Warlock, friend of Delius, wrote wonderful songs, little else, respected musicologist (editions of Purcell, etc.) developed a hearty drink swilling personality and died in Chelsea in 1930 in a gas-filled bedroom.

BOULT AND BARBIROLLI:
6.6.94

I never quite trusted Adrian Boult. Yet there is nothing in the records that goes against him much. The man who was supposed never to lose his temper, did, from time to time. I asked him once if he ever did and his answer was: 'Yes, I do lose my temper sometimes, usually with people like railway porters.' That tells you something about him, doesn't it, as well as dating the offences? He once lost his temper with director Brian Large in a TV studio but it was over a misunderstanding: he thought the rehearsal was to finish at 4 p.m. and that therefore he would be able to catch the 4.40 from Victoria; but Brian had contracted him until 5 p.m. and as a consequence almost caught a right swing to the jaw from Sir Adrian. The conductor failed to land the punch but swept out of the studio followed by Lady Boult saying apologetically, 'I think something has upset him.' Was that typical of a conductor who was more British than the British, apparently unemotional; and yet what came out in Elgar, in *La Mer*, in *Sacre du Printemps*, in *Don Quixote* was not devoid of emotion? But he was content to let it come out of the music without him apparently seeking to touch the emotions. It was further proof of his fidelity to the score. Occasionally he conducted Wagner and it was wonderful. He had more know-how about music and conducting it than anyone: when to take composers' markings at their face value, when not. He set things up as best he could and let them happen. I can see him now conducting *Daphnis and Chloe* making that typical Boult gesture at climaxes of drawing the curtains from right to left. His gestures always meant something. I remember a class at which he condemned the Venetian vase method of conducting when the two hands complemented each other in perfect but meaningless symmetry. I heard so many model performances from him, especially composers and works mentioned. He was the perfect man to do the BBC job with so many scores of different types. He didn't do justice to all of them. The ones that came off worst were the ones that needed style, style of the eighteenth century. Mind you there were times when he seemed dispirited but then after the shabby treatment the BBC gave him, who can blame him? But then in old, old age he came into his own again. Maybe my first sentence was inappropriate, if so forget it.

Barbirolli, now there was a man maltreated. By the critics in America, one in particular. But then who could follow Toscanini? Why take on the job, except it meant big money and the unique chance to prepare works adequately with a great orchestra. He did some good work in New York but not enough to survive the slings and arrows. And he spent the rest of his life recovering, trying to justify himself, often rather conceitedly. Yet his achievement, building a new Hallé from scratch, was vast and a study in human as well as musical achievement. He did some wonderful things at Covent Garden where all his earlier operatic slogging and skilled accompanying sessions for recordings stood him in good stead. His Puccini was perfect. And his work in old age had the Berlin Philharmonic in wonder at his Mahler.

I occasionally saw him socially, notably as a guest in Lady Fermoy's house in King's Lynn. There was no conceit then, as he prepared Italian dishes for us all, happy to be the Italian chef he could have been. After supper he would get out his cello and make music with Lionel Tertis on his viola, Laurence Turner his Hallé leader and our beautiful hostess Ruth at the piano.

Evelyn Rothwell seemed the most unlikely wife for John, tall, gawky, something like Margaret Rutherford and Joyce Grenfell yet serious, friendly, actually the perfect wife for JB. And a wonderful oboeist too.

RAFAEL KUBELIK:
11.8.96

The violist Bernard Shore once wrote that Rafael Kubelik was every orchestra's favourite conductor. He was tall, handsome (v.Czech), athletic and radiated warmth, as did his conducting. The lilt is paramount in the best of Dvorak, Smetana and Janacek – and Kubelik could unleash that joyous lilt. He could also unleash strong emotional currents, tenderness and strength, yes, and enormous power and volume.

At Sadlers Wells after he had conducted a performance of *Kat'a Kabanova* that was a mighty mountain of emotion and power I met a girl in the orchestra, the resident pit band not noted particularly for its excellence. 'I don't know what happened to us,' said this cellist, 'a miracle, because we can't play as well as that.'

I went whenever he conducted: Dvorak 7, Brahms 2, the best I ever heard, the joy of living rampant in his beat. Mozart not so good. Then came his time at Covent Garden. He announced his intention of going to every performance, a promise soon broken. The performances he conducted were good – Mussorgsky, Puccini, Verdi, Poulenc *Carmelites*, *The Trojans*, but only in Czech repertory did he rise triumphantly above the good; so what's wrong with just good? He left to go to Chicago where a woman shot him down, a vicious critic called Claudia Cassidy. He came back to London usually in the summer at Wimbledon time. Accident? No, as I found when I interviewed him at the Westbury. He adored tennis.

He conducted Martinu so well as to convince you of its greatness. But did he agree with me that when Martinu was not inspired he was boring, it was as if the current were switched off? Example? The *Della Francesca Frescoes*? Kubelik agreed, adding that it was an embarrassment for him as the *Frescoes* were often asked for, as they were dedicated to him.

Rafael had met the Australian, Elsie Morison and she was often his soprano in London and elsewhere. She was pretty despite a cast in one eye and as delightful to meet as to hear, although she did her voice no good by trying to make it louder to accommodate larger houses. The most ravishing thing she did was Nanetta in *Falstaff* at the Wells. I was with Donald Swann and when Elsie sang her long top A in her Queen of the Fairies song in Act III he let out a moan of ecstasy that had us nearly thrown out.

After a time Kubelik conducted less and less as he succumbed more and more to some kind of arthritis. They tried wintering in dry California but it was no good. He gave up conducting, housebound in a chestnut haven near Lucerne. Being on the council of the Royal Philharmonic Society I persuaded it to give Kubelik the Gold Medal.

Ronald Smith, the chairman at that time (teacher, not the pianist) came with me to Switzerland to give Raphael the medal in person. Elsie invited us to lunch but warned us of the drastic change in Rafael's appearance. Indeed it was heart-rending to see the once athletic radiant specimen of manhood become now a bony angular cripple in a wheel-chair reminding us of photographs of the old Delius. Rafael was not blind of course and his eyes lit up briefly with the old radiance as we talked of his past achievements. What added to his pleasure in receiving the Gold Medal was the fact that his violinist father, Jan, had received the medal some seventy years previously, the only time a family had received two Philharmonic medals. He excited himself too much in our conversation and had to be hauled upstairs to his bed instead of joining us at lunch. Rafael died just a few weeks after our visit. We were just in time to honour this great musician.

TRIMBLES:
18.6.95

Oh, the pretty Miss Trimbles were a delight playing their two pianos at the National Gallery! Not quite twins but near enough in their red velvet dresses. They had discovered the great secret of piano duet playing: in order to get the balance right, don't play louder but softer. They played all the usual repertoire but enhanced it by playing some of Joan's compositions, always with plenty of fourths (did Bax actually invent them?) and flattened sevenths and that intoxicating lilt that sorted them out from the bangers. Valerie was the other one, even prettier, and she could play a nifty cello I heard but never did hear.

I had a task at that time to research, soon after the war, for a dictionary of musicians (never published) and that gave me the excuse to go and interview Joan (I was infatuated). I was taken in and soon almost became a member of the family with her roguish English husband, Jack, who became one of my dearest friends; he was a doctor of the rare, truly caring type and he cared for his friends too. How did Joan do it all, coping with the phone (busy practice), Jack who was demanding as well as caring, Nicholas the son, Joanna and Caroline daughters?

After thirty or so years Jack developed a muscular paralysis and has got steadily worse. Valerie, incredible though it sounds, got something similar and died quite soon. Now, father W. Egbert Trimble was a rare man, managing director and editor of a local N. Ireland newspaper at Enniskillen, practically on the border, and improbably called *The Impartial Reporter*. It was a family newspaper in the sense that the Trimbles had started it and ran it, with only four editors in a hundred years. Bertie was a 'character', a big man with a booming speaking voice and an eloquent bass-baritone which he would unleash at the drop of a hat. He also earned my envy in that he felt girls' tits like other people shook hands.

One day when he was in his eighties (the family besought him without success to give up driving) he rushed out of his office, late for an appointment, got in his car, forgot it was in gear, so he bashed into the bumper of the car in front, cussed and decided to go ahead. In going ahead he scraped viciously up the right hand side of that same car. At this point his conscience caused him to park in front of the damaged car in order to apologise to the owner, the bank manager next door to his own office. Unfortunately Bertie misjudged the distance and bashed heartily into the bonnet. At which point the bank manager came out, surveyed the wreck of his own car and said, 'Come on now, Bertie, there's one more side to my car that you have yet to hit.' Bertie went home, told them of his little incident and announced his intention of giving up driving.

The Trimbles broadcast during the war every week for a long time on the popular *Tuesday Serenade* but alas! they never made any commercial recordings. But Joan's compositions are being played more and more. At eighty she is a 'celeb' in the Province.

HS: Alas! Jack and Joan are now both up the hill and into the clouds. In her old age Northern Ireland re-discovered its daughter, recorded her works, broadcast them and even commissioned her to write a piece for brass band.

AMADEUS:
2.10.96

What was the collective name of Norbert Brainin, Siegmund Nissel, Peter Schidlof and Martin Lovett? One competitor in Round Britain Quiz buzzed, 'Were they the Tolpuddle Martyrs?' The Amadeus String Quartet thought this was very funny, once it was explained to them who the Martyrs were.

All four of them were around during the latter years of the war. At that time Norbert often played the viola, marvellously; and Peter Schidlof was a violinist called Hans. Sigi was around too, he often played in small orchestras; Martin was younger and I think he occasionally played at Morley College. Morley had been bombed early in the war and what was left consisted of a library, some class rooms, changing rooms and the rather lovely little Holst Room, seating about 150 for the house concerts with Planets (get it?) on the ceiling. That great lady Eva Hubback was the principal and Michael

Tippett director of music. There were classes on various musical subjects. I was in the choir which MT conducted. All the girls were madly in love with him, especially the choir secretary Rose Mori, a dumpy lady with a round face. Among the men were some professional 'stiffeners' like Donald Lea, St. Paul's bass and there was a useful tenor Stanley Etherington. Tony Hopkins was there (later of *Talking about Music* fame, richly deserved) at this time pianist/composer, and at various times P. Racine Fricker, composer, Michael Tillett, schoolmaster, and Anthony Milner, also a composer. Walter Bergmann played the piano for the choir as well as taking recorder classes at other times. Tony's girl friend Alison Purves led the sopranos and sang solos, unforgettably in 'Dear white children, casual as birds' when we did Britten's *Hymn to St. Cecilia.*

There were quite a few house concerts, a haven for people starved at that time of contemporary or baroque and renaissance music. Needed for the baroque music were small ensembles to play a Brandenburg or some Purcell or Gibbons string fantasias, Purcell cantatas or trio sonatas. Sometimes the stunning Maria Lidka would lead, sometimes Norbert. Schidlof, Sigi and occasionally, I think, Martin took part. Coached and conducted by Michael Tippett I am sure this formed an important part in the training of the future Amadeus Quartet.

Norbert was a rough genius, long-haired, stumbling over his English but worth his weight in gold. He was absent-minded and once when he should have been rehearsing a concert in Watford he was found practising in Wigmore Studios. Once at a Purcell rehearsal Michael conferred, as he often did, with Bergmann. They agreed: 'no ritardando' and he turned variously to the soloists, each section of the choir and then to the little orchestra. MT lifted his hands to start the section again. Norbert stuttered into speech: 'M-m-m-Michael, m-m-maybe here there should b-b-be no r-r-ritardando.' One day in a church at Swiss Cottage I heard him give a monumental performance of the Bach *Chaconne*. NW3 was the stamping ground of the not yet formed Quartet. At the houses of rich Jewish enthusiasts there were musical parties, trios (Norbert magnificent in the Mozart Trio for clarinet, viola and piano), quartets, quin-sex-sept-octets. There was Emanuel Hurwitz; Cecil Aronowitz (S. African player who later led the violas for years in the English Chamber Orchestra, was the usual fifth in Amadeus Mozart quintets, he loved music and young girls, rarely practised but if he did, had the TV vision on), and clarinettist Gervase de Peyer.

One of the best houses for these parties was the Loesers. One of the daughters was pretty, slightly vulpine-looking Brigitte, never a star performer on her cello but much in demand. Her mother, we used to joke, must have even gone to bed in her Persian lamb coat. The father was big-faced, a specialist in women's diseases below the belt. Knowing that Gerard Hoffnung was squeamish about such things he would relish describing the removal of a womb while he was carving the Sunday roast, demonstrating by sudden lunges with the carving knife. Gerard would go positively green, only recovering when the well-filled plate was put in front of him.

You arrived at the Loesers – this was wartime, don't forget – and there would be drinks and smoked salmon. Then the meal. After another three-quarters of an hour coffee would come round with all sorts of gateaux, tarts, cakes, everything served with whipped cream. I once commented on this to the gynaecologist: 'Here,' he boomed in heavy Swiss Cottage English, 'here we eat ev-e-ry hour.' (Two syllables like the German 'auer'.) Women were his hobby as well as his job. At a party in Highpoint, in Highgate, he went up to an American girl, pretty Mary Lee Settle, novelist and playwright, and introduced himself, adding, 'You have trouble with your periods, I could fix it for you – no charge.' And he did, like he said – no charge.

The pleasures to be had from listening to chamber music in a chamber rather than a large concert hall cannot be over -estimated. It was from such evenings that the Amadeus was born, private get-togethers, little concerts, working sometimes with Tippett, sometimes with Walter Goehr. The four of them even led the string sections one afternoon in an orchestra I put together for Anatole Fistoulari, the hardly celebrated London International Orchestra. For his opening concert we had a good band (because no other was working that day) what with Dennis Brain and Norman Del Mar on horns, Arthur Gleghorn flute, Archie Camden bassoon, Gervase de Peyer clarinet, James Merrett bass *and* the Amadeus. Brahms 4 was really good. Poor old Fisty, he was looked down on because he was a joke, a Russian émigré entrepreneurial fly-by-night who often didn't pay up, and everybody knew which gramophone records he had borrowed his interpretations from, but he was a highly efficient signaller, a wonderful accompanist, hot stuff on the Russians, and a wizard ballet conductor. He was married to Mahler's daughter, Anna. How had he worked that? He blinked all the time, was a goodnatured creep and was known never to have read anything more cultured than the *Daily Mirror*.

He spoke no language well, including what was supposed to be his native Russian, as I found when I introduced some Russians to him. Long after his first marriage had ended, he married the beautiful Scottish violinist, Elizabeth Lockhart. So he must have had something, shifty Fisty.

It must have been difficult to contain Norbert's genius within the quartet. His character and his ego made him difficult because some things he knew but could not explain. There were fearful rows (I have been present at their rehearsals) and they went for each other hammer and tongs, heavy swearing not excluded. Norbert's genius was instinctive, he could spin a line in a Haydn slow movement to make your heart jump, could fly away in a Haydn finale to make you dance (if Imogen Holst was in the audience, she did).

Sigi's great value to the quartet was his ability to play and listen critically. His playing was sometimes not strong enough: at one time Britten spoke to the boys strongly on this subject.

Peter Schidlof's sound was the most beautiful viola playing I ever heard. He brought a wonderful sonority to the quartet. He looked like an Austrian business man but he was a very attractive human being, a great ballroom dancer incidentally.

Martin Lovett was the only non-Viennese member of the quartet. Rather East Endish in his manner and wit. His father had also played the cello but in orchestras, not chamber music.

It has often been said that being in a string quartet is like being married to three chaps. And perhaps the reason why the Amadeus survived was their consideration for the others. Despite the rehearsal rows they genuinely cared for each other, perhaps they looked after each other better than they did their wives. We shall never know. On tour with them in Bavaria their consideration for each other was noticeable: 'Oh, do you mind letting whichever-it-was sit with his back to the engine; he prefers it that way... . If there's only one portion of Kalbshaxe, could we keep it for whoever?'

The wives survived. Katinka Brainin perhaps the best (at surviving, I mean) – her dressmaking kept her going through the long periods when the boys toured and the girls stayed at home (same trouble as with sailors' wives). Muriel Nissel, the last to become an Amadeus bride, is a sturdy individualist, so determined to maintain her feminine identity that her book on the Amadeus contains almost as many pages about her as the quartet. Nevertheless she obviously had what Sigi needed. Peter Schidlof's wife Margit had perhaps a harder job than the others: being a Swede living outside her own country. A non-musician and remaining, it sometimes seemed, a little apart from the other wives and players. She produced a stunning-looking daughter, Annemarie.

Martin's wife, Suzanne Rosza, had to balance her own career as violinist with being a quartet wife. Suzi is a Hungarian, keenly self-promotional and sometimes awkwardly competitive. She has survived difficult times including Martin's nervous breakdown which threatened the very existence of the Amadeus. It had been agreed that no substitutes were possible. If one of the quartet died, that was it. And so it proved when Peter had a heart attack. Schluss! La Commedia é finita.

But it was a glorious comedy – in the wider sense – while it lasted. You cannot beat constant application. Sometimes they betrayed their common background – studying with Max Rostal – which brought sometimes too schmaltzy an approach – and once they had a period when everything got too polished and thin but generally they brought insight and warmth, expertise and experience to the greatest and most consistent repertoire in the history of music – the string quartet.

HS: Alas! By the time this is published Norbert Brainin has died and so have the wives of Peter Schidloff and Martin Lovett.

CRUISING:
1–13.9.97

At the end of a short holiday in the French Pyrenees prior to joining the *Mermoz* cruise today. Walked in the Cerdagne (does anybody remember an old French film about the kingdom of Cerdagne? – there was a spoof national anthem in it as I recall) staying at Hotel Atalaya at Llo, a name which sounds Welsh but is, I suppose, Catalan. We motored on to stay at les Ornaisons in a valley between Narbonne and Béziers, the object being to find somewhere for a couple of nights enabling us to visit the small town of Pézénas nearby, a charming place with an old quarter, Molière used to have his hair cut there and Clive of India lived there long enough in retirement to install his cook who invented some spicy little pastry number sold to this day in the town as 'Clive pies'. (Cleave peas, they pronounce it.)

Les Ornaisons is built around two blocks of bedrooms spaced around squares of garden. There's a good pool, well cooked food but it's all rather complicated stuff, just a bit 'poncey'. Our host is a burly built chap reminding me slightly of Julian Bream with good English and a rather burly manner too, not aggressive but eyeing you in a manner suggesting don't even think of taking a liberty.

We shall remember him, and Les Ornaisons too, for breaking to us at breakfast the news that Princess Diana was killed in a car crash during the night.

We motor to Marseille, wondering whether the point de départ has changed *again* in which case we are OK because we are in sufficient time to pick up the *Mermoz* at the more usual port of Toulon. All's well, however, lunch on the quayside and then a hello session; ah yes, there's the old girl who looks like Clara Haskil, there's the German mother and daughter (who had a ding with Kissin), the English Chamber Orchestra trickles in, I am honoured to be recognized by Jacqueline Schneider, cruise director, and André Barocz, her husband, the musical director of this cruise, now in its fortieth year. It's a frightfully posh affair, two-star Michelin grub, free booze and the artist list is formidable: Belgian baritone José van Dam, violinists Gidon Kremer and Spivakov, violist Yuri

Bashmet, cellist Janos Starker, pianists Bruno Canino, Christian Zacharias and Turkish Delight pianist Fazil Say, the Keller String Quartet from Budapest and the aforementioned ECO with the genial James Judd flagging them on. Ooh, yes, and the Lord Menuhin, who is to conduct one concert with pride of place, the Scuola di San Rocco in Venice. Before getting to the Edinburgh of the South, or the Athens of the West, we go to Sousse where everybody gets Tunis tummy which rumbles round the ship for days and then to Delphi where there is a concert in the Stadium. Here the programme includes the Mendelssohn Concerto played decently but unmemorably by a nice young Israeli violinist called David Grimal. Lady Menuhin is not with us, she is seriously ill in Gstaad with arthritis where Yehudi has left her to join the cruise a bit late. Next day I begin my interview (I am, nice word, conférencier, talking eight or nine times to the English-speaking sector; there are about forty per cent French speaking passengers so everything has to be double-lingoed) with the noble Lord by asking him if the Mendelssohn brought back memories of playing the work as a child with his teacher Enescu conducting, guessing that the benevolent Yehudi will say a few kind words about Grimal. Not a bit of it; Yehudi is uncharacteristically nasty about Grimal, the performance, the conducting and so on. I wonder whether to pour oil on troubled waters but I stick to my principle, that I am not there to see fair play in my interviews, but to reveal the views and personality of the interviewees. So I let him continue although I can see that he is shocking some of the audience. Goodness (and I do mean goodness), it does flow out of him once he has stopped slating the Mendelssohn (he didn't like the tempi, the phrasing, the interpretation) but he does wiffle, bless his old h.; I try to get him back to music but after a sentence or two he is off again up in the clouds. But it does reveal his personality. And we do (still) love him a lot. His concert is a great success, dare one say it? surprisingly enough, because he does seem to be just standing there and letting it happen. Spivakov plays the Mozart D and the ECO does a lovely Elgar Serenade. Gosh, those Tintorettos are a bit heavy in bulk, though, and I sympathise with the chap who came out of the San Rocco saying that the effect was rather like reading all the Shakespeare plays in one hour.

Next day a trip to Murano and Torcello which I hadn't been to for a quarter of a century. Would like to have lingered and had lunch at the Locanda Cipriani; for a quarter of a century I have remembered the basilica and the gnocchi made with semolina, so delicious and so different from the usually encountered gnocchi made with potatoes. Old age catches up with me but my genteel slash behind a hut is interrupted with 'disgusted-Torcello' who shouts, 'Ché porco!' at me; of course he is right, even if I have robbed him of a thousand lire or two because he happens to be the keeper of the local pissatorium. We are taken to the glass factory where acres and acres of tasteless junk are paraded before our eyes. 'Ché porco!' I continue to echo.

We cannot resist hearing the Charles Ives muddle of two or more bands sounding off simultaneously in St. Mark's Square, even though shamefully enough, the music is all American musicals and Lloyd Webber these days. I ask for Verdi or Puccini but the nice pianist mimes that she doesn't have the music. I start formulating one of those petulant sentences beginning 'You'd think that...' but then I am distracted by the bill that demands about thirty quid for coffee and ice creams. The weather is gorgeous and there is just time to see my favourite Colleone equestrian statue before the ship sails. Damn nearly got lost too.

CRUISING IN RUSSIA:
28.9.–8.10.97

Another cruise! My second in Russia this year and my seventh cruise this year. Last time it was Moscow two days, seven days on the river, canal and lake to St Petersburg. This time we are in reverse, flying to St Petersburg. Funny folk, them Russians, they need tourism and yet the airport welcome is horrendous: the green 'nothing to declare' is locked so we all have to go through the red 'something to declare' door which takes a good hour and a half. We have two sittings for meals on the boat (MV *Kirov*) but fortunately the music room is large enough to accommodate all – last time on the *Tolstoy* we had to do everything twice, which was a drag. The beds are narrow, fornication would be distinctly uncomfortable but there is no temptation anyway. Nice customers, all about my age, patient. Oh, those roads though, bumpitybump and the driver has to watch out for the tramlines which age has raised above the level of the road. My colleagues are Opera Interludes, which are four singers, a pianist and a nanny-manager who also plays the fiddle. Their chief contribution is a semi-staged *Eugène Onegin.* I gave lectures on the Mighty Handful group of Moscow composers, one on Tchaikovsky and one on Shostakovich. Those take place while we are cruising; in the towns, sightseeing is the order of the day and evening. Wonderful to spend more hours in the Hermitage. In the Tretyakov Gallery in Moscow where the basement houses a stunning display of ikons, one lady is asked what she thinks of them. 'Very nice, of course, but a bit old-fashioned.'

What we don't get on these Russian cruises is a symphony concert or opera. All we get is an operatic concert in Petersburg which is held in the superb little theatre in the Yusopov Palace (waxwork of Rasputin being knocked off in the actual basement where it happened) but the programme is disappointing because it is always Mozart, Puccini and Western music which they don't sing all that well, whereas Russian music is what we would all like to hear. But I appreciate that most of the Russky operatic repertoire would call for an orchestra too large to accommodate on the little stage (and more expensive!).

But in Moscow we did get to the Bolshoi Theatre for the ballet. Great thrill to be there for the first time. Disappointment number one: not the Bolshoi Ballet but a visiting company, directed by one Boris Eifman whose choreography we saw in a two act ballet *The Karamazovs.* Disappointment number two: the pit was empty so that instead of an orchestra we had tapes of chunks of Mussorgsky, Wagner and Rachmaninov plus church choral music and some popular (Russian) songs. The story was based on Dostoievsky but the choreography was flash, applause-seeking and gimmicky, lots of ropes and nets. Lots of extended leg stuff, very well danced, especially the girls but the result was a real hodge-podge inflated with symbolism and 'concepts'.

LONG OR SHORT?
12.10.97

'It drips with emotivity,' wrote Virgil Thomson once about the music of Arnold Schönberg. This day I heard *Gurrelieder* in the Festival Hall; it takes a whole concert to perform it and the audience went wild with enthusiasm. Except for one member of the audience who found it mostly overblown Teutonism despite one or two good five-minute stretches, especially towards the end when the composer was several years older than at the beginning. Fischer-Dieskau was his masterly self in the part of the Speaker. The part is notated in such a way that you can say it on pitch or you can almost sing it – and sing it almost was what DFD did, good to hear that voice again. He prudently avoided two or three high notes by singing other notes a bit lower but part of the harmony.

Length appeals to audiences obviously. It is part of the appeal of Wagner's *Ring* surely. (Nagging voice in the rear says why isn't Pfitzner's *Palestrina* more popular then?) Composers who wrote nothing large rarely get into the Top Ten, look at Webern – nothing longer than ten minutes – and Grainger – longest seventeen. Andrew Davies does a great job with BBC forces, fairly good soloists but I don't hear the famous orchestral chains. Early Schönberg always reminds me, even when I like the piece e.g. *Verklärte Nacht*, of pink wall paper and I expect Klimt ladies to shimmy in at any moment. It's precious sometimes, and precious near to sentimentality.

I remember listening first to *Gurrelieder* on 78 records, fourteen of them, which meant getting up about every four minutes to put a new side on. It was conducted by Leopold Stokowski who gave a talk about the work on side one, beginning with the words '*Gurrelieder* is architecture in tone on a vast scale…'

And it is noticeable that, apart from the early tonal works, nothing by Schönberg has become a standard repertory piece – except *Pierrot Lunaire.* But those operas, the concertos, the string quartets! The very idea of a Schönberg comic opera is a contradiction in terms and as for those later string quartets, hearing them is like eating very old ship's biscuits. At one time my mentor, William Glock, was all for the third and fourth quartets; yet a decade later when I suggested programming them at the Summer School he nearly choked with negation.

No, give me Webern every time. Not least for its brevity.

RUSSKIES:
20.10.97

To the Barbican concert hall for the St Petersburg Philharmonic for one of the best concerts I have heard for years. This orchestra is just as good as it was when I heard it in situ under Evgeny Mravinsky in '71, disproving my fears that so many of its members would have emigrated (London is full of such musicians and they have spread all over the world, even to South Africa). The strings are the envy of the world, thrilling. And yet the concert nearly didn't happen: their own conductor Temirkanov had heart trouble; they managed to get instead Rozhdestvensky who also went sick with a dicky ticker; at the last moment they got Lazarev, now conductor of the Scottish National. Liadov's soothing *Enchanted Lake,* then Demidenko flashed elegantly through the Paganini Rhapsody of Rachmaninov, but the real knock-out was the Sixth Symphony of Shostakovich.

A curious shape and many carp that its long meditative first movement (with moments when the action stops and the violas trill for minutes at a time) is followed by two movements of rumbustious good humour, the finale even getting near to aping Rossini and the *Dance of the Hours.* I adore it and so did the audience. Overwhelming virtuoso playing from every department of the band, woodwind excelling, brass now sounding more western in tone and the timpanist making the most resonant sound I have ever heard.

THE TWO MALCOLMS:
21.10.97

Malcolm Arnold is seventy-six today. When we first met he was twenty-three, very young to be the first trumpet of the London Philharmonic Orchestra but the older members had gone to the war. The other outstanding trumpeter of that time was Malcolm's old teacher, Ernest Hall, with the BBC Symphony Orchestra. Both of them made the true trumpet sound, shining and noble brilliance as opposed to the other school of trumpet playing (like George Eskdale of the LSO) which sounded more like a cornet and to my ears, inferior. Malcolm sometimes looked like something out of Disney.

He would play a solo wonderfully and as he played his face would tinge with pink and then, if the solo was long enough, red, through to puce and purple. The solo ended he would regard his instrument with loathing as if it had pooped on the carpet. Then one day he revealed himself as a composer: Van Beinum conducted his overture *Beckus the Dandipratt*, music that was crystal clear, marvellously orchestrated with moods that went from a lovely lyricism to the most uninhibited rowdiness, sometimes it sounded mad. Which indeed Malcolm has been, put away several times, then let out for enough time for him to write nine symphonies, many concertos (composed especially for friends) and a hundred feature film scores, yes, including *Bridge on the River Kwai*. Malcolm loved to entertain, to write tunes and to shock the Establishment. Shocked they were too and he was given the frozen mitt. That's all over now and performances are frequent. There are no less than three sets of recordings of his nine symphonies. But the cost of that intensity and the drinking that followed the completion of a film, left the composer in a state where he now has to have a minder (the heroic John Anthony Day) and has to have everything done for him. No more composing. There are lucid moments when his memory is clear about the past and he is glad to see old friends. But then he may see red, talk gobbledygook and turn abusive. Perhaps years on it may be revealed that his brain was chopped about a bit.

In the afternoon to Wimbledon to deliver the Eulogy at the funeral of George Malcolm, Church of the Sacred Heart. Hadn't realised before now that S.W.19 is a hotbed of Romans: several churches, training colleges and so on. The church is big and spacious, too big to be able to make contact with the congregation; I realise this during the homily, because the celebrant misfired, especially with his humorous bits. Mine misfired too, I thought, but several people at the tea thrash afterwards said they had laughed...but inwardly. Brompton Oratory Choir sang well, Anerio Mass. Dear old George; I had encountered him first when he played continuo and solo for Enescu and the Boyd Neel Orchestra around 1950. Enescu shushed him up whenever he heard him – that generation could not abide the harpsichord – but once the performance started, George pulled out all the stops and let him (and us) have it. George played the piano nicely but the harpsichord brilliantly and he made it sound as interesting as he could, switching about from stop to stop, manual to manual; he could even achieve the impossible and make a crescendo. He was at the top of his profession until authenticity reared its head, then he had to rely on conducting for a living. He was liked well enough by Britten, conducting his operas and première recordings, but he never caught the imagination of the public as a conductor, partly because his body language was not convincing, his elbows were always at right angles which made for a certain lack of legato/flow.

He was a consummate musician, played the organ very well, and could compose pastiche most entertainingly, as in his Mozart Variations for four harpsichords and his hornpipe *Bach before the mast*. But possibly George's most lasting achievement was that he changed the sound of the voices of boy trebles in this country. As opposed to such voices on the continent the taste in the U.K. was for the angelic, rather sugary boy soprano sound, as exemplified in the choir of King's College Chapel, Cambridge. George trained his boys during his twelve-year stint as Master of the Music at Westminster Cathedral to sing with, as he put it, the sort of sound they made in the playground. Britten wrote his *Missa Brevis* for George and the boys, and their Decca recording is superb, George, Britten and the boys at their best. George had duos with several top-notchers, with Julian Bream on guitar or lute, they were star performers for many years at the Summer School at Dartington: George disciplined Julian, and Julian brought George out of his shell. George was a bit of a buttoned-up bachelor, mother-dominated, not at his best with women, with a face that was unyielding partly because of the plastic surgery necessary after he fell out of a first-floor window in the '40s. He had a serious drink problem at that time, partly through repression I have always thought, but possibly because of over-working during the war in the R.A.F. as band master of Bomber Command. But despite everything, George could be great fun and was a loyal friend; he could always be relied upon to speak the truth as I knew very well. After studying for five years in the '60s I wavered between believing my teachers and some friends that I was a good singer, and taking in the fact that all my auditions failed. George let me sing to him and then said, 'John, it's not good enough.' So I quit.

George also had duos with two violinists: Manoug Parikian, who eventually found that, although George could be so eloquent on the harpsichord, his piano playing lacked character; and Yehudi Menuhin. Programmes with Yehudi were all, I think, baroque music and at a time when the violinist was having great problems with his bow arm. Yehudi's pride as a performer only cracked once, George told me: after a particularly disastrous performance YM said as they entered the artists' room: 'Oh, George, that was terrible.' Enter a member of the audience with fulsome compliments and Yehudi's mask was back in place: 'I'm *so* glad you liked it.'

Once George and Julian had an appointment with a lady photographer near Aldeburgh for a record sleeve. George was, of course, on time; Julian was, of course, late; and so was the photographer (her name was Sandra Lousada). George was understandably a bit testy with her until Julian pointed out that she was heavily pregnant. Telling the story later that day Julian said, 'Poor old George. When he realized that, he was desiccated with remorse.'

SANDOR VEGH:
22.10.97

Concert in St. George's, Hanover Square in memory of Sandor Vegh who died in January, aged eighty-four. A great violinist and equally great as string quartet leader and teacher, and in his late seventies he started to make some fine records as a conductor including Mozart concertos with Andras Schiff. Many of the recordings he made with the Vegh String Quartet are fine too, especially the late Beethovens. But there are only moments in his *solo* records that reveal the greatness of his violin playing. Like another favourite artist of like vintage, Vlado Perlemuter, the recording studio did not suit their artistry, which makes it all the more necessary to write about them.

Sandor (like Perlemuter) was in a way the last of the line; he had studied with Hubay and had worked with Bartok and Kodaly; his playing and teaching embodied the best of the nineteenth century. What Sandor taught was imagination and colour, with the bow especially, to make music sound fresh, spontaneous and inspired, so that performances were not manacled to the printed notes but

186

took off into the air. And spontaneity also included the use of experience, never let it be forgot.

Sandor was a vast man, his face not unlike a ghoulash version of Charles Laughton (whose 'autogram' he was often asked for in America). Hungarians rarely lose their colourful accent, with a firm biff on the *ini*tial *syll*able, no upbeats in their music which is one way of distinguishing between the genuine stuff and the gipsy. In Sandor's case, however, living in German speaking countries had also left their mark on his speech, particularly in the matter of grammar. Sandor was magisterial, genial, generous, devious (in small quantities), fun-loving, big-hearted and in touch with matters of the heart and spirit. He used to teach in master-classes at the Summer School at Dartington in Devon and later at Prussia Cove in Cornwall, and I found his teaching so moving that I sometimes wept because he seemed literally to refresh one's love and understanding of music. He loved good food, wine and pretty girls and on all three his inclinations were monitored by his beautiful, volatile, former actress wife Alice, a true Hungarian blonde with a formidable sense of humour. She was present at the memorial concert together with her artists' agent daughter Alya. Cellist Isserlis played the 'old growler' F major Sonata of Brahms opus 99 with an excellent pianist Alexander Lonquich. There followed a tribute by Myra, Lady Verney, done well, and made more entertaining because the dear girl could never find the right next page. Alexander Janiczek was an outstanding leader in a performance of Schubert's C major String Quintet, all the players drawn from amongst the musicians of many nations who continue to go for teaching and chamber music playing to Prussia Cove.

At some point in the evening I recalled a paprika pandemonium that occurred at the Summer School at Dartington. The scene is the artists' room where the Vegh Quartet is three-quarters assembled and practising madly in different keys and tempos (this is one scene that Charles Ives omitted to compose). The only thing the three players have in common is that they are all wearing dark lounge suits.

Enter the second violin – in full soup and fish, white tie and tails. No language is better for having a row in, it seems to me, than Hungarian. And a devil of a one now ensues; from which it gradually

187

emerges that leader, viola, and cello think they arranged to wear lounge suits whereas the second violin maintains they agreed on tails. No, he cannot go and change into a lounge suit because he hasn't brought one. So, we had six concerts in which the second violin was dressed up to the nines with the rest of the quartet somewhat less so. During the month they played all six Bartok quartets quite wonderfully.

The quartet by this stage in their careers expressed their feelings about each other in that Vegh lived in Zurich, Janzer the violist in Geneva, Szabo the cellist in Basel whilst Zöldy, the one in tails, was resident in Paris. This made crucial the question of the location of the next rehearsal: 'Your place or mine?'

DONALD SWANN:
24.10.97

To the Astor Theatre, Deal, to give the first public performance of a show I have devised about Michael Flanders and Donald Swann, a kind of *Drop of a Hat* affair but without the two departed protagonists. It's about the two of them, their work and their lives. The music comes up perennially fresh, so do the words, as sparkling and clever in their own way as Cole Porter or Noël Coward. Donald's music is several cuts above the usual revue song, tunes that satisfy everybody and musicianship that lifts them up; he makes the love that the Armadillo feels for a deserted tank on Salisbury Plain feel real and touching; little things creep in too, I like a sly reference between verses to *Coriolan* Overture. Richard Lloyd Morgan sings with wit and a pleasing baritone voice; Christopher Ross has the measure of the music and puts no foot or hand wrong at the piano.

I could never quite cross the barrier between me and Mike's wheel-chair but we were always on friendly terms. Donald was at my Prep school in Dulwich and we remained friends ever after except that he sometimes blew cold, perhaps part of his tendency towards manic-depression that forced him into retreat once in a while. Until he was eighteen or so his muse was classical, true to the long stay in the Baltic that his forbears had made; Rachmaninov, Tchaik. and Medtner were his loves. At Westminster School he was put down to play the third Beethoven Piano Concerto, made a mess of it and thereafter renounced the classical stuff, having it in for Beethoven ever after. In the Friends' Ambulance Unit in Greece he was captivated by the local songs and folk music, adored the irregular rhythms; he also wrote some light music songs for his mates in the Unit. When he came home he met Flanders again. At Westminster they had written a few songs, put into a revue for end of term, stage-managed by Tony Benn. By now Flanders had been forced by polio into a wheel-chair, his dreams of an acting career shattered. The pair wrote a few songs for intimate revue and graduated to performing them themselves and that led to eleven years of *At the Drop of a Hat* and world wide (English speaking) success.

Donald Swann's music-making, especially his piano playing shows his spirit, his usual spirit, wonderfully warm and with a fine ear for dynamics, knowing how loud he can play a line without it becoming harsh. I agree with Leslie Howard that Donald was one of the great pianists of our time. Great? Well, significant and life-enhancing, especially when playing one of his more and many inspired songs. There was such a one on this tape, one I hadn't heard before, one that reminded me of his setting of a poem by Father Michel Quoist which is 'Lord, why did you tell me to love all men, my brothers?'. This is the last of a clutch of settings of Edna St. Vincent Millay: 'I have no time to hate'. Donald's last decade brought forth songs based on Emily Dickinson, Tennyson, Rossetti, Hardy, Blake and others, many of them I believe at the suggestion of his young art historian wife, Alison. Some of them are first-rate art songs, in the line of Ireland, Warlock et al. Donald's setting of 'The Fly' of Blake, for instance, is a gem and, for my money, a more penetrating setting than Britten's; it has only a right hand piano part, as quickly drifting as a fly's flight. On the other hand Donald's setting of 'A Time there was' doesn't work at all, like a rightly rejected revue number and vastly inferior to Britten's version. But there are superior and inferior Wolf and Warlock songs and, if prejudice could be overcome, I think Swann could become better known as one of our better song writers. Of course, I am a believer.

My mind goes back to meeting Alison and Donald one day; they had been to their favourite little cafe in Battersea High Street, a greasy spoon of the sort that he loved (after a performance of *Drop of a Hat* with Flanders, Donald would return to Battersea by bus for an egg on toast, all by himself and quite happy). But this day something in their expression warned me of some dire calamity. I believe it was the day that Donald was told his fate, incurable cancer.

Some of the happiest moments of my life were when Donald asked me in to the music room on the first floor of Albert House to listen to new songs. He was as nervous and tense as I was.

One day when the diagnosis had been confirmed and he was already on one of his sojourns to the Tooting Hospice I asked him why he and Alison didn't marry. He said that she did not approve of marriage. I argued that it would be prudent because if anything happened to Donald the legal complications might prevent her easily receiving anything he left her in his will, house, royalties and so on.

A week later Donald rang me from St. Thomas's Hospital to say that he and Alison had just got hitched in the hospital chapel.

Not that these jottings prove it but Donald was something of a saint; a wonderful pianist and composer (although his output varied in quality; I don't fancy some of the longer pieces, operas, cantatas, etc. – he didn't have a wide enough spectrum, enough musics to deal with many situations), a loyal man and good.

RUGBY AND LEVY:
29.11.97

Was persuaded by Jo-burg friend Alec Grant to watch the All Blacks playing Wales. Am not really a rugby fan but this was something else, the New Zealanders won 42-7 but, although they were vastly superior, it was by no means a walk-over. The Welshmen played as though their lives depended on it, aggressive and tough but they were outclassed. Naturally I couldn't help seeing the game from a musical point of view. As performers the All Blacks, like the best musicians, always seemed to have time and space on their side, the result of meticulous practice obviously. The action of the three-quarters was a pure joy to watch, there was always another one in the right place to accept a pass, even, and especially, one going the other way. Their overlapping and the amazing athletic speed in running, dodging and feinting reminded me of the overlapping of stringed instrument entries in the quartets of Bartok, likewise the melee of the forwards; and the reverse passes seemed to me like enharmonic modulations (there, if that doesn't qualify for Pseud's Corner, nothing will). And there was one incredible moment in the second half when the All Blacks forwards in a scrimmage walked the Welshmen backwards for something like forty feet, an unbelievable and probably unique happening (against the rules?). Don't know how it happened but this game, before seventy-odd thousand at Wembley took place simultaneously with another match at Twickenham where England were licked by South Africa before a similarly large crowd. Both were covered on TV, the Twickenham game shown at a later time, overlapping with Wembley by a quarter of an hour. But the second game to be shown was not a patch on the first: Dohnanyi compared with Bartok?

Ooh, have suddenly remembered there is a piece by Honegger, *Rugby*, number two in a set of three orchestral works of which number one is *Pacific 231*. I think both pieces are excellent, good music; but Honegger got lambasted when they came out in the '20s for imitating a train and football. So he then said they were not imitations, which was silly, 'cos they are...as well as being good music...but they are both rarely played now. And the third in the set is never played, just called *Symphonic Piece number 3*. So the poor old Schweizer just couldn't win.

Once upon a time there was a canny little East End cockney muzo called Louis Levy who graduated from pit work for silent movies to being Music Director of Gaumont British and he didn't half give himself airs. Honegger did the music for a picture here and was present at the sessions but Levy conducted. From the podium Levy telephoned the control room: 'Is that you, 'Onegger? *Mister* Levy 'ere.'

And on another occasion when conducting he said to the orchestra, ''Ere, give us a bit more, will you?' and the leader said, 'But Mr Levy, it's marked *morendo*.' 'All right,' said Levy, 'let's have more of it then, but don't let it die away.'

PAST AND PRESENT:
3.12.97

This morning the regular nine o'clock presenter on Radio 3 referred to Korngold's opera *Die Tote Stadt* with tote pronounced in one syllable as if it were an abbreviation of totalizator.

But later, before Debussy's *Trois Chansons de Charles d'Orléans* the fascinating information was given that the poet was taken prisoner at the Battle of Agincourt in 1415 and was a p.o.w. in England for twenty-five years. Then went back to France and lived a similar period before handing in his dinner pail. Not many people know that!

ADVENT:
30.11, 3, 6, 7, 8.12.97

Church crawling in the cause of writing a piece for *The Tablet* (I've been its music wallah for nearly a decade now, circulation 25,000 including, they tell me, some 2,000 Anglicans). My S. African friend Ba Bailey always does the rounds when she comes to London because she loves church music and she thinks the standard of singing is very high. And she is right: people who worship at the Abbey, the Cathedral, St Paul's and the Oratory all get wonderful value for what they put in the collection plates. They get a wide variety of music, all of it good, occasionally something new and the standard is absolutely first class, utterly professional. Which is more than could be said of the clergy who frequently mumble their jumbo (there, now it's out: I am not of any faith, save in men and women, some of them, and their spirituality and their art works; I can't believe in a god with arms and legs; and I can't imagine one without). The Bishop of London was a notable exception and the Dean gave a good sermon; but the Oratory preacher, or homily giver (the Oratory mistakenly doesn't give you a printed order of service) fairly awful: this was the Mass of the Immaculate Conception so he went on at great length about Mary, quoting theological tracts of 1858 and 1870, and ending by exhorting us all to tell our beads (cf jujubes in the jungle). At which point I think I heard some derisory shuffling of feet from the choir. If the homily giver was a canon, he should have been fired.

192

The high point of my visits was a Palestrina mass at the Cathedral (James O'Donnell is the director of music) and I think they are the tops: partly, I guess, because the acoustics are better than at the other churches I visited, and the choir is placed so that the singers can hear each other properly which they cannot, for instance, at St Paul's where any note below middle C is a willowy wobble, magnified by the echo. But Walton's *Coronation Te Deum* still sounded grand at St Paul's with organ accompaniment and the proper brass fanfares and parts.

The occasion was the tercentenary of the opening of Wren's work; the Queen was present and all the city big-wigs – I was shown under the dome into a row 'reserved for Livery Ladies'. At the Abbey (Martin Neary) we had good old Stanford in B flat and a choral chunk of Britten's *Saint Nicolas*, the 'piety and works' bit with its haunting harmonies. The Brompton Oratory choir (Andrew Garwood) sang beautifully two Bruckner motets but also sported an orchestra to give the first performance of a Mass by Frederick Stocken. This young man achieved notoriety a few years ago by shouting abuse and disaffection at several performances in London. His Mass was nothing to shout about, however, except that one moment, an Agnus Dei, had a certain charm about it with skeins of woodwind sound rising above four soloists, very calm until the sounds of war broke in (as they do in Beethoven's *Missa Solemnis*).

In my five visits there were three new or newish pieces to be heard: the Stocken; a new anthem by Philip Moore at St Paul's and some Responseries by Francis Grier at Cambridge (the most interesting of the three and the most taxing). The Cambridge occasion was the Advent Procession (so-called because the choir sings in different places of King's College Chapel).

THUS SPAKE...
11.11.97

Dear old Isaiah Berlin has died, wise, lovely man.

It must have been in the '60s that he came to give a talk at Dartington (Summer School) in the Great or Banqueting Hall. He was to start at 5.30 on a Sunday evening and he arrived at 5.29 and a half (panic stations), having gone to sleep on the train, therefore did not change at Newton Abbot and had taxied from Torquay. Now the big hall was the only venue large enough for the talk but the acoustic, so good for music, is lousy for speech. As is well known, Isaiah spoke very fast indeed, if he had not been so distinguished a man, one would say he gabbled; try as we swine would, it was difficult to catch the pearls. Ten minutes into his talk, a lady in the audience:

'Mr Berlin, could you please speak a bit slower?'

'No, I can't; I'm like an aeroplane: if I go too slow, I crash.'

For years after this, whenever I encountered Isaiah at a concert or opera, he mumbled further apologies for having been late.

Some time later I got him to tape a story about the Stravinskys which he agreed to do with the proviso (perfect gentleman that he was) that I should not broadcast it until after Vera, Mrs Stravinsky, had died. The tale went like this:

'One day Igor rang up: 'What is playing May 24 at Covent Garden?'

'*Nozze di Figaro.*'

'Ve vill com: Vera, Bob and I'

'But Igor, it's a routine performance and in English too, you won't enjoy it.'

'Ve vill com.'

Why did Igor want to come? All became clear when Isaiah discovered that on that very day, May 24, Monteux was to conduct the London Symphony in a fiftieth anniversary performance in concert of *Sacre de Printemps*. At the premiere in 1913 Stravinsky had embraced Pierre Monteux: 'it was the saltiest hug of my life' but since that time he had become disenchanted with Monteux and his rendering of *The Rite of Spring*. He not only was not going to attend the performance in the Royal Albert Hall: he wanted to be seen in public in another place, as a further snub for the conductor.

Then Boosey & Hawkes, publishers of *Sacre*, intervened, arguing that Igor's presence at the Albert Hall would be good publicity, they would surely sell more copies of the score, etc. The idea of more money always carried the day with Stravinsky so he agreed to attend, or rather, to take a bow at the end of the performance. But he was certainly not going to hear Monteux's performance and a car to the Albert Hall was ordered for the end of Act One of *Figaro*. Igor had worked out that the first act would take so many minutes, the journey would take so long and by these means they would arrive for the bow, having missed the music.

So the Stravinskys, plus Robert Craft, attract the right amount of attention as they enter the Royal Opera House and sit down for Mozart's first act. At the end of the act they get up to go but an attendant tries to prevent them leaving. 'You can't go now: the first interval is not until the end of act *two*. And indeed the lights have only been raised a little. 'But,' says Stravinsky, 'we all have diarrhoea.' The attendant lady cannot take the risk and lets them go.

RVW'S PROGRESS: 3.11.97

Vaughan Williams called *The Pilgrim's Progress* a Morality, avoiding the term opera. When it was put on at Covent Garden in 1951 it was botched and VW did not help matters by asking that a young conductor should take charge; because the music is non-operatic in style and pace, with vocal writing that almost entirely lacks characterization, the work needs careful handling by a very experienced conductor; Boult or Barbirolli would have been a better choice. VW was bitterly disappointed.

Friends told me that the staging in 1952 by Joseph Ward at the Royal Northern College of Music in Manchester was revelatory and successful, likewise a concert performance conducted by Richard Hickox at the Cornish St Endellion Festival earlier this year. Ward and Hickox with the resources of the Royal Opera put on a semi-staged performance that I went to in the Barbican Concert Hall. There were walkways and costumes and this seemed a satisfactory way of performing this work which has a great deal of strong and beautiful music in it. The weakness of the piece still seems to me to be the fact that for a dramatic work of this kind the composer needs to have different kinds of music at his disposal, he has to be able to illuminate many moods and to have a sufficient variety of musical substances. This is what Britten had in abundance. The comic scenes have some variety but on the whole there are only two or three kinds of music: the baddies have woodwind and brass, often in unison and with plenty of augmented fourths, the rest is noble and good but monotonously diatonic. They all sing the same kind of vocal line.

The choral bits contain some of the best music. Hickox did a good, committed job. There was a good deal of doubling in the personnel and it was confusing that one moment a singer was Obstinate, the next Watchful, another, Heavenly Being II soon became Madam Bubble. Gerald Finley, fine baritone, was Pilgrim; if he can colour his voice more he will be one of our best singers.

GIVING TALKS:
1.10.91

I'm on the 16.35 to Newbury. Met, taken to Downe House girls' school to give a talk supposedly to the inmates plus staff and a few friends. I slightly know Sue Cameron, the headmistress, who wonderfully looks the part, tall, serene, sensibly dressed, quietly in charge. Bit of hole-and-corner changing into my glad rags, try out the machine for the tapes I use in my talk Amiscellany (amazing how people can't say it, or misspell it). One switch won't go on and two of the music staff and Sue are as hopeless with machines as I am. Michael Meyer gave me a useful word: technophobe. The light meal promised does not appear; twiglets and crisps!

My talk varies but it is about my life and my work, bit about *My Music* usually and then some bits about Beecham, Donald Swann, Joyce Grenfell, Peter Ustinov, Eric Fenby about working with Delius, Percy Grainger, Alfred Swan (Donald's uncle) about Rachmaninov, Diana Menuhin on being the wife of a star, Gerard Hoffnung and me doing *Punkt Kontrapunkt*, a skit about avant garde music from one of the Hoffnung Festivals.

Over the twiglets it emerges that the whole damned school will be present. Now I'm chary about talking to children because they've not come of their own accord. Usually my audience has come because it has heard of me or *My Music* and they are on my side to start with. Kids don't laugh at the same things as adults and of course I have to vary the show to make sure that they know who and what I'm gassing about. Fortunately on this occasion something drops into my lap. I've started with Donald and happen to mention the Hippo Song; one little girl starts whistling it. So I suggest we all whistle or sing it and after that things go, well, not exactly swimmingly, but at least I don't sink or drown. Afterwards there *is* a meal, buffet supper (oh dear, I said 'no meals, didn't I?) with staff, some male, and three sixth form girls who are charming and articulate (though I gather afterwards from Sue that one of them is a thorn in the side of, or has been). I am taken to a teachers' hostel house, no heating and fairly basic, lavatory down the corridor; but lovely view from my bedroom in the morning.

Taken to Reading Central Station (I always think how silly that 'Central' is, even if it does differentiate it from Reading West) for a train to Newport across the Severn. Taken north to Dulas Court which is the 'other' residential home of the Musicians' Benevolent Fund, just in England, not too far from Hereford. Fine house in many acres where some eighteen musicians are retired, one or two were not actually in music but were relatives. I had been to the other home they have near Bromley to talk to the inmates and thought I had better finish the job and come to Dulas. They're mostly in their eighties, some sadly crippled but mostly quite bright and obviously well cared for. Léon Goossens was here for some of his last days, also Stanford Robinson the conductor. I manage to chat to most of them: the first wife of John Barbirolli, very pretty old lady, widow of singer Henry Cummings, the soprano Margaret Field-Hyde, a countertenor from St Paul's, a double-bass player, the widow of Redvers Llewellyn walking with a frame and others. I notice how if one cuts in while I'm talking to another, the first person goes away until he or she can command my complete attention, just a touch of second childhood about. I was reminded of that French film with Michel Simon and Louis Jouvet about an old home for actors: Jouvet every week gets a scented letter to the envy of the other old jossers until one day he is rumbled in the post office mailing one of the scented letters to himself.

My room is comfortable, only lacking a loo or bathroom 'en suite' (that descriptive phrase that we suddenly couldn't do without although it is new in our vocabulary) but all that is about to be changed, which means that the poor old dears will have to leave Dulas for local digs for four months while the place is kitted out with 'en suites'. Take a walk in the fields and beautifully kept garden before setting off for my home.

CZECHS:
16.1.98

The BBC begins a mini-festival weekend of the music of Bohuslav Martinu. This Czech composer wrote some 276 catalogued works. You might guess that that is too much and you would be right. He was a compulsive writer with scarcely a moment for anything except that he had a devoted French wife and a mistress. His first ten years were spent at the top of a church tower, his father being a watchman and church minder. So the boy had a clock ticking at him day and night and the townspeople must have looked to him like so many L. S. Lowry figures, only smaller. He was apparently the world's worst student and was even thrown out of the Prague conservatory, but he did manage to get a job for a bit in the second fiddles of the Czech Philharmonic.

As soon as he could he went to Paris, lived in poverty relieved somewhat by his seamstress wife who brought in the bread. In seventeen years in France he managed to get known a bit as a composer. Came the war and with great difficulty the Martinus crossed to America where he blossomed and flourished. From the '40s date his symphonies of which numbers 2 to 6 are some of his finest work, masterpieces of the first order, I would call them; and so did Virgil Thomson.

How great is Martinu? Oh dear, value judgments. Well, I rate his best work very highly, below Britten and on a par with somebody like Copland. Martinu's music is busy music, not very dissonant but highly original, easily identifiable. Scoring excellent, piano often used in the orchestral palette, strings to the fore, woodwind for contrast, brass in moderation with a predilection for cymbal and bass drum sounding together – crump! His tunes are not memorable but often they soar high and jubilant in the strings, usually syncopated. A certain set of chords and a particular modulation haunt his later music; they came first in his almost successful opera *Julietta*. The earlier Paris music contains some splendid charlestons and the like.

Fortunately the BBC chose good pieces like those later symphonies (No. 6 is life-enhancing and lives up to its alternative title *Fantasies Symphoniques*) with their curious but convincing logic. The trouble is when you come to those works which go through

198

similar motions as the good ones but seem to lack electricity. The Field Mass was one dud performed during the weekend, the Cello Concerto another.

CATHOLIC MUSICIAN:
29.1.98

To Westminster Cathedral for a Requiem Mass for George Malcolm. He was Master of the Music here for over ten years, from 1958, during which time he changed the sound of British Cathedral music by training the boys to sing in a more natural way.

Many chums and mutual friends of George were there: Neville Marriner read a lesson, Dame Janet Baker read some responses, Ian Partridge sang Schütz with John Elwes, and the Cardinal, Basil Hume, officiated. A St Martin-in-the-Fields group played the first movement of Mendelssohn's Octet (George would have appreciated that use of his favourite nineteenth century composer) but they had to play in the nave because the choir had of course bagged the best, their usual, place in the cupola. High fiddle notes, even with Ken Sillito playing, failed to come through, but what a piece it is! One of the most amazing works of the nineteenth century and one of the most amazing works by a teenager, far superior to anything, for example, of Mozart. Mind you, there is Shostakovich's masterly Symphony No 1 at sixteen.

When I first went to the Cathedral many years ago the little Baptist/C of E British boy (apologies to Taki) thought that the interior was vulgar and Roman. Now he thinks differently, finding that central array of yellow columns most attractive and decorative especially with the blue upper work contrasting with the yellow and non-coloured bit in between. Funny though, how sometimes one doesn't even see that enormous Crucifix, something to do with eye-lines.

I remember once that George played a bit on the great organ to show me how the sound came back about seven seconds later by which time he was playing something quite different. I recall too the premiere of the *Missa Brevis* which Britten wrote for George and the boys, a kind of leaving present. The choir sang the Sanctus and Benedictus from it during this Requiem Mass. Those D major scales with Lydian fourths (G sharps) are an emotional knock-out and the boys really relished them. The rest of the music featured Victoria (sixteenth century).

The Cardinal was the only one of the priests with the manner born, the only one who *belonged* and was able to speak and move naturally. There was a binge afterwards and I had the pleasure of shaking him (tall man) by the hand. 'Marvellous to find a man of God who is also a real pro' ,I stammered. 'A *what?*' said he and then smiled as he realised I wasn't being snide or disrespectful.

GRAPPELLI AND NIGE(L): 1.12.97

Stephane Grappelli has died (nearly ninety). He was inspired as a child by hearing records of Joe Venuti and taught himself to play the violin, inventing his own unique style of arabesque, including all the devices of which the instrument is capable: double-stopping, harmonics, glissandos, portamentos, near and far from the bridge, pizzicatos, spiccato, staccato, swooping down to the G string, the whole gamut of effects. All this plus a fantastic sense of rhythm which would really swing. And his playing had a beguiling innocence about it. Once in a radio programme I played one of his choruses at slow motion speed, an octave lower, and you could hear all the devices clearly and also tell that every note was bang in tune.

In an interview he was asked if he warmed up before playing. No, he said, he warmed up *while* playing. Did he have a secret then? Grappelli then said that he used a special elixir: a liquid made exclusively in Scotland and named after its people. On the TV they showed pictures of Grappelli playing including some with the infant Nigel Kennedy. Nige has recently, as I forecast, made a return to the public sector but renouncing his first name. Bit silly really. Like, man, squire, monster, his slang words and his cockney accent. Incidentally I knew Nige, sorry, Kennedy, before he had acquired his cockney accent; which was not surprising since at that time he hadn't then learnt to talk. His father John Kennedy was a first-class cellist, leader of the cellos in Beecham's orchestra, the Royal Philharmonic. John was fun, although a compulsive joker and it

200

was sad that he smoked and drank himself to death. Nige's mother, Scylla, is a darling and is now seeing a lot of Nige. Nige's absence from the platform for some years, incidentally, gave Tasmin Little the opportunity to step in as England's foremost fiddler, delightful girl and superb player. Now they will be encouraged, I hope and expect, to new heights to try and outdo one another.

TORTELIERS:
15.12.97

A two-hour chat show with Yan Pascal Tortelier for Putney Music Club interspersed with tapes and CDs, including, at my request, part of his orchestration of Ravel's Piano Trio. It really works and turns this monumental chamber music piece into the Symphony that Ravel omitted to compose. Ingeniously what Yan Pascal did was to leave more or less intact the violin and cello parts, augmented often to full strings, and to orchestrate the piano part. This works particularly well in, for example, the closing pages of the finale where, as a trio, the piano part is so full that the strings are left just trilling, there are no harmonies left for them to play by the dominating piano. But the heart of the work is the slow movement, the *passecaille*; at the third repetition of the ground the harmonies, lean, virile and piquantly dissonant, the music is Ravel at his greatest.

Tortelier Non Papa (cf. Clemens Non Papa 1510-56), as I sometimes call him, was quite happy to talk about father Paul and his adorable mother Maud (also a cellist) who could have had almost as starry a career as Papa except that she sacrificed her career to be mother and wife. I used to call her 'La petite ange du 17me arondissement' an error which Paul never forgot because, owing to a stupid quirk of the French language, 'ange' happens to be masculine, not feminine. I first got to know the whole family when I did the chat and interviews for a BBC Monitor item. Humphrey Burton directed and we went to Paris to film this great cellist with the charismatic personality.

It is strange how both father and son have flourished most in the U.K.. Papa broke through by auditioning for Beecham. Paul was an early performer way back in 1929 of the Elgar Concerto and his second recording of the work with Malcolm Sargent is the best version I know (yes, despite Jackie's). His command of sound, technique and music made totally satisfying his performance of the sonatas by Beethoven, Fauré, Debussy and Brahms; not forgetting *Don Quixote*. He composed a *Hymn for the United Nations* 'to give that organization a soul' and a group of twenty-four cellists played for our cameras a special version of it. It has a rousing quality that the best hymns have; Humphrey and I can still sing it right through at the drop of a hat.

I have followed YP's later career as a conductor through his Toulouse days, directing opera at Wexford, the Ulster Orchestra (who recorded the Ravel Trio) and his seven years with the BBC Philharmonic. He is a hard worker, everybody likes him and his strong point is his intuition and his love shown in his performances of the best music of our century.

DOWN AMONG THE DEAD MEN:
April 12, Easter Sunday 1998

Decided to have another butch at the composer deadies in Vienna. Took tube and bus to the Zentralfriedhof. At the entrance I saw somebody buying what looked like a guide to this vast cemetery; it was and I bought one too. With this in hand I found my way to the composers and musicians either buried here or, in the case of many of the most celebrated, their Denkmals/ Memorial stones. Beethoven and Mozart, for example, have nice memorial headstones but their bodies or remains are elsewhere, whereabouts known or, famously in Mozart's case, unknown for he was put in an unmarked grave. Salieri also has a Denkmal, well away from Mozart's (just in case there was any bad feeling as appears in Pushkin's *Mozart and Salieri*; envy, rage and situation that Peter Shaffer cleverly stole without acknowledgement for his play and film *Amadeus*). Mozart, incidentally, looks here very prettily nineteenth century as if he only wrote what Charles Ives described as 'ladies' finger music'. Most of the nineteenth century Denkmals are on the pretty side; it isn't until you get to Schönberg's memorial that you find one that is suitable. Old Arnold's is a big rectangle, not properly squared off, resting awkwardly and patently not fitting into its frame on the ground.

Even posthumously S. was what my mother used to call an 'awkward squad'.

Wolf's Denk is carefully positioned so as not to be visible to Brahms, nor either to Richard Wagner, but as it is not the famous Richard but another of the same name, it doesn't matter. There are many composers near to the great ones, but who ever heard of, for instance Adolf Müller (1801-86), Anton Rückauf (1855-1903) or Karl Komsak (1850-1905)? Never mind, they R.I.P. almost next, as they are, to Johann Strauss senior who only wrote one well known piece (*Radetsky March*) but begat some clever sons: Johann junior (or as we could call him Strauss Non Papa, like Clemens), Josef (whose music I prefer to his famous brother, much more interesting musically, his introductions are quite symphonic) and Eduard, schöne Eddie, they called him. But I call him Shitty Eddie because he committed one of the greatest musical crimes I know. When his brother died he hired a furnace and burned all the manuscripts he could find, plus all the orchestrations for the band that he could lay his hands on. People implored him not to, but he persisted and it took some five hours before he had completed the spiteful deed.

I could not find Pfitzner but Krenek is there, Schubert, Gluck, cataloguer Köchel, Hanslick and all the light music boyos like Lanner, Kalman, Müllocker, Stolz and Francesco Ezechile Ermenegildo Cavaliere Suppé Demelli (obviously more Poet than Peasant). Also Julius Bittner, Egon Wellesz and Alexander Zemlinsky; but no Mahler, Berg or Webern.

There are many singers who have a place in the myriad avenues and groups including Lotte Lehmann, Hilde Konetzni, Eberhard Wächter and, from the jazz scene, a 'musiker' known as George Fatty.

One curiosity: there is a large tomb inscribed for the family Wittgensteins, including Ludwig and his one-armed pianist brother, Paul, who commissioned works from Ravel (whose Concerto he tried to rewrite), Prokofiev (which he never played, couldn't make head or tail of it), Benjamin Britten (played occasionally) and Hindemith (who wrote his Concerto in 1923, his opus 29, not only never played but not published because the Wittgenstein heirs are sitting on it and nobody else has a copy, neither Hindemith's family nor his publisher). But the curiosity is that nowhere in the official printed guide to the Zentralfriedhof is the Wittgenstein family tomb (No. 34) listed or mentioned. Rum! (Perhaps because they were Jewish? But then, why is Schönberg there?)

HOWARD HARTOG:
14.5.98

Go to lunch with pianist Margaret Kitchin, widow of Howard Hartog, important figure in postwar German and British music. Sad how the world is full of widows of men who die too soon, leaving grieving dames. Why was Howard important? He was English, born of Dutch parents, educated by others at public school and university, educated himself by reading, studying paintings (Klee he adored) and listening to music. Prewar gobsmacked by concert performance of *Wozzeck*.

After signals duty in N. Africa and Italy (going to lots of opera) he found himself by a series of flukes in charge of the music of the radio station in Hamburg, Nord West Deutsche Rundfunk. He did it, he said modestly, because it was there to be done. He helped that fine conductor, Hans Schmidt-Isserstedt to make the NWDR orchestra one of the best in Europe. Of course things were difficult, scores to be found, singers to be transported, problems of denazification; musicians were hungry, fees mattered less than dinner. Howard, bulky, rotund, high forehead, explosive temper, a laugh likewise that went off like a bomb, just one cataclysmic shot of mirth. His influence was great, his industry likewise; he put on *Peter Grimes, A Child of our Time* (a pacifist oratorio in English in Germany in 1946), got Gunther Rennert engaged as Intendant of Hamburg Opera in one morning, and Philipp Jarnach as head of the Hochschule. Got Rosbaud and Furtwängler to come and conduct. Dr Hans S-I wouldn't do Elgar but took to Tippett. And in fact it was his performances of Tippett with the Hamburg orchestra in London that made the break-through, showing us English how, for example, the string Double Concerto 'went'.

Howard wasn't sure if he would stay in music but took a job with the music publishers Schott in London. They were Tippett's publishers and their friendship was of great value to them both although in old age Howard would enthuse about the early works, not the late.

Later Howard took over the running of the concert and artists' agency Ingpen & Williams where he looked after, among others, Solti, Boulez, Söderström, Sutherland and Brendel. Hartog always said what he thought, no nonsense; he was famous for his letters which rarely contained more than two sentences; he could be brutal on the telephone. (Once a BBC booking lady I knew rang me up in a state of elation; 'You will appreciate this,' she said: '*I* put the phone down on Howard Hartog.') Of all the people I have known, Howard was quite the dirtiest; his handkerchiefs were disgusting and with him the usual question was reversed: with Howard it was not 'how many shirts do you wear a week?' but 'how many weeks to you wear a shirt?' He smelt of the interminable cheroots or cigars he smoked and he was the messiest eater any of us knew. Yet once you knew him, you loved him; and he was generous.

One day Howard and Margaret and Pierre Boulez motored up to stay with the Harewoods in Yorkshire, lunching on the way. At dinner that evening an object broke loose from Howard's corsage and rolled to the floor. Blades the butler retrieved it and it proved to be a parsley potato. 'How odd,' said Patricia, Countess of Harewood, 'because there are no potatoes on the menu tonight.'

Another time, Howard and Margaret were staying somewhere in Southern Italy. In the middle of the night Howard farted so loudly that he woke himself up, shouted, 'Come in,' and immediately went back to sleep.

BANNED MUSIC:
16.11.98

An evening of Banned Music at the Union Chapel, Islington (Canonbury, to be exact) which seats 1800, an enormous octagonal building with good acoustic. It was completed in 1876, designed by James Cubitt, very imposing. The pews allow of no kneeling because it is Congregational in denomination. All the composers represented were said to have been in some way censored. In fact neither Alan Bush, Nancarrow, Poulenc nor Shostakovich had their works actually banned, not the ones in the programme anyway. Since

Messiaen wrote his *Quartet for the End of Time* in a German prison camp no doubt his score was given the once over by the Stalag commandant before he allowed four prisoners to perform the work to the prisoners of war, but I doubt if an Oberleutenant could read the score well enough actually to censor it. Alan Bush of course was due to be banned by the BBC but Vaughan Williams read the riot act to Broadcasting House; and Bush's works were not performed as much as they should have been (on merit) because he was a member of the Communist Party.

Bush's work in this programme was his *Voices of the Prophets* settings for tenor and piano of words by Isaiah, Blake, Milton and a toshy West Indian poet called Peter Blackman; beautiful music, a fine mix of head and heart, the style rather like John Ireland at his best, tempered with Alan's own toughness and mastery of counterpoint. Philip Langridge and David Owen Norris gave it their best and the result was affecting. Jill Gomez sang songs associated and arranged with or by Casals (who exiled himself and whose music was not played in the Franco era), and also two Poulenc songs including the magnificent 'C'. Robert Lloyd sang eloquently *Four Monologues* based on Pushkin words by Shostakovich, whose music definitely gave Conlon Nancarrow (1912-97) a hard time and he consistently gives his listeners a hard time. He found a way to greater complexity by writing works for the pianola so that the piano sounds as if Charles Ives and Art Tatum were improvising at the keyboard, scudding all over it most of the time. He has been hailed as a genius but I hae me douts.

The performance of Messiaen's *Quatuor pour le fin du temps* was impassioned and performed in a masterly way by Tasmin Little, violin, Anthony Pay, clarinet, Lynn Harrell, cello and with Sir Simon Rattle at the piano. The first three of course are masters of their instruments; to single out one player I would have to mention Pay not only for his command of the notes but for his variety of wonderful sound. As for Simon Rattle, he has no business to play so well, dammit he is a conductor. This performance was truly committed. As I listened I recalled going in 1974 to Bournemouth when Simon won a conductor's competition. He was then nineteen, head and shoulders above all the others. I remember Sir Charles Groves, one of the judges, saying then that 'This boy seems to know by instinct things that it has taken me thirty years to learn.' He also added that he thought there would probably be several Lady Rattles. Well, only two so far, but he has got his knighthood and he is still only forty-three. As remarkable as his talent for conducting (and piano playing) is his talent for managing his career, doing the right thing at the right time and resisting many offers that would have been short-term prizes. Famously Simon resisted the recording companies when they wanted him to go to enwax this with the Concertgebouw, that with the Los Angeles and so on; whereas he said he was going to stick by, at, and with, Birmingham and if they wanted him, they could come there. Wise chap, not big-headed either.

After the competition in '74 I invited Simon to come to the summer school at Dartington and he directed a good *Soldier's Tale* in '75. I asked him if he would like to conduct the amateur choir that we used to form each week. He demurred as he had never conducted a choir but he consented when I suggested that Dartington was a good place to dip his toes into choral waters. He did in '76, with Janacek's *Glagolithic Mass* (no orchestra but two excellent pianists). The first rehearsal found Simon making a few slight errors of judgement owing to his ignorance of the psychology of conducting amateurs. By the next day he had sorted it all out in his mind and was in complete command. Another year he conducted Britten's *War Requiem* (two pianos still) and in the first half of the programme he had a bash in the Bartok Sonata for two pianos and percussion. The Rattle family came in force with the lovely mother, Pauline, and Dad Dennis, good jazz pianist, excellent cricketer and with a feeling for the girls (so they told me). By 1977 Simon was away to fresh fields and better paid pastures.

Simon was and is delightful to be with, so talented and unspoiled. I remember that in the '80s when André Previn was asked his opinion of Simon he singled out three things: firstly, he is young, which is bad; secondly, he is talented, which is worse; thirdly, he is very nice, which is unforgivable.

His manners are good but you soon realise that you don't mess about with Simon. He can tantrum to good advantage when crossed. He is quite obstinate.

HS: 1999, appointed to Berlin Philharmonic. 'Das Land ohne Musik?' And in 2001 he was contracted for ten years.

CONSTANT LAMBERT:
15.12.98

Listening to old BBC tape of Constant Lambert on *Music Magazine*, 'Cat, friend of man, what a splendid phrase.' He goes on to say that although Rossini once kept a friend waiting while he played his dog a piano piece written for its birthday, although Ethel Smyth was devoted to her large Marco, although Elgar had written a variation in the *Enigma* for the dog Dan, yet on the whole composers had preferred cats: the Egyptians worshipped them, the Russians admired them for their qualities of wisdom, enterprise and virility. Would we ever have remembered the verse 'hey diddle-diddle, the cat and the fiddle' if it had been 'hey diddle-diddle, the dog and the fiddle'? There is a charming BBC photograph of CL in shirtsleeves making advances to a mogador with a pencil. He loved talking to cats, stopping often in the street to do so, usually stray cats. He was like a cat himself.

A friend describes Lambert as being 'glamorous', not in the cliché Hollywood sense but in the truer meaning of glamour as 'magic entertainment' or 'alluring charm'. I used to see him in a pub near to the old Queens Hall and Broadcasting House, called *The George* but nick-named *The Gluepot* by Sir Henry Wood because of the way his musicians got stuck in it. Many of his cronies, musicians, writers and producers used to congregate but if there were none around and I was there, he would talk to me as he knew me as a fan and as a member of the staff of the London Philharmonic. He always spoke as though in public: I don't believe he ever looked me in the eyes. Apparently he was also a public drinker; at home the only drink available was bottled cider. When he had done a conducting job (most evenings) he had a drink at the pub, came home and worked through the night. It was not until his last days – he died of drink and undiagnosed diabetes in 1951 at the age of forty-six – that he fell down, sometimes literally, on the job. Sometimes though, after a party, he would arrive – I saw him once at the BBC Maida Vale studios at five to ten in the morning trying unsuccessfully to walk in a straight line from the studio door to the podium. Drinking was in his genes although what he passed to his son, Kit, was not only his looks but a taste for drugs. I guess he drank partly because of his failure as a creative artist. He filled up his life with conducting (which he did extremely well) partly to earn money but partly (like Boulez?) to avoid composing. He was bitter, friends said, about his lack of success as a composer and, probably, because he knew that his range as a composer was too limited: 'too few shots in his locker'; the harmonies and rhythms that are so vital in his best known work *The Rio Grande* of 1928 are used again and again in subsequent pieces until they become stale and threadbare. And there are too few moods that he can portray, the alternative to the jazzy 'Rio' being the chromatic mix of fourths and sevenths as heard in the work he thought his best: *Summer's Last Will and Testament*. CL had good taste and strong creative friends in Walton, and Rawsthorne; he must have seen how his own oeuvre paled beside theirs.

He remained loyal to his composer friends but loathed Britten and Tippett when their stars rose during the Second World War. In fact, it was the discovery that I was a friend of Tippett that caused him abruptly to finish his drink at the Gluepot one day, turn on his heel, never to speak to me again. But he conducted an excellent early performance of Britten's *Sinfonia da Requiem* at the Orpheum, Golder's Green, so he could swallow his resentment.

Lambert was also a highly literate, perceptive and witty critic who wrote for many journals, a weekly column for the *Sunday Referee* at one time, and the book *Music Ho!* A survey of contemporary music. In his writings Lambert talked a lot of sense, some non-sense, flew kites and ground axes, all in a beguiling, entertaining way. German music in general he could not abide although he did not usually say it was bad, except for his noirest bête, Brahms: whereas other composers have composed at the piano, it was obvious to Lambert that Brahms composed at the double bass. About the old translation of Verdi's Requiem into English he said that, for example, to render 'Dies Irae' as 'day of trouble' was to reduce it to the level of spring cleaning. Tovey's Cello Concerto, performed by Casals, he was 'compelled to leave at the end of the first movement, which seemed to last as long as my first term at school'. He delighted in the works of Satie, Chabrier and his friend Lord Berners, slated Stravinsky for his postwar pastiches and, rather bizarrely, pointed to Sibelius as being the road to the future.

'Glamorous' is a good description of Lambert the man, despite the fact that, already by the time I knew him, when he was in his early forties, his complexion was slug-white and raddled by booze, he was fattening dangerously and his lameness much in evidence. His conversation sparkled and it was clear, as his friend Frederick Ashton told me, that Lambert knew not only the full range of music, but also of literature, painting and architecture. He used to say that he was the only Francophile English composer-conductor of an Australian painter father born in St Petersburg who could play God Save the King by ear, i.e. through a hole in his eardrum.

IRELAND AND JOYCE:
9.12.98

Playing through the old early wartime recording of John Ireland's Piano Concerto with the Hallé Orchestra conducted by the brilliant Leslie Heward, who died middle-aged of tuberculosis, with the solo part imaginatively and virtuosically played by Eileen Joyce. When it was issued it fell to me, reviewing for the Monthly Letter of E. M. G. Handmade Gramophones, to write about it. A few days after my review appeared, Dr Ireland comes into the Grape Street shop in a paddy. 'Who is this Harris that reviewed my pianner concerto?' he demanded. Much to the amusement of my colleagues in the shop, who were a little jealous that I and not they had been chosen to help out Tom Fenton with the compilation of the Letter. It seems that I had praised the work but left in some faint-hearted statements with that awful 'perhaps' in it: 'Ireland's Concerto is perhaps (or maybe I had written 'arguably': just as silly) the finest British piano concerto etc.' Anyway Dr John went for me (quite rightly) and I defended myself as best I could and I managed to mollify him enough for him to calm down a little and ask me out for a cup of tea. He was a nice old thing, although he could not have been more than early fifties at the time; but he seemed older. He had built up a grouchy persona and loved to grumble. Later he kept on asking in the pubs around Broadcasting House, 'What's the BBC going to do about my fiftieth birthday?'

Eventually Auntie put on a John Ireland concert at the Proms at the appropriate time but that did not stop the grumbling: 'The BBC is trying to kill my music by putting on a whole programme of it.' You could not win with Dr John. However, he was very pleasant at our tea together. But then he was partial to young men: that was the story of his life. Although he did in fact get married; and that proved a disaster. The story goes that he walked out, or was pushed out, on his wedding night and went home in the middle of the night. He talked in a growly gravelly kind of near cockney although he was born in Cheshire.

I suppose that the most popular pianists during the Second World War were Myra Hess and Moiseiwitsch of the old generation (with Leff Pouishnoff as a third) but of the younger ones Eileen Joyce was number one. She played a lot in London and slogged round the provinces doing concertos and recitals, working very hard until she began to elicit harsh criticism on three counts: limited repertoire, diminished technical ability, and sartorial. I am fairly sure that her repertoire was largely dictated by managerial demands, the public wanted the same old concertos that they knew; this undoubtedly blunted her ability. The sartorial criticism was because if, as she often did, she played two concertos in one evening, she played the second one in a different coloured dress from the first. I think it livened things up for her, and also she had started to associate various composers with colours.

In the late '40s it was part of my duties as concert manager of the Royal Philharmonic Orchestra (Beecham's orchestra although rarely, if ever, did *he* conduct for Eileen) to look after the soloists at concerts, make sure they were comfortable, and push them on-stage at the appropriate moment. At one concert in the Davis Theatre, Croydon, Eileen had played the Grieg Concerto in a green dress and was due to play César Franck's *Symphonic Variations* in the second half. I was standing in the wings during the work before the Franck when I became aware that she was standing beside me. 'Oh,' I said, 'you've changed your dress.' (This was one of the first occasions on which she had started this habit.) 'Well,' she said, 'I couldn't play the Franck in green, could I?'

Eric Blom, who edited the fifth edition of Grove's Dictionary of Music, actually made snide remarks about her changing her dress in the article on Eileen in Grove. Not a nice or proper thing to do. And it wasn't as if Eileen was the first artist to change dresses in mid-concert. Certainly the Spanish mezzo-soprano Conchita Supervia was doing it way back in the '30s, as Ivor Newton once recounted.

Eileen Joyce once told me about her early days. She was born into a very poor family in Tasmania. Her first recollections were of living in tents with her mother and father, later in a shack in the gold fields of Boulder City. Her uncle owned a rough pub that had a tumble-down piano in it that was her first musical experience. She badgered her dad until he bought the piano for a small sum and wheeled it home. Later Eileen went to a convent school where she persuaded her mum to pay 6d a week to a nun for piano lessons. She went in for examinations, higher and higher, until a priest wrote to the *Loreto Comet* newspaper in Perth asking for a convent to take her in and educate her. During her two years there Percy Grainger visited Perth and not only gave concerts but allowed budding musicians to come while he practised. He also came to play to the nuns and school and was persuaded to hear their star pupil play the piano. He didn't say anything to Eileen but he wrote to the Perth newspapers saying she should be sent away to study. A little later Wilhelm Backhaus was in Perth, heard her and pronounced that she should go to Leipzig to study with Backhaus's teacher, Max Pauer. She was the youngest of a dozen or more students and was not at that stage sufficiently advanced to cope. Fortunately a visiting couple from New Zealand took her under their wing, encouraged her to go to another teacher, Teichmuller. Eventually the benevolent couple set her up in London, got her a Blüthner piano and she started up on her own. Enterprisingly Eileen decided she wanted to hear herself so she managed to arrange to make a record at her own expense for £7.10. Her technician thought she was wonderful and persuaded one of the bosses to listen to her single-side of Liszt's Study in F minor. They asked her to come to hear the disc, what did she think of it? It was the first time she had heard herself play and she said that she thought it was wonderful too. The boss agreed with her but said that now Parlophone were going to pay her instead of her footing the bill. And that is how Eileen Joyce got launched.

Her career tapered off after the success of some twenty-five years but she lived comfortably enough, latterly in a house near Chequers. I saw her one day at Glyndebourne a year or two before she died, went up and talked to her, and she was pathetically glad to find that someone recognized her and remembered her. She remained a handsome woman, elegantly dressed. I arranged to go down to see her but she had to postpone my visit, she asked me to wait until the spring when the flowers would be out. Next thing I heard was that she had died.

Another visit that got postponed, indefinitely as it turned out, was a proposed interview with John Ireland who had moved out of London to live at Rook Mill, near Pulborough in Sussex. Norah Kirby, housekeeper and minder, rang up to say that Dr John was ill, could we postpone? And in fact he died on the day originally fixed for the interview.

PANUFNIK:
2.1.99

Took train to Richmond as I was needing a walk and as I climbed the Hill towards the Star and Garter passed Petersham Common at the bottom of which lies the parish church in the village. A few years ago I went there to take part in a recording of Panufnik's *Thames Pageant*. One of the movements is about the Oxford and Cambridge boat race and it features a narrator giving a quasi BBC commentary. This movement has one aleatoric feature, just one word where the commentator is allowed to decide whether to announce in a shout that Oxford or Cambridge is the winner. In between the rehearsal and the 'take' I was subject to attempted bribery. The work was written for children's chorus from local schools of Richmond and Twickenham. One by one, four small boys came up to me. 'Jolly good, sir, would you care for a sweet, sir? Oh, and by the way, sir, you will let Oxford win, won't you?' and the next one, proffering liquorice-all-sorts asked me to let Cambridge win. I thanked them but said, quite truly, that I hadn't made up my mind yet who was going to win, I would decide right at the last moment.

Andrej Panufnik was a local man, living in a lovely house down by the river between Richmond and nearer Twickenham, with his equally lovely wife, Camilla (not that she looks like a house, anything but, she is a beautiful woman, good photographer and produces excellent children's books). Coming out of the brackets I say also that she was the perfect wife for Andrej, adoring him, looking after him, protecting him and generally being a model composer's wife partly because she did not ram his works down your throat (as, for example, Ming Tcherepnin did). I think I first met the Panufniks at a Boosey and Hawkes thrash organised by Janis Süsskind. Soon I was on the dinner list, Polish vodka, the best steaks in London, what a butcher there must be locally! cooked to a T, usually just the three of us, houseful of treasures but I was never allowed to visit the stables where the Master did his compo. There is a little bridge in the garden over the road onto another small garden on the banks of the Thames. In those days they had a little boat which chugged up and down the water, Andrej at his most masterful playing the part of the captain, whilst Camilla was in command of the galley, preparing supper. But one day she was not in total command of the galley for, as I, bad guest that I was, pointed out to her, one of her red Creuset saucepans was floating away with our haricots verts on its way to Greenwich and Southend. I was sworn to secrecy about that in case the Captain should find out.

As a result of being bullied and threatened in Communist Poland about worse things than errant Creusets Andrej got into a sweat if anyone tried, as I did for the radio, to interview him. However I did try to get his works performed. At that time, he was persona non grata with the music department of the BBC: Howgill had been sympathetic but William Glock would not allow his music on the air, not even the magnificent *Sinfonia Sacra* despite its having won a prize in Monaco. Under Glock and his sidekick, Hans Keller, many distinguished writers, such as Frank Martin, Roussel, and Honegger were unofficially declared non-composers. Either serialists you have to be or weirdos like Varèse or Ives or you didn't get played, a throttling blanket that would have done credit to an Iron Curtain country. Many composers were in despair and financial trouble. It was great to hear all that Webern and Berg, and Debussy scraped through, being dead, and Stravinsky having in his old age become serially respectable but otherwise it was a kind of teutonic totalitarian situation.

However, the Glock iron fist did not grip television and in the

214

early '70s I was editor and programme maker of a music magazine, called in its first year *Music Now* and in its second *Counterpoint*, the change in name thought up by my boss John Culshaw being fatal. Anyway I managed to slip twenty minutes or so of Andrej's vast *Universal Prayer* into one of my programmes, unleashed in Twickenham Parish Church and conducted by his patron-saint-conductor, Leopold Stokowski. Because of arranging this I had to go and see the great conductor and look after him at the tele-recording. I had interviewed him for radio years before that, when he was lying on his bed in the Stafford Hotel. The narrow bed had a shiny, silky cover on it that kept slipping and I feared for his safety and spoke thereon. 'Ah,' said Stokey as orchestral musicians called him rather maliciously, 'you hope that I will fall and injure myself.' He kept up this rather unpleasant *de haut en bas* attitude until the next time I met him when he was all sweetness and light. The only time the claw showed was when, crossing the grass and gravestones between his car and the church, some innocent passer-by fan took a photo of him. He went berserk. I could not understand how a man who had had thousands of photographs taken of him should object to a snap. Was it because he wasn't sure if the lighting would show his profile to best advantage? After that he went back to being the benign uncle. To the vicar Stokey said that in his Anglican church he, Stokey, was a sinner, a lapsed Catholic. 'Never mind,' said the vicar, 'if you are a bad Catholic, that might make you a good Anglican.' Thirty-fifteen to the vicar, I thought. Stokey conducted inspiringly, patient with his musicians, though demanding.

That piece, *Universal Prayer*, has sunk without a trace, despite a recording made in Westminster Cathedral. To my mind it shows a debilitating fault present in most of Andrej's later music where the inspiration seems to be channelled not into the music but the geometrical schemes around which the music is made to fit. This involved a lot of symmetry, so that the repetitions become predictable and boring. Also the idea of dissonant and energetic strife followed by sweet, slow harmonies always with major and minor thirds clashing become predictable. In his finest works, like the *Sacra*, the overtures and some vocal pieces, it all works (just as it does in the fifth *Tre Re* symphony of Honegger, a composer whose influence on Panufnik I have always thought palpable).

These misgivings I suppose I must have hinted at in conversation with Andrej and Camilla. And so the invitations to dinner floated away from me down the river like the cruising Creuset. But he was a very likeable man, with his impeccable manners and his unique hissing way of laughing. Very Polish, I have always thought, although only because the manner and the manners were somewhat similar to the only other Polish composer I knew of the same generation, Witold Lutoslawski.

Luto, as we called him for short, was also full of charm, a smaller man that Andrej, small enough to be called dapper, again with a rather hissing laugh. His command of English was first-class, he said he could learn a language in a matter of weeks. No more than Andrej did Luto ever unburden his soul or his inner thoughts, maybe that was something to do with having to play your cards according to the rules of totalitarian states, rules that shifted like sands. Luto managed the system pretty well which was amazing considering that he came from the aristocratic class. He had had his times in the political doghouse, but on the whole he wrote the music *he* wanted, conducted it well and managed to get abroad (Dartington '64, for instance, and a passport for his loving wife Drusina – they were introduced by Andrej). Panufnik (always called Panicfuk by the British orchestras) and Luto had teamed up during the war to play two piano duets. Concerts for Poles were forbidden but they played in cafes, played a large repertoire, arranged and sometimes improvised by themselves.

Like Andrej, Luto liked to build his music on ground-plans but whereas Andrej turned to geometry, Luto invented strictly musical games (Hesse's *Glass Bead Game* comes to mind). He liked to reverse the Haydn symphony plan and start with a gay movement and gradually get more serious; so that just when the listener is wondering where things are going, the musical matter comes to a head and the work is satisfactorily clinched. Luto's use of aleatoric procedure is, or was at one time, part of the scheme and he managed that particular trick better than anyone else. Earlier in his career he had contrived to steer clear of the danger area of big symphonies and choral works, areas controlled by policy makers, by concentrating on folk and children's music, stuff badly needed just after the war. Later Luto never went with serialism or other fashions, he toyed with them, incorporated them into his work but on the whole he was a lone wolf or should I say, more like himself as a person, like a cat that walked by itself. He ought to be played more than he is, because his music is of our time but, mirabile dictu, enjoyable. Mind you, Luto was lucky in having two champions in Esa Pekka Salonen and Simon Rattle. Whereas some older conductors liked his music but found it difficult to rehearse, these two younger men took to Luto's music like ducks to water, no problems for them.

KISSIN:
6.1.99

Just round the corner from where I live in London I encountered two ageing Russian ladies, the mother and teacher of the great Russian pianist, Evgeny Kissin. Four years ago he was on the good ship *Mermoz* for the floating music festival I have attended as music lecturer five out of the last six years. Up to that time I had heard about this phenomenal boy wonder, then seventeen or so. Phenomenal he certainly was: the most remarkable technique you can imagine plus a musicality and poetic imagination that could make you cry. He would play a Chopin Waltz or Prelude for an encore, a piece everyone has known from childhood, so familiar and yet he had everyone in tears. Mozart, Prokofiev, Rachmaninov, Scarlatti, the whole range marvellous. And one time the director of the cruise, André Barocz, put together Accardo and his string quartet, three quarters of it, with Philip Simms of the English Chamber Orchestra, to play the Schubert *Trout*, which Evgeny hadn't played for eight years; it was perfect.

Genia is a nice looking boy with a mass of dark hair but his appearance sometimes marred by a facial tic of the jaw. Apparently there is a sister who is mentally disturbed. Always, except once, the boy is heavily attended by the mother and the teacher. He sits with them at meals, they come while he practises, they shadow him on the trips ashore. After he has given a recital of exquisite perfection, half an hour later there he is in the concert salon, empty except for him, mum and his teacher putting right what he had apparently done wrong in the concert.

Just once we managed to pry him out of their company and took him down into the ship's bowels to the quasi nightclub. Evgeny drank, told stories and picked up a nice German girl, had a whale of a time. Just that once. But he was allowed later in the year to date the girl a few times. She told me a year or two later, that they had nice times together, the only trouble being that he was conditioned to ring mum'n'teacher every two hours, so every two hours he started getting anxious to find a phone. It would be easier now, what with mobile phones. Somebody on the cruise asked Evgeny once why he was always with his mum'n'teacher and he replied, 'It's a lonely life, being a concert pianist.' Which is no doubt half the truth. The other half might just possibly be that, as with Wolfgang Amadeus, that he is a meal ticket for the whole family, including Papa who is some kind of Boffin (which is why he wasn't let out of Russia for a long time).

The family now mainly lives in New York (with Papa and Sister when possible) but they also have a flat in Ashley Gardens facing what a friend of mine once called 'that vast dissenting tabernacle' (Westminster Cathedral).

Sadly this was the day of the funeral of André Barocz who so brilliantly directed the Menton Festival and forty sessions of the floating music festival, held latterly on the cruise ship *Mermoz*. André was a picaresque character, looking like a goulash version of Popeye the Sailor, but it was his personality that enabled him to persuade artists like Rostropovich, Bashmet, Vengerov, Menuhin, Ciccolini, Penderecki, Stern and Kissin to join the cruises.

FISCHER-DIESKAU:
7.1.99

Fischer-Dieskau on Radio 3 talking to Joan Bakewell. In 1951 he made his debut in the UK singing Delius's *Mass of Life* under Beecham who had heard about this fabulous singer (b.1925). A mere two years later, before his fee shot up too much, we got him to come to the Summer School in Dartington to sing a *Schöne Müllerin*, two years after that a *Winterreise*. Did he want Gerald Moore? No, he was happy to have William Glock both times; William played very well, apart from one or two booboos, usually in the easiest passages.

William knew his Schubert and he made a truly beautiful sound on the piano. Dieskau's voice was also beautiful and his musicality was immense. He stood still (he started to throw himself about when his voice deteriorated) and the drama was all around.

Even at that age he was apart, a kind of head prefect with wings. He didn't join in the summer school at all, didn't come to a class or anybody else's concerts, stayed quietly in a house put aside for him and listened to gramophone records all day. His only request was for the loan of more records.

At the concerts his behaviour was impeccable, thoroughly professional, not more friendly than he need be. He didn't say anything to William about his performance. The only surprise was when asked, in the interval, if he wanted anything, a drink perhaps? 'I am dying for a cigarette.'

His career spanned four decades during which time he had done much for Lieder, put it on the map and made it possible for other singers to do a little map-making. He was aloof with most people, a sort of de haut en bas atmosphere prevailed. He would only be interviewed when it suited him: zum beispiel when he tried conducting. That did not last long, although I thought his Schumann 3 and the *Unfinished* at Edinburgh not half bad. Unfortunately after some thirty years before the public he started to force his voice and one began to think that Hector might have been a more suitable first name than Dietrich. But those first thirty years were sensationally good and deeply satisfying: a complete artist with a wonderfully lovely voice.

Britten was smitten with his performance and they collaborated in the *War Requiem* (1961) and superb records of Schumann's *Faust*. Britten also wrote the Blake *Songs and Prophecies* 'for Dieter' (1965), but since those songs are rather gruff and charmless I wonder if the magic of their friendship wasn't wearing off by then; because later BB wrote in a letter that Fischer-D was like a school bully. It was interesting to hear the retired F-D (sounding much less arrogant on the radio today) say that his favourite operatic part was the Count in *Figaro*. There's a bit of unexpected self-knowledge in that choice, I think, because the Count is an arrogant bastard if ever there was one.

POULENC:
9.1.99

A centenary concert of unaccompanied choral music in St John's, Smith Square, London to celebrate the birth of Francis Poulenc on 7 January 1899. That year saw also the birth of Noël Coward and it seems that the two met, because a journalist in San Francisco sent me last month a cassette of the pair of them performing the composer's *Babar the Elephant*, a joy to hear, not on Coward's part because he is too stiff-upper-lippish (probably a bit scared), but for Poulenc's piano playing which is not 100 per cent accurate but for élan and imagination it is perfect, 100% proof. But how did the recording come into existence? No one seems to know; no mention in any biogs. or letters that I have come across. Sheriden Morley does not know (I wrote him). The only ref. is in a letter of 1957 (or it might be '59) to his London publisher, R.D. Gibson of Chesters, asking when the record will be issued. But it never was, although Sheriden M. wonders if it wasn't on the back of the recording of Saint-Saëns *Carnival of the Animals* (probably the commentary of Ogden Nash).

The singers performing were the Exmoors, named not for the place but their founder/conductor and they are amateurs conducted now by James Jarvis. He did a magnificent job, for the programme was fiendishly taxing and, in fact, they only flagged once, in the last piece, and I think that was because of a hesitant beat by JJ, otherwise they could not be faulted either for notes, sound or spirit. The Poulenc works were: *Sept Chansons* (1936), *Figure humaine* (1943), the *Four Motets pour un temps de pénitence* (1938-9) and the Mass in C (1937). Interspersed were Stravinsky's somewhat penitential Credo, Pater Noster and Ave Maria and three pieces dating from 1907-8: Debussy's Orléans Songs, Schönberg's *Friede auf Erden* and Webern's *Entflieht auf leichten Kähnen*. Crikey Moses, what a programme!

Forty or fifty years ago any of these items, except perhaps the Debussy, would have been sung with frightened, constricted throat sound and a look on the faces of the choristers showing how agitated they felt. Nowadays there are smiles all round and the music comes out as easily (after adequate rehearsal) as if they were singing No 396, A & M. I was particularly struck by the beauty of the Webern and Schönberg pieces that I used to think were so dry and ugly. As for the Poulenc…already in the *Sept chansons* the tears were pricking the back of my eyeballs and once or twice I nearly shouted for joy and pleasure. But one thing; we are always told of the perfection of the settings of the surrealist poets Eluard and Aragon. Word setting, yes, but it seems to me that although some of the songs reflect the zaniness of the words, yet the choral idiom is scarcely, if at all, different from the religious music – not surrealist at all. It was a warm-hearted evening. The only possible cavil was that the tone of the sopranos tended, though not always, to harden above the stave. The alto soloist in the Debussy, Janet Willink, had a lovely voice, easily produced. I gather she is wondering whether to turn professional; she should.

Poulenc's first appearance in England towards the end of the war was, I think, at the National Gallery concerts in '45 when he did concerts with Pierre Bernac and with the young violinist Ginette Neveu. At the same time, maybe even before Nat. Gall., FP and Bernac gave a recital at the Wigmore Hall; when they came on the platform the entire audience stood up. On another visit Poulenc's Concerto for 2 pianos was performed in the Royal Albert Hall with Benjamin Britten on January 6 1945. What a star Neveu was! She had a face like a horse (that's not an insult) and in general she behaved rather like a colt. Poulenc looked incredibly like Fernandel, whose films were all the rage just then. He spoke not a word of English but he obviously understood it quite well as when he understood the two old birds at Glyndebourne in the coach. Before the first concert at the Nat. Gall. he demanded a cushion. This took some finding because they don't have cushions at institutions like the Nat. Gall. By the time I got one and returned to the concert platform he had already started playing without anything under his bum. I thought that he was terribly selfish, the way he left the platform as soon as he had finished playing and made one perfunctory bow, leaving Bernac there all on his lonesome. His playing lacked total accuracy but he clicked totally with Ben Britten and they gave a fizzing performance of his Concerto, a work that he described in a letter as having 'blythe bravura'. Ben was quite nervous.

In the '70s when Denis Moriarty and I made a film about Poulenc,

Darius Milhaud fortunately was in France and cooperated generously. I was a bit frightened to interview Milhaud again for the previous time he was awful, not feeling well, maybe. I had been suddenly asked to do an interview with him about a programme he was doing in Maida Vale studios with the BBC orchestra. I didn't know the works, a concerto for one or two pianos, and his *Music for Texas* and his *Music for Oregon*. I am not 100 per cent sure of those titles because I have not a complete list of Milhaud's 441 numbered works. He was very bad tempered and gave me a hard time. But he did explain that when he had composed twelve symphonies he became suPERstitious (that's the way he stressed it) and so called his future symphonies by the name of the place that commissioned them. Hence Music for TexArse and Music for OreGOHNe. Floundering for further questions, I asked if any of these places were in sonata form. 'There is no such thing as sonata form, so I consider that a rather stupid question.' Ouch!

But when I interviewed him for the Poulenc film Milhaud was all sweetness and light, sitting there very benign in a black suit and Panama hat. 'When I hear the telephone in France I always think that it may be Francis calling, as he did every day.' When I asked him about some works of Poulenc, the piano pieces for example, were they not inferior to others? 'You know, Francis was like a brother to me and I like everything that he wrote.'

After the interview, I asked him if there was anything that he could like me to send him when I returned to London. 'Yes, there is a work for forty parts by your Thomas Tallis [pronounced the French way] which I would dearly like to see.' I sent it and got a charming postcard from him, just a few weeks before he died (1974).

TCHEREPNIN:
21.1.99

The centenary of the birth of Alexander Tcherepnin although it is possible, I understand, that Russians born in the nineteenth century can have three birthdays nowadays (if they be still alive) because a) of the difference in the calendars (remember 'give us back our twelve days') between Russia and the rest of the world and b) because the Russians made 1900 a Leap Year whereas the rest of the world did not. Stravinsky was suddenly aware of this when he was asked to conduct a concert on his seventieth birthday. Commanding a large fee for such an appearance he was thus able to have two such concerts and, no doubt, if his health had permitted it, he would have had a third.

Sasha's father, Nikolay, was a respected figure in the Old Russia and he composed *Le Pavillion d'Armide*, the very first ballet performed by Diaghilev's company. Sasha was a tall, gangling figure of a man, stooping somewhat, perhaps because his Chinese wife, Ming, was a foot shorter than him. Although there was never any difficulty in hearing her, for she spoke clearly and often. She was a composer's wife par excellence except that she drove most people mad because all her utterances revolved round Sasha and getting his works performed. One day at a party at their house in Marlow several of us were talking together, recounting our various routes. Ming joined our group just as somebody mentioned catching a 49 bus; '49', says Ming, 'is the opus number of Sasha's Duo, Menuhin and Tortelier just played it, I get you score.' Actually if you could get her off the subject of Sasha, Ming was an interesting and kind person, wonderful cook. Sasha had met and married her in a protracted visit to China in the '20s. The family, including the father, had left Russia to settle in Paris.

Sasha told me that as a child he once prayed in front of an icon in the family home in St. Petersburg, where he was born, 'Please make me composer.' He had his wish, he also became pianist and conductor. Some of his first compositions were written as inexpensive presents for friends and relatives. When he started to have lessons with the famous French piano teacher Isidore Philipp he showed them to him. Philipp took the bundle and parcelled them out saying, 'Right, this lot you will call *Feuilles d'album*, these you will call *Morceaux de concert*, these become *Petite Suite* and those will be *Bagatelles*.' Strangely enough it was only the *Bagatelles* opus 5 that had success, were recorded, orchestrated, etc. Sasha came to London in his early twenties and was taken up, particularly by the fashionable and enterprising sisters, Jelly d'Aranyi and Adila Fachiri, both giving concerts with him at the Wigmore Hall.

By the time of Sasha's seventieth birthday (he died in '77) he had clocked up well over a hundred works in every genre. But he never made the headlines. A composer's success can often be discerned through the list of his publishers: if he has one or two, that usually means that he is too valuable a commodity to let go. If he has at least fifteen, like Sasha, it means that publishers have chanced their arm but withdrawn it when no big money-spinners ensued. There is a fine article in Grove by the late and still lamented Christopher Palmer which sums up aptly the few of Sasha's works that have come my way. At the beginning the witty and intriguing *Bagatelles,* towards the end the boring Piano Concerto No. 5, in the middle some boring string pieces. Then I was sent two pieces Sasha composed in 1957-8, taped at performances by Fritz Reiner and the Chicago Orchestra (after how many phone calls from Ming, I wonder?) soon after their premières, *Divertimento* and Symphony No. 4, opus 90 and 91 respectively. I have been playing tapes of these for a whole month and I am continually delighted with them. Palmer writes of 'Tcherepnin's quicksilver, egregiously cosmopolitan musicality, which, though recognizably Russian at base, conspicuously lacked the nostalgia and melancholy of other expatriate Slavs...the influence of Prokofiev is discernible (motor rhythms and a mordant though fundamentally good-tempered wit); but T. was already experimenting with new scales and a new species of counterpoint.' Well, there may be theories at work in opus 90 and 91 but inspiration and imagination are what keep me listening; and I wish someone would have a go at these works. When Sir William Glock was at the BBC he persuaded Sir Colin Davis to air Symphony No. 1, the one that caused a scandal in Paris in 1927, partly because the Scherzo was scored only for percussion. Sasha (and the affable but boring Ming) came to the Summer School at Dartington several years running, brought their avant-garde composing sons Serge and Ivan with them, too.

Sasha was a most stimulating lecturer, affecting for that purpose a swiftly flowing delivery that was full of charm, strong Russian accent, every aitch a catarrhal ch, and no definite articles from beginning to end. In private he talked at a normal pace, saving his energy for the lectures, no doubt. He was charm itself. It was interesting to see them at work at parties. First Sasha would talk to people in a captivating way. Then he would move on while Ming moved in to the group with a hard selling technique and leaflets lest we forget. For many years he had lived in New York as an American citizen but he still kept on his apartment in Paris.

CONDUCTING MYSELF BADLY: 31.1.99

Chastened. Was asked to conduct *Casse-Noisette* Suite on an open day of the Kensington Symphony Orchestra. These open days are held every year I think and serve as a kind of public service advertising display. The venue is Whiteley's store in Bayswater and the public mills around, mums with prams, etc. So, having looked at the score during the three days after having been invited and the event, I went along and...and whatever talent I have, it is not for conducting. The idea makes me nervous and I don't look at the orchestra with any confidence. In fact I make the mistake of not really taking in where everybody is. At the beginning of the 'Valse des fleurs' I turned to the brass but the horns were somewhere else. So I started again. Starting, in fact, was a hazard. Twice I gave (I thought) upbeats and nothing, but nothing, happened.

Ever since that day I wake up, hearing in my mind the preliminary upchuck-chuck chords before the horn entry in the Valse. Fortunately *Casse-Noisette* is full of repeats so I was able to have a second go. I don't think I made a complete fool of myself; just showed that I have absolutely no command of an orchestra. For example, I started off the afore-mentioned Valse too slow. But could I get the band to go faster? Could I hell! If I pushed on the tempo, everything got ragged because most of the band stayed at the tempo I had started at. So I went back to my sluggish adagio. I did, however, manage to do a ritardando in the last bar but one. But when the rhythm goes hemiola-like into three lots of two within the three-four rhythm I found myself beating the twos instead of maintaining the threes. At least, the first time; the second time I managed to keep in threes. Oh well, I suppose it is good to be chastened occasionally.

I had been hoping that Lucy Waterhouse would be leading the orchestra, she is rather attractive, but she was off that day. Becca Walker was there on the third desk of cellos. She hasn't spoken to me since. I don't blame her.

The Kens were playing all day. Some of the conductors paid. Me, being a lower case celeb, didn't. I should have done. The chap before me did rather well, I thought. But then I realised he was standing in for someone who hadn't turned up. And 'he' was Russell Keable, the regular conductor of the orchestra. No wonder he did well.

My very first attempt at conducting was way back during the war when some guardsmen mixed with amateurs got fed up with inactivity and started some rehearsal sessions. Karl Haas, of London Baroque Ensemble fame, and Richard Temple-Savage, librarian and bass clarinet of the LPO were also on. How I was asked, I don't know, but I was. I was given the first two movements of Borodin's Symphony No. 2, which starts off full of pitfalls, with a pause on practically every other bar for minutes on end. Very difficult to negotiate. The lead was Dea Gombrich, sometime professional, wife of the art historian. I remember she at the first desk had brought with her a cumbersome and heavy metal stand. I knocked it over five times during the first movement.

The second movement is marked prestissimo, one in a bar. Same trouble as with the 'Valse des fleurs': couldn't get it to go faster. During a tacet one of the trumpets shouted to me: 'Bit faster?' I shouted back, 'I'm trying.' But the prestissimo was stuck in the treacle of my slow beat.

As I walked past Bayswater Tube on my way home after the rehearsal I recalled one evening arriving at the station and seeing on the stairs a Gents with a notice on the door saying:

TOILET CLOSED
London Transport regrets any
Inconvenience

and that in turn reminded me of a sign seen in Gillingham Street outside a recently arrived ethnic tailor's which advertised:

TROUSERS LOWERED WHILE YOU WAIT

and I guess that last statement describes my conducting caper.

PUD:
3.3.99

At the Coliseum during the interval of *Otello* the neighbour on my left suddenly proffered me her programme open at a blank page and a pen saying 'Could I have your autograph, Mr Mortimer?' This has happened to me many times (and to *him* in reverse a few, as we discovered at a party some years ago) so I said sorry, I wasn't John Mortimer. She snatched back pen and programme. Half a minute later after a nudge and a word from her companion she re-proffered pen and programme with the query 'Kingsley?' 'No, again, I'm afraid, my cousin Kingsley died nearly three years ago.' This time she fairly grabbed her pen and programme back and said not a word further.

My features, I can see, are a bit like John's although he has a sag in his underlip on one side, and he is much less tall than me. The shape of my head, though is quite similar to Kingsley's although our features were not similar. I sometimes think my face has got into print but after half a second I realise my mistake.

As children we were not alike; he seemed then to take more after his mother whom we all called Rosie. Curious that in Eric Jacob's biography of coz Kingers (as his beautiful and intelligent Elizabeth Jane Howard, No. 2 wife always called him; how I wish I liked her novels!), she is always called Peg. Rosie was a creature of nervous quick movements and speech, quick to laugh in spurts. And she always smelled of a certain type of face powder, I see her face vividly when I come across that, or a similar smell.

I used to think it odd that, although I went to see him in Norbury, he never came to see me. But then I walked a lot (three or four miles from W. Norwood across Streatham Common) and Pud never went anywhere on foot. No wonder his legs packed up in the last decade of his life. We used to have lunch about once or twice a year during that time, sometimes at Simpsons in the Strand, once at the White Tower, last time at Mon Plaisir. Pathetic the very last time, because he could hardly stand and he nearly fell over in the street waiting for his taxi. That last time I rang up in the morning only to find that Mon Plaisir didn't stock his favourite whisky Highland Park, so I bought a half bottle on the way which emptied itself quite soon. K was quite touched. He was also terribly apologetic at one point. He had been sounding off about things he hated particularly at the moment and one of them was corduroy trousers. I removed my right leg from under the table and shook it. He was properly mortified to see corduroy. We also discussed what might have happened if Rosie had not refused to go to South America where Uncle Bill had been offered promotion by Colman's Mustard as their rep. there. As it was, Bill was subsequently thought rather little of by the firm and not offered promotion again. A case of not cutting the mustard.

When *Lucky Jim* came out I wrote him a congratulatory letter which was replied to after some weeks in a gracious way except for telling me not to call him 'Pud' any more. So called because Rosie was always telling him to go and wash his puddies before meals. Forty years on he relented and even signed letters in that way. Incidentally I relished his 'quite liking' my autobiography *Amiscellany* with the remark that 'it wasn't badly written, either'.

As a teenager he was further into twentieth century music than I was, making me listen to records of RVW4 and Walton's Viola Concerto, works I at first balked at. Strange to say, we never discussed books or writing. From Oxford, or maybe at some time before that, he sent me some prose poems à la Rimbaud for me to set à la Britten. One of them began 'He sees immortality in the eyes of a virgin'. I preferred 'and he finds fresh isles in a negress's smiles, the poxy-doxy dear'.

DAD:
1.12.99

There was a theory that the Amis family were originally Huguenots. It seemed likely, as our name was French and we all knew that our ancestors came from Norfolk where Huguenots settled after the Edict of Nantes was revoked in 1685. However, this theory was upset in 1947 when Mrs Blanchard an American, whose great-great-grandfather was an Amis, was given a reception by the English Jockey Club. She stated that her ancestor, William Amis owned the racehorse Sir Archie, son of the first Derby winner, and she presented the Jockey Club with a portrait of that famous animal, which had been taken to America and founded American horseracing under the auspices of the Amis family. This lady was writing a book on the history of the family and their connection with horseracing and hunting in the United States covering over 150 years.

'During her trip to England she visited the small Norfolk village of Barton Turf where the Amis family originally hailed from. Shortly after her I visited this village and inspected the chapel in which are the brasses erected to Thomas Amys and his wife Margerey in 1445. (Norfolk was then the centre of a very flourishing woollen industry.)

'My own records go back to 1780 when William Amis, my great-grandfather was born in Norfolk. He lived 100 years. His son was also a William who married Harriet Preston (hence my second name, Preston). Wm. Amis jnr. was the father of J. J. Amis, my father and another son of his was George Amis, father of Thomas who became a U.S. citizen eventually when his family emigrated to America.

'There is little doubt that we are descendents of Thomas Amys; the registers in Barton Turf have been kept for over 500 years. So, we are of French origin but not Huguenots.'

(this page was written by my father, James Preston Amis, 1886-1980)

HS: Alas, Jimmy A. was not quite correct. From information received subsequently it seems that Amis, Amyss, Amies, etc (I once got 'Dear Mr Anus' on a letter) is/are probably derived from the Celtic Ennis, a name meaning 'Uncle'. But the earlier part of the spiel is, I believe, correct.